How to Live. What to Do

How to Live. What to Do

In Search of Ourselves in Life and Literature

JOSH COHEN

Pantheon Books
New York

Grateful acknowledgment is made to Alfred A. Knopf for permission to reprint
an excerpt from "How to Live. What to Do" from *The Collected Poems of Wallace
Stevens* by Wallace Stevens, copyright © 1954 by Wallace Stevens and copyright
renewed 1982 by Holly Stevens. Reprinted by permission of Alfred A. Knopf,
an imprint of the Knopf Doubleday Publishing Group,
a division of Penguin Random House LLC. All rights reserved.

Library of Congress Cataloging-in-Publication Data
Name: Cohen, Josh, [date] author.
Title: How to live. what to do : in search of ourselves in life
and literature / Josh Cohen.
Description: First American edition. New York : Pantheon Books, 2021.
Includes bibliographical references.
Identifiers: LCCN 2020057288 (print). LCCN 2020057289 (ebook).
ISBN 9780593316207 (hardcover). ISBN 9780593316214 (ebook).
Subjects: LCSH: Psychoanalysis and literature. Fiction—History and criticism.
Fiction—Psychological aspects. Identity (Psychology) in literature.
Conduct of life in literature. Characters and characteristics in literature.
Classification: LCC PN3352.P7 C58 2021 (print) |
LCC PN3352.P7 (ebook) | DDC 809.3/9353—dc23
LC record available at lccn.loc.gov/2020057288
LC ebook record available at lccn.loc.gov/2020057289

www.pantheonbooks.com

Jacket illustration by Miki Lowe
Jacket design by Emily Mahon

Printed in the United States of America
First United States Edition
9 8 7 6 5 4 3 2 1

For Abigail, obviously

Contents

Author's Note

Writing about cases confronts any therapist with irresolvable difficulties. If rendered too accurately, they compromise patient confidentiality; too loosely, and their clinical value becomes suspect. As I'm writing for a general rather than professional readership here, the purpose is to put flesh on the dilemmas of life rather than to provide a significant contribution to clinical knowledge. The result is that the cases I discuss are composite figures, with the basic details of the source cases heavily disguised. It's not an ideal solution, but there is much more to lose on the side of confidentiality than of strict accuracy.

Introduction

These days I'm often regaled at the kitchen table by "origin stories" of how some Marvel character or other attained their superhero status. I sometimes find myself wanting to ask the boy telling them why use of this phrase is so restricted, why superheroes and ancient divinities should claim exclusive right to stories of their origins. Don't we all have our own private myths of how we became who we are?

Mine, for example, begins aged six, with the return of my parents from a two-week holiday in the US. Having left my elder brother and me with our grandparents, they came back bearing gifts and guilt in abundant quantities. Of the gifts, there's only one I've kept, or even remember: a volume of *Peanuts* cartoons, its deep red cover depicting an evil-tempered Peppermint Patty at a school desk alongside an impassive Charlie Brown, the title emblazoned above their heads in that unmistakably rough typeface: DON'T HASSLE ME WITH YOUR SIGHS, CHUCK.

If I had an origin story, *Don't Hassle Me with Your Sighs, Chuck* would be the Ra's al Ghul to my Bruce Wayne, the radioactive spider to my Peter Parker. Until I received that gift, the best I could say about myself was that I was there and contented enough. I was small, I went to school, I liked *Top of the Pops* and *The Big Match*, or my brother did, which felt like more or less the same thing. But if there was anything that made me properly distinct from the kids around me, I had no idea what it was.

Until I walked up to my room, sat on my bed, drew my legs up and, resting the book on my lap, turned to the first strip, featuring the bald kid with two squiggles of hair matted to his brow talking to the cross-looking girl. I knew the dog's name, but not theirs. Nor did I know the word "psychiatric" written across the top of the booth she was sitting in, so that scanning it produced something like "Pssitchric Help 5c" in my mind's ear. Happily, the base of the booth read "The Doctor Is IN." Well, I knew what a doctor was.

The boy was sat atop a stool on the other side of the booth as the girl told him, "You need to improve your character," before elaborating: "Once a child is five years old his character gets to be pretty well established"; to which he replied, arms raised high in frustration, "But I'm already five, I'm *more* than five!"

"That's right," she said, every inch the poker-faced shrink, "You are, aren't you?" before coming back with, "Too bad, that's the way it goes." Her patient winced in despair.

I read this strip a few more times, each time a little more breathlessly alive to something happening in me. It didn't matter that my cognitive grasp of their exchange was limited. I somehow knew exactly what was being said and heard.

These days we might say that I found Charlie Brown "relatable." But I don't think the word captures the unsettling and exhilarating surprise I felt at this moment. Relatability describes the reassurance of seeing familiar feelings and traits of our own reflected in someone else. The little jolt I got from this strip came, on the contrary, from being told something new and unsuspected about myself. Until this moment, I'd had no awareness of the frustration I now felt so palpably, the frustration of *my* character not being established despite being already five, *more* than five.

In simply naming my barely felt sense of not being quite sure of who I was and what I was supposed to be doing in this world, the *Peanuts* strip offered a remedy of sorts. Lucy's psychiatric booth created a space in which Charlie Brown's and therefore my own confusion and anxiety could be heard.

That strip ignited a passion for Schulz's creation, not to mention books more generally, that abides to this day. Reading it through the course of my childhood gave shape to my inadequacy, insecurity, rage, cruelty, envy, self-regard and desperation, as well as to my occasional joy and hilarity—in short, to the whole landscape of my inner life. It's when it unsettles rather than confirms our pictures of the world and of ourselves that a book is most thrilling and most transformative.

But the strip was still more than the sum of its characters and stories; it modelled an orientation to life rooted in careful attention. Its observation of the languages of gesture and expression was so close and precise and yet so gentle, it seemed as though a benign adult friend was listening to me intently without intruding or judging or imposing his own interpretation on what he heard. *Peanuts*, you could almost say, was my first psychoanalyst.

Having always been wary of books (and people) that tell us how to live and what to do, I'm alive to the irony of having written this one. It's a book that comes out of many years of listening to people and reading fiction. But can these occupations be the basis for general guidance on how to live? What do the best novels and psychoanalysis have in common if not a suspicion of reductive generalisations, ready-made answers and one-size-fits-all prescriptions for life?

Literature and psychoanalysis are both efforts to make sense of the world through stories, to discover the recurring problems and patterns and themes of life. Read and listen enough, and we soon come to notice how insistently the same struggles, anxieties and hopes repeat themselves down the ages and across the world.

A lifetime reading fiction and fifteen years practising psychotherapy have given me a small window into our common experience: I am clear that even a childhood rich in love and security will see its fair share of sadness and pain; that no one passes through adolescence without being flooded by confusion; that there is no purely happy marriage or family; that no one can get old without confronting the looming spectre of their own death.

In fiction as in the consulting room, different life stories abound with mutual echoes and resonances, bringing out not only what our lives have in common, but what sets them apart. And this is where fiction and psychotherapy come into their own. We may recognise aspects of ourselves in a fictional character or psychotherapeutic case study; but we will also be struck by the singularity of each of them, their tenacious attachment to being themselves and no one else.

The self-help genre, it seems to me, goes awry when it tries to override the distinctness of our selves and our stories and prescribe rigidly generalised rules and formulae for how a person should be. Something similar could be said for psychotherapy: a patient wants above all to be heard as a person rather than a case, an individual with a unique history and personality, not an impersonal cluster of symptoms. Psychotherapy is about discovering *this* person, not a composite type.

When psychotherapy is successful, it works in much the way that great fiction works: that is, it induces the near-miraculous sensation of the very core of ourselves being seen. It sets a mirror before us, in which we see not only the self we know, but the self we don't. We discover regions of ourselves we were barely aware of, to sometimes exhilarating and sometimes distressing effect. The *Peanuts* gang had helped me discover strange, barely acknowledged layers of my internal world. In my subsequent reading life, a host of fictional characters—Emma Woodhouse, say, or Hamlet, or Joseph K. or Willy

Wonka or Emma Bovary—have had the same effect, confronting me with the same, perpetually surprising question: am I really like that? Which is the very question, of course, that repeatedly arises in the course of a psychoanalytic treatment.

What cuts across these two very different vocations of fiction and psychotherapy is the supreme value of listening. A psychoanalyst must make herself receptive to many different currents of communication, verbal and non-verbal, conscious and unconscious. She must attend to what her patient says as well as to the stray and often surprising thoughts and sensations he evokes in her. A fiction writer must be similarly attentive to his own creations, eking out the nuances and rhythms of speaking and moving and feeling that make his characters who they are. And this too requires a stereophonic listening, to others and to himself.

All this is as true for the person on the couch as it is for the person behind it, and as true for the reader as for the author. Being in therapy is an extended exercise not only in speaking freely but in listening to oneself do so, noticing how we get stuck down habitual, ossified paths of thinking and attempting to find ways to open up new ones. And what is reading a novel if not opening our mind's ear to other voices?

Listen. This is the indispensable lesson psychotherapy and fiction can offer in how to live and what to do. If we can't listen, we can't be surprised, by ourselves or anyone else, nor can we make ourselves available to new thoughts or feelings or perceptions or desires. Listening is the engine of curiosity, and so of change and growth.

"How to Live. What to Do" is the title of a poem by Wallace Stevens that can be found on page 329. Separated from the poem, it seemed an obvious title for a book offering "life lessons," which is one reason I poached it.

But in poaching the title, I also had the poem itself in mind. It's a short yet enigmatic poem, made of simple words, elemental images and steady, stately rhythms. Among its many puzzles is its relationship to its title, which announces a didactic agenda the poem itself seems to withhold. If you come to the end of the poem not much the wiser as to how to live and what to do, it's not because you're being obtuse.

It tells a bare-bones story of a wandering man and his companion seeking the extravagant spectacle of the fullest, most fiery imaginable sun, and stumbling instead across a massive, tufted rock. Resting before it, something unexpected is revealed to them—the high, bare mountain, its ridges "thrown like giant arms among the clouds." Notice the Hemingwayan* austerity of that image, a concentrated expression of the poem's stripped-back sensibility. But more than the sight of this plain, unadorned mass of rock, there is the sound of the wind

---

* A fun if irrelevant aside: in Key West, where they both owned homes, the usually stiff, mild-mannered Stevens once got into a drunken and very ill-advised fistfight with Hemingway. No prizes for guessing who came off worse.

blowing through it, "heroic sound / Joyous and jubilant and sure." It is with this sound that the poem ends.

What does the poem teach us about how to live and what to do? Clearly there are no simple rules or programmes to be extracted. But it offers a life wisdom nonetheless. It presents us with a search for a "sun of fuller fire"—some ultimate object of worship. What if, instead of searching vainly for an elusive entity ahead of us, we stopped at something in front of us, and rested, and listened?

What would it mean to live this way?

This, the focus of meditation, yoga and other Eastern disciplines, is also the aim of psychoanalysis. The difference is that in encouraging us to step back and listen, psychoanalysis isn't directing us to transcend the mess of the world but to deepen and enrich our involvement in it.

Psychoanalysis is not a way of distancing oneself from life but, on the contrary, of feeling more alive in it. It nurtures a receptive curiosity and concern for all the colours and textures of life, an availability to the full range of experience rather than the edited highlights in which we look prettiest, happiest and most youthful.

In the chapters that follow, we'll explore how this orientation to living can be facilitated (and frustrated) in eight stages of life, from childhood to old age. Our companions in this task will be major characters from over two centuries of fiction, alongside some of the men and women I've worked with in psychotherapy.

We will listen closely with them to the dramas and difficulties of life's stages. In so doing, we'll inevitably find that some lives are more meaningful and fulfilled, while others are more impoverished and frustrated. This is where the value of listening comes into play. However, taking the time to listen to ourselves, whether in psychotherapy or some other form, will not inoculate us against the numberless ways we can be blindsided and deceived by our own unconscious. Who, after all, doesn't regularly wonder why on earth they did or said something, or failed to do so?

But more modestly perhaps, in listening to ourselves we become attuned to at least some of the tricks we play on ourselves. Listening can help us notice especially those errors we can't seem to stop repeating—the bad choices, misjudgements and self-delusions that can make us feel like the hapless annual victims of the same April Fool's prank.

Part of the problem is that we're trapped inside our own heads, unable to see ourselves from the outside. This accounts for why we're so much more adept at pointing out the habitual mistakes of others than our own. Here, fiction can help in ways real-life experience usually can't. What the best fiction does—which is also, hopefully, what the psychoanalyst would do—is help us to experience the same errors and illusions from the inside rather than to view them from on high, to enter the world of the person who made them for long enough to understand why.

This is the viewpoint I'd like us to take up in the course of this book, as we follow twenty-four fictional characters, as well as some non-fictional ones, across eight stages of life.

The first six of the eight chapters that make up this book take us through some of the key phases and milestones—playing, schooling, rebelling, falling in love, nurturing ambitions and marrying—that form the person we become. The last two chapters, on midlife and old age, focus on life after the most urgent questions— what we do, who we'll spend it with, the values we live by—have been settled.

For each chapter, I've chosen three fictional characters reasonably close in age in order to give a loose sense of life as it unfolds for most people. As I see only adults clinically, this has been neither possible nor especially desirable for the psychotherapy cases I discuss. The value of a patient's insights into school or ambition or marriage rarely correlates to their age. It is in their shared life problems and dilemmas, rather than their ages or specific life circumstances, that the fictional characters and psychotherapeutic cases overlap. Fictional characters offer us ways of attending closely to the questions that confront nearly all of us by virtue of the simple fact of being alive: what kind of person would I like to be? What kind of life would it be worth living?

While the youngest character discussed is aged six (characters any younger are rare in fiction), the centrality of our earliest years in forming who we become is a basic premise of this book.

The lessons that follow are journeys into the dilemmas, confusions, desires and hopes that make a life, and reflections on how we can best live with and make use of them. While they may offer little in terms of moral instruction or practical life hacks, I hope they prove useful in a different, perhaps more durable way.

How to Live. What to Do

I

Childhood Part 1: Play

i "Let's pretend": Alice

A, seven, was notably excitable throughout today's assessment. Parents described her in state of heightened confusion following an outdoor sleep in yesterday's unusually warm afternoon sun. Spoke rather breathlessly of series of peculiar exchanges and adventures with domestic, wild and extinct animal species, as well as a range of evidently thought-disordered and verbally abusive adult men and women, raising possible safeguarding concerns. Given many incidents she describes incompatible with laws of gravity and biological development, likely that heatstroke has affected apprehension of space and time. Seems nonetheless to have emerged from these experiences relatively unscathed, describing them as "silly" and "curious" and giving surprising impression of being amused by them. Long-term monitoring advised; delayed trauma cannot be discounted.

I was ten by the time I came to read *Alice's Adventures in Wonderland* (1865) and *Through the Looking-Glass* (1871), three years older than Alice herself. School at the time seemed to me like one long, perpetual demand to "be sensible." The imaginative anarchy of play was giving way to the competitive rigours of sport, a fairly disastrous development from my perspective.

No sooner was I following the White Rabbit down the hole with Alice than I knew she and I would be lifelong companions. While the adult world was sending me the message that I needed to start placing truth above fiction, the real above the imaginary, *Alice* was showing me that, in the words of Picasso, "Everything we can imagine is real."

Twenty-five years later, at the first parents' evening of my first child, I realised not everyone feels the same way.

From the moment we sat down, the early-years teacher seemed distinctly nervy and apologetic. Walking across the scratched parquet floor, I'd already felt a little as though I were approaching the dock at my show trial, anticipating the teacher-judge looking down from on high and pronouncing her terrible verdict: "You are the most pathetically inept parents in recorded history," adding with a finger pointed my way, "Especially you."

But as she stumbled her way through our son's reassuringly unremarkable termly attainments, my dread gave way to concern. Why did she seem so distressed? What terrible truth was it her burden to reveal?

"Look, he's a lovely child!" she blurted, nodding furiously, as though having to insist on this point in the face of our vehement denials.

A silence followed, a Mexican stand-off in a gunfight no one could remember starting. And then she stood up, toppling her low schoolroom chair, clomping to the nearby wall. She pointed to a drawing: a long oblong outline randomly patched with red crayon, a smiley face hanging off one end of it. It was much like the thirty-four drawings around it, if decidedly at the lower end of the scale of technical accomplishment. At the base of the paper were a few lines of adult handwriting.

"Look!" she ordered. "We asked the children to draw any animal they liked, then we asked them what it was. Do you see? We wrote down the conversation here, at the bottom." Pointing to and enunciating every word in the same loud monotone, she read, " 'What is it?' / 'It's a crac-prac!' / 'What's a crac-prac?!' / 'A crac-prac is a croc-proc!!' " And with that, she raised her forearms and eyeballs heavenward and cried out, "That makes *no* sense!"

I glanced over at my wife. Her brow was knitted so tightly I wondered if it would ever unravel. My mouth opened, emitting sound but no words.

The story of my son's picture and its caption came to mind as I was thinking about the wisdom of the *Alice* books, most obviously because of those nonsense words, with their echo of "Jabberwocky," in the sensuous mouth-pleasures of sound we discover as babies and rediscover in poetry and song.

I tend to think of that parents' evening as something like a preposterously banal episode of *Alice's Adventures in Wonderland*. Surely verbal nonsense is the very stuff of daily life to a primary school teacher? Isn't a Reception teacher who complains about small children talking nonsense worryingly nonsensical herself, a little like a Year 11 teacher lamenting his pupils being sullen or self-conscious?

Our son's teacher struck me as a kind of anti-Alice. She left me wondering how the world would look and feel if schools trained children from the first to renounce nonsense, play and disorder. She speaks for just the kind of joyless pedantry overthrown with such wonderful abandon by both *Alice* (the book) and Alice (the character).

There's nothing all that exceptional about Alice. Unlike a lot of Victorian child heroines, she's no paragon of angelic wisdom and delicacy. She is stubborn, awkward, impatient, often daft; she is, in short, a kid. But then why is she the first stop on our literary life journey? What does a kid like Alice have to tell us about how to live and what to do?

Perhaps the most important insight into childhood we glean from psychoanalysis is that we forget most of it, particularly the parts that most matter. The years up to three or four tend especially to be shrouded in a fog of amnesia. Our childhood feelings become ever more inaccessible to us. The sheer intensity of our daily life experiences come to seem to us comical and alien. We laugh at the sobbing, screaming, tyrannical monster we once were, as though they had nothing to do with who we are now.

This chasm between adult and child is as much a problem for adults as it is for children. The Hungarian psychoanalyst Sándor Ferenczi called it a "confusion of tongues"; adults and children seem to speak the same language but are separated by a cognitive and emotional chasm that mires them in permanent misunderstanding. The child's world is too elastic and excitable, the adult's too rule-bound and repressed. The child doesn't yet know what an adult mind is like; the adult has forgotten what it is to inhabit a child's mind. That teacher was right in a way: it *doesn't* make any sense.

This might be one explanation for why we write and read stories. Stories, and especially the ones we come to love as children, loosen the grip of logic and law on our inner lives. They help us reach the child still lurking in us, whose playfulness hasn't been entirely crushed by the demands of the adult world—don't make up silly stories, don't excite yourself, don't be childish.

One of the most common ways this conflict between child and adult realities manifests itself is in our different experiences of time. "Not being childish" means conformity to a regimented clock-time, adapting oneself to rhythms, schedules and speeds imposed from the outside. When I recall my own childhood, it often comes back to me as a relentless montage of irritable adults telling me to hurry up, get on with it, stop dawdling.

When I talk to a friend about this, she relates an exchange with her daughter, then aged about six. Anxious to get to a scheduled appointment, my friend told her daughter to hurry up, they had to leave, that moment. Her daughter remained impassive, sitting on the carpet absorbed in the intrigues unfolding between the various toy farm animals she was playing with. "Come on, Rosie, we must go!" Still no answer. "Rosie!" she shouted. "Stop taking your sweet time! Stop being so childish!"

Rosie turned her clear blue gaze on her mother and said, "But, Mum, I am a child."

Rosie's gentle protest illustrates more lucidly than any theory could the value of a child's right to inhabit the time and space of play. In Alice's dreamworlds, time won't be pressed into a single, uniform rhythm. It can pass with breathless speed or easy leisure, collapsing anarchically at one moment, expanding languidly the next. Every character, every region of these imaginary worlds, forges its own rules of time and space.

One of the most reliable ways to reconcile this conflict of perspectives is to read a story together. When bedtime rolls around, we may be itching to recover our own time and space. We will often have spent the entire day trying to impose adult rules and disciplines and agendas, to cajole our children into conforming to the world as we see it, into moving at our pace, only to be left reeling with exhaustion and defeat. Story times create a space in which we're licensed for a while to suspend the conflict between our reality and theirs. Parent and child alike can forget all we've told them about the impassable laws of physics, morality and self-preservation, and enter a world—like Wonderland, or the Looking-Glass—where none of these apply.

At seven and a half, Alice is well past early childhood. Very much the older child forever protesting that she's not a baby, she likes to assume an exaggeratedly sensible posture while remaining a child nonetheless. More than anything else, what separates her mind from an adult's is her casual indifference to the boundary between reality and illusion.

Alice's favourite phrase, we're told, is "Let's pretend." It's the one phrase I recall from first reading *Alice*. The world seemed to me at that time to be brimming with adults telling me to stop daydreaming. Schoolteachers warned my parents that if I didn't drag my head out of the clouds soon, I'd continue to underachieve.

Twenty-two years later, I began psychoanalysis, which led in turn to my starting the long process of training to be an analyst. It strikes me that through all these years on either side of the couch, that daydreaming child has never been far away.

The people I see in analysis are adults rather than children. They come with all kinds of troubles and maladies. But it's surprising how often the same inchoate feeling will be expressed by otherwise very different individuals—of being blocked or inhibited. "It feels like I no longer know how to be who I am. Almost like I don't remember," a patient says to me in a first meeting. When we're in this state, the world seems rigid, a series of roadblocks in the face of every change or development we try to effect, so that we too end up feeling perpetually stuck and anxious.

What if this feeling has something to do with no longer being able to say, "Let's pretend"? This is a question posed by the British psychoanalyst Donald Winnicott, whose thinking had a profound and immediate effect on me when I first came across it, around the time I began my analysis.

A paediatrician as well as a psychoanalyst, Winnicott was gifted with an almost eerie capacity to attune himself to the ways in which children think and feel. His most important insight is that play is the basic mode of a child's existence. For a child, the imaginary world feels at least as real as the "real" world, and probably more so. We cannot feel properly alive in adulthood, he suggested, if in early childhood we've not known what it is to pretend, to experience the intimacy and permeability of real and imaginary worlds.

To say we're blocked or unable to be our true selves is to realise we've lost contact with the impulse to play, that the dividing line in our own minds between what is real and what isn't has become too stark. The effect of this line on imaginative and creative lives is debilitating. This is why Winnicott insists that a child's adult carers should never dictate to them what is real and what isn't.

Telling Alice that her kitten doesn't know how to play chess won't help her grow up. On the one hand, she knows that perfectly well. On the other, if she's allowed to reserve a space in herself where her kitten *can* play chess, her imaginative range and curiosity will only be enriched.

This is how she's able to move with such open curiosity and easy acceptance through the anarchic and disturbing dreamworlds of Wonderland and Looking-Glass. She simply has no use for the objection that this or that isn't real. In Alice's world, reality and illusion are intimate friends.

This isn't to say she doesn't protest against the anomalies and oddities of Wonderland and Looking-Glass. But it's not their unreality she objects to. At tea with the Hatter and the March Hare, she takes in her stride the fact that time is stuck permanently at six o'clock; she is bothered only by their rude and inhospitable behaviour. "It's the stupidest tea-party I ever was at in all my life!" she complains, reacting to a violation of the laws of the physical universe with the kind of offhand dismissiveness you might recognise if you've ever watched kids' reactions to a poor birthday party entertainer.

When, without warning, the White Queen metamorphoses into a sheep, who happens to be a clerk in a shop, whose sale items float away the moment Alice looks at them, she says ("in a plaintive tone"), "Things flow about so here!," sounding roughly as alarmed as someone who's found a stray melon in the dairy section.

Alice doesn't need the world around her to conform to the logic of ordinary reality. She just prefers it not to be annoying. In small, everyday matters, children demand consistency, reliability, regularity. Objects should be easy to pick up, people (and animals) should be nice; they will be upset by even minor aberrations from these norms. But in large matters, like reality itself, they are far more receptive, and more generous towards change and disruption, than we are—or perhaps just more unbothered by them. The Caterpillar smokes a hookah and talks? No big deal. He's short-tempered and haughty? That won't do.

But while expanding exponentially our sense of what's possible, *Alice* also draws a vivid symbolic landscape of what we might call the ordinary madness of childhood. Lewis Carroll employs wild exaggeration and distortion to render childhood experience more precisely. Take physical growth: adults are prone to remember a sentimental and sanitised version of the whole thing, as though our massive, unpredictable gains in height and weight, the elongations of trunk and limbs, the fluctuations in tone and pitch of voice and bodily coordination, all occurred smoothly and evenly.

Alice's Adventures in Wonderland brings to life the experience of growth as a bewildering and disturbing shock to the system. Alice stretches to double her height after eating a small cake and weeps inconsolably, flooding the hall, at the thought of her feet feeling lonely, writing to them to assure them they're not forgotten. As poignant as it is bonkers, Alice's tearful letter to her feet is a reminder of growth as a kind of universal human trauma. Only yesterday, every growing child might want to say, my feet seemed so nearby, and now they've moved all the way down there. Wonderland gives us a wonderful image of how sad and frightening this might feel.

More than one writer—the French poet Stéphane Mallarmé, the Argentinian writer Jorge Luis Borges—has advanced the exhilarating idea that each book is an infinitesimally small piece of one single, endless Book. I've always felt that this idea, unlikely as it might sound, makes perfect sense if you read enough novels. The incidents, descriptions, phrases and images in the book you're reading will always recall the incidents in another, and those in turn will call up the incidents in another, so that even as you're reading one book, you're reading countless others.

For example, I pick up *Through the Looking-Glass* and suddenly find myself reading Kafka.

In the second chapter of *Looking-Glass*, Alice makes a series of frustrating attempts to find her way from the house to the Garden of Live Flowers. She tries one path that seems to lead to it, only to find its arduous twists and turns send her back to the house. So she tries another way, and another, but "do what she would," she is led back to the house each time.

In the opening chapter of *The Castle*, Kafka's K. takes the path that seems to lead toward the Castle, only to find the path turns away from it "as if deliberately . . . and though it did not lead away from the Castle, it got no nearer to it either."

The incident in *The Castle* eerily repeats the one in *Through the Looking-Glass.* In both, the protagonist finds that the very path they thought would take them to their destination instead diverts them from it.

Who hasn't felt the agonising frustration of lighting out for a destination only to find themselves returned, again and again, to their starting point? We can hear this question literally, or at least I can. Mercifully, I have lost count of the number of times I thought I'd driven out of a neighbourhood, only to pass the same kebab shop—which, by this point, has become the undeserving target of my overspilling rage—for the fourth time in ten minutes.

Read more figuratively, Alice's and K.'s predicaments offer us startling reflections of the near-universal feeling we call "stuckness." It may be the single most commonly expressed frustration in my consulting room, partly because it can take on infinite guises. One patient says of her husband, "I keep thinking we've got somewhere, that he's finally heard me, and then he says basically the same, totally enraging thing and we're right back where we started." Another says of his job, "I was offered this crazily good redundancy package—this was my chance to get the hell out—and I turned it down to stay in the exact same job I've hated for so many years."

Alice and K. offer us two very different ways of responding to this predicament. Alice rails against the house for getting in her way (as I do when I see that kebab shop a sixth time). But seeing the garden before her once more, she determines "there was nothing to be done but start again," and this time manages to break through the obstacle to her destination. K., exhausted from the fruitless effort of walking the same endless circuit, "suddenly came to a stop, and could not go on."

In Alice and K., we can see two different ways a child might experience the world and its dangers. Alice seems never to feel herself to be in real danger from anything in her dreamworlds. She is nonchalant before obstacles, frustrations and threats, knowing that she can abolish them at a stroke, in one grand act of imaginative will. The Looking-Glass can't stop her going through it, the house won't get in the way of the garden—under her imagination's imperious rule, the things of the world are her servants, not her masters, even if it can sometimes appear otherwise. Perhaps, deep down, she knows that it's her dream to do with as she chooses.

But not every child will feel so free and secure inside their own minds. The imaginative verve and confidence we see in a child such as Alice can very easily be damaged by material and emotional impoverishment, violence and persecution. The dream of Wonderland and the nightmare of K.'s village are psychological neighbours. As a certain world leader reminds us many times each day, fantasies of omnipotence, of total control over the world, are never far from feelings of total impotence and inadequacy. Of course, this is something we all know deep down. Is there an employee or parent or any other human being who hasn't experienced that alarmingly rapid internal shift from feeling like a seasoned professional to feeling completely useless?

Alice's dreamworld shows us a child's inner landscape writ large, where she reigns supreme. But the village in which K. arrives is the projection of a more traumatised inner world, infused with the sense of his own helplessness and despair. When he fails repeatedly to reach the Castle, he doesn't have the childlike optimism that would spur him to "start again," but simply falls into exhausted resignation.

Perhaps, then, we should use these books to cheerlead for Alice's "positive" against K.'s "negative" thinking?

If literature and psychoanalysis have taught me anything, it's the importance of being in touch with the full range of our thoughts and feelings, not just those that make us feel good. Sometimes the feeling of being stuck can be the prelude to an imaginative leap like Alice's, leaving us feeling like the superhero child triumphing over the world. At others it can leave us feeling like the helpless child defeated by the world. Perhaps you can grab that redundancy package with both hands and reinvent your life. Or perhaps your unhappiness at work has come to feel so much a part of you that you can't imagine life without it. A fully lived life will be open to both kinds of experience.

Alice's capacity to say "Let's pretend," to be imaginatively receptive to any possibility, however strange or outlandish, starts to look peculiarly like an indispensable life skill, a source of adventurousness and courage.

The problem is that age will inevitably make us wary of imaginative leaps, and more willing to stay stuck in the known malaise of the present than to leap into an unknown future.

As life goes on, we complain about the unavoidable effects of ageing—on our adolescent skin, our middle-aged memory, our elderly bones. We tend to be less vocal about its corrosive effect on our imagination. Perhaps we are pleased to be rid of our topsy-turvy, whimsical childhood fancies, to leave them behind along with Santa Claus and the Tooth Fairy.

We may be relieved above all to settle into a world of *sense*, the one so prized by my son's Reception teacher, in which what we say is what we mean. Carroll opens the door to the child's experience of language as pleasurable nonsense, a triumph of sound over sense, where there is no necessary correlation between words and things, where crac-pracs are croc-procs. As adults, we tend to use words to secure and clarify our knowledge of the world around us—the objects on which I'm now sitting and writing feel more solid and real when I call them "chair" and "desk." For those who have grown up a little too much, there's something frightening about imaginative play and its capacity to make all that's solid dissolve into air.

In Alice's dreamworlds, as Humpty Dumpty famously says, "when *I* use a word . . . it means just what I choose it to mean." In the constrained reality of adults, we expect words to have fixed meanings so that we can understand one another. But in the imaginary play of the child, words can be used to make and unmake the world at will.

In growing up, we railroad our words and minds into accepting a constricted version of "reality." This guarantees a certain level of social conformity and life competence. Neither of these benefits should be dismissed. We need to live in a world that is reliable and secure, that will look and feel tomorrow much as it did today. But lose contact entirely with the wild chaos of Wonderland and we cut ourselves off from the fundamental sources of creativity and invention.

In embracing the robust clarity of adulthood, we lose the very thing that can make adulthood rich and meaningful. There is no better way to sap a person's vitality and creativity than to renounce one's "childish" imagination in the name of a grey "realism." That realism, sometimes confused with "normality," is not as natural to us as we might believe. Think of the gleeful pleasure we take in the nonsensical narratives and words of our dreams, or the numerous strange ways our unconscious minds express themselves in our "slips" and inexplicable actions.

In other words, we all think and do crazy stuff, even if we dismiss such things as accidents, stuff we didn't really "mean." Perhaps our creative and imaginative lives—not just in the form of art, but of science, the built environment, business, even politics—would be enhanced if we related to this inner craziness with the unjudging curiosity of Alice, rather than the corrective wagging of a Reception teacher's finger? Perhaps we might just be saner as well as more creative if we could embrace the illogical and the impossible, instead of dismissing them as aberrations from adult "normality," mere childishness.

The world today, however, seems to be firmly under the sway of the grey realists, for whom the rearing and education of children are matters of their eventual entrance into a society of productive and solvent adults. In this and many other countries, children are subjected to attainment targets in literacy and numeracy from the moment they enter nursery. In the course of schooling, subjects that cultivate imaginative and creative life—art, music, drama, dance—are being squeezed out of curricula in favour of the practical disciplines that better serve the needs of the future economy.

This conception of childhood as adulthood in waiting, a kind of proving ground for the assumption of skills, competencies and responsibilities, is hardly confined to education systems. Childhood as a space of play and unstructured exploration is being lost every day—to child labour and war in poor countries, to the growing pressures of familial and societal expectation in rich ones.

Lost childhood, and its effect on the adults we become, has turned out to be one of the most insistent themes of my daily work in the consulting room. I'm not sure I've ever felt the force of that loss more palpably than with

Ernesto, a high-flying junior executive in a shipping corporation.

Before completing his American MBA and moving to London, Ernesto had grown up in a wealthy suburb of São Paulo. When I asked him about his earliest memories, he struggled to recall the smallest detail. When I pressed him, he said, "I can see myself, maybe two or three, sitting on the carpet of our living room, staring out at the sun on our perfectly manicured lawn." Over the years that followed, he and his older sister were told never to run on the grass—"You'll spoil it," his father explained.

His detailed memories began only from the age he was old enough to sit at a desk and work. From around the age of five, his parents had instituted a demanding and carefully monitored regime of homework and extracurricular activity—English, Japanese, cello, judo, chess—that left no time for outdoor play or indoor loafing. "I remember hearing the doorbell ring and coming out of my bedroom onto the landing," Ernesto told me. "I could hear the voice but not the words of a kid from down the street on the doorstep, and then my mother's response, loud and clear: 'No, Ernesto is busy. He can't come out to play now.'"

"Coming out to play" became the source of a distressing split in Ernesto's mind, between the child who longed to claim his own childhood and the compliant miniature adult who had to make his parents' denigration of play his own. When he dared to ask why he couldn't occasionally say yes to the visiting kid, his mother looked stricken with disappointment: "All these opportunities we give you and this is how you repay us? You want to run around with this kid!"

Ernesto learned to expunge from the repertory of possible occupations anything that fell short of a maximally productive use of his time. No play, but also no laughter, no boredom, no staring out the window or lying on the grass, nothing that could conceivably interfere with the regime of training in seriousness. For this legacy, Ernesto insisted, he was very grateful to his parents; they had taught him the value of hard work and responsibility.

I caught the true measure of just how comprehensively this regime had shaped Ernesto's character early on in our work. He arrived one morning visibly fuming and related an abortive effort at starting an office romance. The young woman in question had clearly responded to him, and it wasn't difficult to see why: he was a model of professional dynamism, chiselled features and sharp tailoring, not to mention impeccable manners. It took still less effort to see why this figure of the corporate knight might be as comical as he was attractive—at least for anyone other than Ernesto himself.

"So I asked her if she would like to accompany me to dinner," he told me, fixing his gaze on mine, "and *she laughed in my face.*"

"Hmm. Just laughed? No words?"

"Oh yes, words! You know what she asked me! 'Why? Do you need accompanying to dinner?' Do I need accompanying to dinner!" he repeated, then sat for a moment, wide-eyed and open-mouthed. "Like she was trying to humiliate me. Do I look like I need accompanying to dinner? I had a mind to tell her no, I certainly do not. I am not a child, I can assure you! But I was unsettled. I just smiled weakly and said, 'Well, let me know,' and walked away."

I was aware of just how close I was to playing out a version of the same scene by bursting out laughing. I was rescued only by the intense and entirely real distress and fury I could see in his face as he now sat silently, eyes boring into the floor. I remarked that she seemed to have left him feeling very angry indeed.

Radiating incredulity, he replied, "You were expecting perhaps a different reaction, Dr. Cohen?" Ernesto's English, like everything else he'd learned, was just a little too immaculate, as though he'd acquired fluency purely by binge-watching 1950s government information films.

I paused. "Well, it sounds to me like she was having fun. You, on the other hand, were not."

"On that point you are most certainly correct! But perhaps this is a failure of mine? Perhaps if you asked a lady to dinner and she laughed in your face and made a sarcastic remark, you would think it was all great fun."

We were silent for a while and he shuffled agitatedly in his seat, evidently as furious with me as he'd been with her. Eventually I said, "You seem to be enjoying this exchange about as much as you enjoyed that one."

He looked by this point like a man holding on for dear life to the last, fraying thread of his courtesy. "It seems as though this is some kind of a joke to you. Perhaps you're trying to make a point, but I'm afraid I am not grasping it."

"You feel I'm just teasing you, just like you felt she was."

This seemed to stop him in his tracks for a moment. "Aren't you? And wasn't she?"

I was quiet again as he rubbed his palms together, looking agonised. "I just think that if you ask a simple question, you should be able to expect a simple answer. But in my experience, and I mean no disrespect to them, this is not what young women do. You know, this is not the first time this has happened! I have asked other young women to dinner since I arrived in this country, and almost every one of them has laughed or said something that sounded mocking. From which I have reluctantly concluded I hold no appeal for the fairer sex. I sense this amuses you."

I'm tempted to say that Ernesto was formulating a theory of verbal communication here, the basic outline of which was that there should be no gap between what we say and what we mean. To be ambiguous, to play with the meanings of one's words instead of stating them as plainly as possible, was a kind of wilful cruelty.

Never having learned to play, Ernesto was another anti-Alice. He clung to his rigidity of thought and action as though his life depended on it. The strict correspondence between words and meanings was a principle of quasi-religious faith for him. Jokes offended this principle, so any joke addressed to him could only be at his expense; he could never hear in it an invitation to laugh with it or to participate in it, to join in the game. But then, how could he? He had no idea how to play it, barely an idea it was a game at all.

Once I got past the comic absurdity of this predicament, I found it made me deeply sad. Ernesto's character, it seemed to me, had been formed by a profound emotional deprivation, an exclusion from his daily life of a basic human impulse. Now he was a handsome and successful young man who couldn't get a date. Having been conditioned to disdain play, he was unable to see why it was so central to human relationships, especially the kind driven by sexual desire. "She just teased me," he complained, apparently deaf and blind to the possibility of teasing as a vehicle of mutual interest and seduction.

Ernesto gave me some sense of what can happen when parents or other adults denigrate play. The teasing that upset him so much was a kind of verbal sport, playing on the different ways he might have taken what she said. On the surface, "Do you need accompanying to dinner?" signifies "Are you a little boy who can't eat by himself?" This was all Ernesto could hear—no wonder he was so affronted. Lacking the feel for play, he couldn't pick up the more seductive undercurrent: "Or are you a man asking out a woman?"

Childhood play, in other words, doesn't end with childhood. And it's no coincidence that it persists into adult life most palpably in our erotic lives: playing, teasing, cavorting, frolicking, messing around—these are words that simultaneously evoke the excitable, competitive and occasionally cruel world of the children's playground and the pleasures of the adult bedroom. Play is the source of many different modes of aliveness.

Ernesto's mother had taught him to be wary of girls, and he was beginning to understand why. He would present them with the seriousness and sincerity of his desire for them, and they responded with giggles, smiles and oblique words. Having concluded his terminal lack of appeal to "the fairer sex," he recalled his mother's warning about girls and lamented its prescience: "Just remember, Ernesto, to them everything is a game."

"And that's a bad thing?" I said.

"Again, you sound like you're playing with me, Dr. Cohen. You seemed to me to be a serious man, but I'm frankly beginning to doubt it."

"Well, maybe we're getting somewhere then."

He remained silent for a few moments, as though trying very hard to understand what I'd just said. Then, with an unmistakable look of surprise, he laughed out loud.

ii "Now you've spoiled it!": Bunny Morison

BM, eight, appeared sullen and fearful from beginning of assessment. When asked why he seemed so upset, shed a few tears but otherwise did not respond. After waiting a couple of minutes, said he wanted his mother.

But reassurance he would surely see her soon only amplified distress. After some gentle probing, spoke of his unhappiness at home. Father liable to impatience with him, felt rejected by brother for being "weak" and a "cry baby." Only when asked about his mother did mood perceptibly lighten. He felt safe with her, she appreciated his jokes and games. Then paused and became melancholy again, saying he was worried about her, but declining to say why.

Donald Winnicott talks of "transitional space," the area of early life experience in which the real and imagined mingle indistinguishably, as when a toddler talks to his teddy. Ernesto was deprived of any feeling for what Winnicott calls the value of illusion. A certain kind of adult—Mr. Spock, say, or Ernesto's parents—might chide him for his silly delusions, explaining that teddy bears don't speak or have feelings; a more attuned adult would show discretion and leave the child to his tête-à-tête, seeing that he is opening a space for his imaginative life inside the external, objective world.

Reading *Alice* is exhilarating for the sense we have of its author as someone in constant contact with his own spirit of play. Much of what happens in psychoanalytic work, as in Ernesto's case, is about what follows when this contact is prematurely curtailed.

The eight-year-old Bunny Morison, one of the three protagonists of William Maxwell's novel *They Came Like Swallows*, is an anxious and delicate boy whose imaginative life is a fragile retreat from the hostile world around him.

The first part of Maxwell's novel is narrated from Bunny's perspective. In the second we follow his elder brother Robert, a boy both emotionally and physically more robust than Bunny, despite the loss of his leg in a buggy accident caused by his aunt's reckless boyfriend; in the third, the focus shifts to their grieving father, James. The book, in other words, is about members of a family whose individual and shared sense of security is menaced by external dangers and internal fears. And lurking behind all these threats is the 1918 Spanish flu pandemic, creeping ominously through the household.

It is difficult to write those words without feeling deeply unsettled by them. I chose to write about *They Came Like Swallows* long before the coronavirus unleashed terror and misery on the world. Rereading it in these times has been a strange and eerie solace, a reminder of how different both art and real life can look when cast in one another's shadow.

In March 2020, as the coronavirus raged, must-read lists of dystopian novels from Camus's *The Plague* to Emily St. John Mandel's *Station Eleven* began to spread alongside it. With uncanny percipience, these books anticipated the damage wrought by an imagined pandemic to the fabric of civilisation.

They Came Like Swallows appeared on none of these lists. Published in 1937, it doesn't predict an imagined future horror, but memorialises an actual and recent one.

Its canvas is not the broad one of a total society but the miniature one of a single family. As sparse in external incident as it is rich in interior drama, it explores how the basic security of our relationships and our sense of self can be irreparably damaged by events beyond our control.

In the weeks following the outbreak of the virus in the UK, the resonance of this theme hit me hard. Lockdown conditions forced me, like all my colleagues, to move my psychoanalytic practice out of the consulting room and onto a digital platform. Having conducted no more than a handful of phone or teleconferencing sessions annually over the last decade, I was now listening and speaking to pixelated men and women in an empty room for eight or nine hours a day.

Psychotherapy ordinarily offers a space of continuity in an unstable world. Now it was as helplessly swept up in the crisis as everything and everyone else. So many of the elements that ensure its atmosphere of safety and reliability disappeared overnight: the therapist's physical proximity, the sealed-off privacy of the consulting room, its sense of insulation from the world outside. Many of my patients were now bringing acute distress and anxiety to a screen, as small children and pets hovered agitatedly outside bedroom or study doors.

What was happening in psychotherapy was only a concentrated instance of what was happening everywhere; the world we had long taken for granted was being withdrawn from us. The fears that devil so many children at night—that their parents will go out never to return, that a monster or ghost will steal in and do them evil, that the world they know and love will simply evaporate overnight—were becoming the fears of our daylit reality.

Clare, isolated and alone in her flat, seemed to edge closer with each session to the state of this frightened child. She was ravaged by fear for her elderly, frail father, whom she couldn't stop from going out and who surely wouldn't survive the virus if he caught it. Her face was much closer to mine than it would have been in the consulting room; yet as she sobbed uncontrollably, lamenting repeatedly that she just didn't know what to do, the space between us felt like an unbridgeable chasm. Her distance from me only amplified her fright at being cut adrift from everything that had kept her life in place.

But this wasn't everyone's story. Some patients spoke of lockdown as a surprising rediscovery of what really mattered to them, of the strengthening of frayed marital bonds, of their children's delight at the sudden glut of parental presence and attention, of the unanticipated pleasure of enforced stillness. Remote psychotherapy for these men and women, while frustrating, wasn't unbearable. As Harry, a married father in his forties, said to me, "After coming to you for so long, I feel like I've got enough of you stored up in me to fill in the gap between the screen you and the real you."

Isolation was a radically different experience for Harry than for Clare. Where Clare had severed her connections to the world beyond herself, Harry was surrounded by a family who filled his days with ordinary pleasures and irritations, helping him to feel loved and needed. Harry continued to feel a sense of his own substantiality, where Clare was being rapidly emptied of herself.

Winnicott talks about psychoanalysis as two people playing together, and this creative quality of the work was nicely preserved in Harry's remote sessions. He could joke mordantly about the prison of his present, remember and reinterpret various stages of his past, project different possibilities for himself into the future. Clare, on the other hand, could not think or feel beyond the immediacy of her crippling fears for her father. She could use her sessions only to give voice to those fears. Psychotherapy as a space for imaginative play had been indefinitely suspended.

They Came Like Swallows offers a lot of insight into this difference. The novel revolves around Elizabeth Morison, whom we see only through the eyes of her children and husband. She is the centrifugal force of their world, shaping their everyday lives through the love and care she daily bestows on each of them. More than this, she is the source of their very sense of reality.

Winnicott suggests that the strength and depth of our creativity are determined by the quality of the maternal presence* in our early lives. Our sense of permeability between the real and imaginary worlds is nurtured or

---

* I say "maternal presence" rather than "mother" because this function can be fulfilled by adult carers other than a mother.

diminished by the adults who care for us. A child can discover in her mother a companion in imaginative life, someone who can listen to and participate in her stories and ideas of imaginary friends and secret, invisible places; or, like Ernesto, she can find an antagonist of her inner world who tells her she must face reality "like a grown-up" and stop messing about.

Maxwell has a similar sense of the place of a mother in her children's inner lives. Bunny's capacity to play with, explore and remake the reality around him is entirely dependent on his mother's presence.

A mother's emotional steadiness and reliability provide a kind of lining for the agitations and uncertainties of her child's feelings, enabling him to explore his inner life without being hampered by fear and anxiety. But for Bunny, this feeling of imaginative freedom is entirely dependent on his mother being around.

When a child invests so totally in a single human being, everyone and everything else is bound to become an object of fear and suspicion. Bunny's mother is quite literally the centre of his world:

> If his mother was not there . . . nothing was real to Bunny—or alive . . . The vermilion leaves and yellow leaves folding and unfolding upon the curtains depended utterly upon his mother. Without her they had no movement and no color.
>
> . . . All the lines and surfaces of the room bent toward his mother . . . And in a way he was more dependent

upon her presence than the leaves or flowers. For it was the nature of his possessions that they could be what they actually were and also at certain times they could turn into knights and crusaders, or airplanes, or elephants in a procession. If his mother went downtown to cut bandages for the Red Cross (so that when he came home from school he was obliged to play by himself) he could never be sure that the transformation would take place.

If his mother is not around, Bunny's rich imagination and emotional security evaporate. Without her presence, life becomes a torment of deprivation and anxiety:

> If his mother were not there to protect him from whatever was unpleasant . . . what would he do? Whatever would become of him in a world where there was neither warmth nor comfort nor love?

We only realise the terrible poignancy of that question later, when Elizabeth succumbs to the Spanish flu. Bunny's horror of his mother's even temporary absence looks in the light of her eventual death like the expression of an eerie foreboding.

But in asking himself what he'd do without his mother to protect him, Bunny isn't prophesying her death. A child who feels his mother single-handedly holds his world together is bound to feel perpetually apprehensive about the possibility of a world without her. All separations, even her spending a couple of hours away from

the house, stir up this anxiety, and every new development in his life is filtered through it. When Elizabeth
hints at her pregnancy, hoping to enthuse him with the
prospect of a new playmate, his immediate thought is
"His mother was not satisfied with just him." For Bunny,
the world is a big conspiracy to divide him from the one
person he loves and needs.

Imaginative play, even in as basic a form as staring
into the living-room curtains, is the means by which
Bunny can feel the fullness of being alive. But his mother's absence makes the world seem empty of anything to
play with, a cold and loveless void.

We have all had at least some intuition of this terrifying void as children. But if we can feel we have a
place in the minds of those around us, we are less likely
to be overwhelmed by it. When her dreamworld is at
its most sinister and threatening, Alice can survive and
even thrive by playing her way through it. Even as her
reality is erased and remade, she retains her capacity to
wonder, question and laugh. Bunny's sense of his place
in the adult world is far more fragile and precarious. He
has the fearful sense of existing only in the mind of his
mother, so that as soon as she disappears for him, he
effectively disappears for himself.

The difference between Alice and Bunny correlates
strikingly to the different ways my patients experienced
the crisis of the coronavirus. While in touch with his fears
of danger to his family and an uncertain future, Harry
could put enough psychic distance between himself and

the virus to perceive its imaginative and emotional benefits. In stark contrast, Clare's field of vision was filled almost entirely by the prospect of losing her father. In her mind, his loss would empty the world.

Elizabeth protects Bunny "from whatever was unpleasant": that is, "from the weather and from Robert and from his father." It can't be a coincidence that these three "unpleasant" entities will each assume some responsibility for Elizabeth's death. The weather triggers the epidemic; Robert fails to prevent his pregnant mother from entering Bunny's bedroom when he is sick with the flu himself; and, ironically, in taking her on the train journey to secure a safe hospital birth, his father likely causes her to catch the fatal infection.

Bunny is morbidly sensitive to anything that might endanger the continuity of his world. The assurance of Elizabeth's presence frees him to wander through the wilds of his own mind. But the corollary of this freedom is the brittleness of his mood whenever she's not there. Later in the book, we see this from his older brother Robert's perspective, after Robert makes "adjustments" to his younger brother's cardboard creation.

Robert tries to enthuse Bunny about his transformation of his "Belgian village," a First World War battle scene, into an airfield. The younger boy's reaction offers insight into the incessant squabbling of siblings: perhaps the possibility of being displaced or usurped in their parents' affections implants an enduring seed of mistrust of a sibling's every little gesture.

Robert tries to insist that his adjustments to Bunny's cardboard creation are a way of joining in with his game. But Bunny sees Robert's changes as malevolent: "My village . . . you've torn up my Belgian village!" He will not be consoled by Robert's assurances that it can be fixed. "It can't, either. And I wasn't through with it. I was going to play with it a lot more and now you've spoiled it!"

The American developmental psychologist and psychoanalyst Erik Erikson, in his discussions of play and early childhood, pointed to a kind of duality in the function of play. In this regard he followed Freud, who posited one version of play, in his early book on jokes, as a kind of overbrimming, innocent exuberance, a joy in the pleasures of nonsense and make-believe that evokes Alice's dreamworlds.

But there's another side to play, which Freud would discover fifteen years later. Play helps us to take imaginative control of the world. If a bully threatens and humiliates us at school, we can reverse the scenario a few hours later on our bedroom floor; the bully becomes a toy infantryman cowering in terror before the might and rage of the Hulk. This is what Erikson called "prestige through mastery."

If play is a means to such prestige, it becomes easier to see why so much is at stake for Bunny and Robert in their struggle over a length of cardboard. What complicates this struggle is that the siblings yearn to trust one another, even as they're wary of doing so. The sadness of the scene is only deepened by Robert noticing that

Bunny, just before he howls in protest, is "hovering on the edge of pleasure."

As the younger of two brothers, I'm spooked by a flash of recognition of this moment: that pregnant pause in which I tried to work out whether I should be pleased or sad, grateful or furious at my brother's latest antics. Like Bunny, I often chose fury, swerving away from the edge of pleasure and plunging into the depths of pain.

Why should we, or Maxwell, make so much out of a fraternal scrap? But this points to his understated brilliance as a writer: Maxwell introduces us to ordinary domestic life as a crucible of the most intense and dangerous passions. He alerts us to our liability as adults to forget how charged and traumatic our emotional life as children could be.

Perhaps we laughingly dismiss our own children's distress and rage because we can't bear to contemplate the possibility that their pain is real. From the outside, it looks as though Bunny is working himself up over a bit of cardboard. But Maxwell places us inside the long-forgotten inside perspective on this scene, helping us see that the rip in the cardboard is also a tear in Bunny's sense of continuity. Precisely because he longs to believe his brother wants to play with him, he falls prey to the anxious suspicion that his brother is trying to humiliate him. It's a painfully familiar scene. Gripped by the righteous conviction his older brother has spoiled his play, the younger brother can't see the spoiling effect of his own tantrum: "Robert sighed. All he ever wanted to do was play with Bunny. And whatever he did, the result was always the same."

The scene reminds us that when it comes to sibling interaction, we're never quite in control of what we're doing. Robert tells himself he only wanted to make his brother happy; but do we not see an edge of subtle mockery in his "improvements" to Bunny's creation? After all, who knows better than an older brother the sensitivities of the younger one? Bunny, on the other hand, investing his entire faculty of trust in his mother, can only see the cruelty in his brother's intentions.

It's no coincidence that this meltdown occurs just before his mother's departure from the house. Perhaps he intuits that her temporary loss will turn out to be permanent. This is more than enough to undo the coherence and integrity of his world, to create the conditions under which play ceases to be safe. Between them and without really knowing it, Bunny and Elizabeth have forged a dynamic of airless dependency. Its consequences alert us to how risky this kind of dependency can become, for it stakes the child's emotional health entirely on the love and care of a single person, where it too easily becomes stuck. I find it hard not to wonder what kind of love the adult Bunny could bestow on anyone else, or how he would be able to extricate himself from a state of permanent fear, anger and isolation.

The last part of the book points us subtly in this direction. The disintegration of Bunny's world anticipates the hollowed-out grief of his father in the last part of the book. All the anxieties Bunny has secretly harboured of the thinness of his father's love for him are devastatingly confirmed. While his mother was alive, his father's severity and dryness had been lifted by her lightness; after her death, his emotional emptiness becomes fully apparent.

With Elizabeth's death, James's sole line of emotional contact with his children is abruptly eroded. Without her, he can no longer disguise his alienation from them, his total incapacity to enter their world. "In the long run it was a mistake to have children," he reflects. "James did not understand them."

But what is the chasm separating him so definitively from his children? The clue, at once ordinary and terrible, comes as he walks through the burial grounds at Elizabeth's funeral and recalls how, when he was Robert's age, his parents had taken him south for winter—that is, during the years following the Civil War: "They rented a farmhouse on the side of a hill overlooking a Confederate cemetery. And he had no one to play with, being a Northerner, and he wanted to go home."

James's loss of his wife, like Bunny's of his mother, drains his world of colour and light, transporting him back into a place of comfortless isolation, where no one wants to play with him. But it's worth noticing that this personal wound of exclusion is linked by Maxwell to a profound national trauma. A Northern child abandoned to himself by a Confederate cemetery; this is an image of a landscape ravaged by pain, hatred and resentment.

James has invested himself so totally in Elizabeth that he can love his children and even his own life only through her. Perhaps he finally rejects Bunny because he can't help seeing in him the agonising reflection of his own child self. Seen alongside one another, Bunny and his father suggest a lifelong pattern; once total dependency takes hold of a child, it can be fiendishly hard to shake off.

There is not the smallest aspect of personal relations, Maxwell hints, not even the play of children, that remains untouched by the North's humiliating defeat of the South's feudal, slave-owning society and economy. James Morison is just one of innumerable minor casualties of the raging anger and hurt pride tearing through post–Civil War America.

A wounded nation is one whose different factions will not play together, who reject one another's stories, ideas and languages as alien and hostile. The absence of play creates an atmosphere of rejection, suspicion and prejudice.

We can hardly fail to hear the echo of our own societies, the UK and Europe as much as the US, in such a description: rigid lines of demarcation between us and them, the included and the excluded—whether in the form of blue against red states or multiculturalists against nativists. And this atmosphere is felt as much in intimate personal relations as it is in the air of public life and language.

The subtle parallel Maxwell draws between the slights of children and the hostilities of adults has much resonance for me as a psychoanalyst. It's rare that a day passes without the resentments and divisions of the outside world intruding into the consulting room—although perhaps it's wrong to talk of intrusion here, as though the therapist's couch should or could be kept clear of the fault lines running through every other part of our society.

I have sat in silence as a young American woman wept her way through an entire session the morning after the 2016 US election. When I tried to say something about the echoes of the bitter end of her marriage, she told me to shut up: "Don't interpret my rage as being about anything other than what I say it's about. Even if that's true, I'm not ready to hear it. I need to hold my anger close. It feels like it's all I've got right now."

I know how debilitating this kind of rage can be, as though it's jamming up my entire emotional circuitry, cutting me off from empathy and curiosity.

When it overwhelms us, anger blocks our capacity to play. I'm reminded here of Grete, a patient who seemed to want to stretch my capacity for non-judgemental empathy to its very limits. Grete would find occasion repeatedly to interrupt her discussions of her marital and family difficulties and launch into invectives against the "hordes" of Muslim migrants flooding Europe. "I am serious," she would say at these moments. "Deadly serious. This is not a laughing matter."

"I bet you're among the nice liberals," she said to me one morning, seething with savage irony. "You think we have to be kind to the poor refugees. You get taken in by the sad-eyed little boys and girls, the same ones who'll be nursing their hate for you every day, who'll be blowing themselves up on your bus in another ten years. There's nothing worse than a kindly fool."

These words were pure and unambiguous bigotry. And yet I felt inexplicably tender towards Grete at this moment, as though she were less a responsible adult than a vulnerable adolescent resorting to making herself as hateful as possible in some desperate attempt to be noticed.

"Hmm," I said eventually, "you must feel I'm the worst sort of kindly fool, welcoming you in here just so you can nurse your hate for me and blow me up."

A tense pause followed. I had the momentary sensation of hearing her mouth clamp tightly shut, the air steaming out of her flaring nostrils. But what I heard instead was genial laughter. "I know, I'm terrible!" she said, a surprisingly open smile in her voice. "Sometimes I think I just say this stuff so someone will listen. And you, you're stuck here, so you have to listen."

"You imagine I wouldn't listen otherwise?"

She sighed. "I was the kid at primary school no one wanted to play with. Always vying for attention, always desperate to be liked, but always getting it wrong. I would come up to a group of girls and instead of trying to join their game I'd say, 'No, let's play this way!' And they'd tell me to stop being so bossy, go and play with someone else. I'd go to someone else and the same thing would happen . . ."

"And at home?"

"Yes, the same thing, both my parents. 'Mummy, Daddy, can we play?' 'Ach, Grete, not now! Can't you see I'm busy?'" Grete had gleaned early on that her conception had been an "accident." Her parents were always exhausted from gruelling work, and everything from their social lives to the arrangement of their house suggested to her from the youngest age that a child had never been in their plans. The fact that no sibling came after her only confirmed the intuition.

Grete's rage was hardly going to evaporate in a moment, but the tight knots of our interaction began to loosen after this session. She had grown up with no one to play with and so had never learned how to play. In the soil where imagination and empathy might have grown, a brutal "realism" about the essential self-interest and venality of people had taken root.

Psychotherapy introduced her to her own mind, its capacity to imagine and interpret herself and others in different ways, to question her own rigid convictions in how things are. Raised to be compliant and unquestioning, Grete had never known anyone, including herself, to be curious about who she was. From a childhood poor in play, she had grown to an adulthood full of creative and emotional disappointments.

She remembered that exchange about bombs on buses years later. "I was sure even as I said it that this was it, now you'd really hate me and find a way to get rid of me. Instead you made me laugh. I feel like I started learning to talk to people that day. I stopped taking myself so seriously."

"Kind of," I said. "But you also started taking yourself seriously for the first time."

"Yes, true." She paused. "You bloody shrinks. Always have to know better."

iii "Dined on raw squirrels . . .": Scout Finch

SF, six, proved a challenging though rewarding case for assessment. Spoke at great speed, speculating extravagantly about reclusive occupant of neighbouring house, including a suggestion he was eating live animals. Given frequent references to beating others up, including a threat to do same to assessor, these fantasies are likely projections of her own aggression. Death of mother aged two, with unusually strong attachment to father as result, and corresponding idealisation of his intellect and attitude. One elder sibling, to whom she is evidently very close, as well as a male best friend to whom she refers as her fiancé. Notwithstanding concerns about lack of structure in household, coupled with exposure to disturbing material regarding racial and sexual violence in environs, a surprisingly well-adjusted child.

Our last child character in this chapter can hardly be said to suffer from a lack of parental interest or attention, like Bunny (or Grete). And yet she breathes an air dense with hate and mindless prejudice, just the kind of atmosphere that conspires to stifle a child's openness to the world. For Scout, the narrator of Harper Lee's *To Kill a Mockingbird* (1960), the carefree joys of endless childhood summers are revealed in retrospect to have been subtly menaced by racism and intolerance.

Perhaps what makes these glaring contrasts of innocent pleasure and unspeakable horror bearable for us as readers is the sense from the outset that the funny, feisty child Scout has survived in the adult telling her story, which she begins by baldly stating its denouement: "When he was nearly thirteen my brother Jem got his arm badly broken at the elbow." The cause of this break, we're then told, was a subject of debate between Scout and her elder brother for some years after.

We'll eventually discover that the arm was broken by the dirt-poor, racist drunk Bob Ewell, who had been attempting to kill Jem in an act of revenge against Jem and Scout's father, Atticus, who had been acting as attorney for Tom Robinson, the young black man Ewell had falsely accused of raping his daughter. In retrospect, it is evident from this first page that the naive view of young Scout and Jem sits uneasily alongside the perspective of the narrator Scout; for the adult Scout, the injury symbolises the racial and class divisions of the South in the 1930s.

The novel's storytelling masterstroke is to put into practice Atticus's counsel to Scout that she won't understand a person "until you climb into his skin and walk around in it." In other words, she must cultivate empathy, the generosity and expansiveness of her feeling imagination. *To Kill a Mockingbird* is a kind of living testament to this advice, an act of imaginative solidarity by the adult Scout with the child she was, feeling herself into the skin of her younger self.

This generosity must be wrested from the impoverished imaginative life of Maycomb County's white citizens. This isn't to say that Maycomb is poor in stories; on the contrary, the town gossips readily conjure up all kinds of extravagant speculations about their neighbours. But these are not the kind of empathetic gestures Atticus is looking to encourage in Scout, and in fact the wild tales she and Jem pick up about Arthur "Boo" Radley ("about six and a half feet tall . . . dined on raw squirrels and cats . . . a long jagged scar across his face") are more about demonising him than understanding him.

By painting the disabled, housebound Boo Radley as a monster, the Maycomb citizenry's collective imagination serves to stifle empathic curiosity rather than encourage it. In repeating the myths about him, Scout and Jem invert their father's counsel. Instead of walking around in Boo's skin, they shrink from it in fascinated disgust.

This grotesque version of Boo betrays the broader mindset of Maycomb. The gaze that turns Boo into a depraved monster is informed by the same ugly prejudice that fuels racism. As Grete reminded us, prejudice teaches its exponents to see the world with a kind of joyless rigidity. It traps its perpetrators as much as its victims in impoverished forms of thinking and relating. We see this in gross forms of racial hatred and cruelty, such as the threat of the white mob to storm the jail in which Tom is being held, but more subtly in the pinched, defended mindset of the more genteel white citizens. *Mockingbird*, we might say, is about how racism impoverishes our capacity to play.

Scout intuits something of this mindset in the way she's treated in comparison to her brother. The death of her mother, when Scout was aged two, has led to widespread lamentations about the absence of a feminine influence and paternal overindulgence of her tomboyish aggression and smart mouth.

Some decades previously, Mark Twain had railed against the Southern obsession with chivalry as a pernicious collective delusion, ensuring that every kind of cruelty and injustice could be preserved under a veneer of impeccable courtliness—the gentility of curtsying, raised hats and "Why thank you, ma'am." The cornerstone of this culture was the ideal of the pure Southern lady.

More than a sentimental myth, this stereotype was a central plank of the racism that saw black men lynched in their thousands. This virginal maiden required constant, vigilant protection against supposedly marauding, voracious black men—the very trope, in fact, that leads to Tom's false conviction. Twain noticed that this injustice was rooted in a kind of imaginative poverty, in a desic-cated and redundant culture's vision of itself.

Looking askance at her childhood, the adult Scout might be channelling Twain in her mordant observations of Maycomb's narrow-mindedness: "In Maycomb, if one went for a walk with no definite purpose in mind, it was correct to believe one's mind incapable of definite purpose." This little dig points to the suffocated state of the town mind, its incapacity for flexibility and change. Twain's point was that racism ensured the South was mired in lifeless, empty traditions and rituals. Racism is both cause and symptom of an airless culture in which every walk is known in advance and grinding predict-ability squeezes out every possibility of surprise. It is an atmosphere that gives no quarter to play, or to the pos-sibilities of imaginative invention and transformation.

It's worth asking how Scout manages to resist this demand for compliance and hold on to a mind of her own. Like Bunny, she has lost her mother; but unlike James, Atticus is ready to step into the void left by his wife. Bunny's suspicion that it is his mother alone who could love him is confirmed when his father aban-dons him.

Although she is also motherless from an early age, Scout is spared a similarly loveless future. There is no avoiding the impact of this loss; Atticus can't conjure away his wife's death and assume two parental roles in one. But he is able to take on the role of lone parent with his own singular personality, in all its eccentricity. While losing her mother is a deprivation, being the child of her widowed father turns out to be emotionally and imaginatively enriching for Scout.

Instead of trying vainly to mitigate their mother's loss, Atticus stays firmly inside the limits of his own character. In practice, this means leaving his children to discover themselves through play, their elaborate make-believes and games stretched over the duration of long, hot summers. He even allows Scout to fight and court danger with the boys around her.

Atticus has a way of assuming paternal authority without resorting to sentimentality or condescension. His mode of parental education brings to mind the sequencing of the phrases in the title of Stevens's poem and this book. Good little Southern girls, we might say, are told what to do and to comply. Scout is told how to live and is thereby freed to learn under her own steam what to do.

When Atticus tells Scout he's defending Tom, she asks him why he's taken on a case he knows he can't win. He tells her that if he refused he could never again hold his head up in public, or maintain any authority as a father: "I could never ask you to mind me again." Even though he's fighting a losing battle, this is no reason to give up: "Simply because we were licked a hundred years before we started is no reason for us not to try to win."

As soon as you give up the fight, in other words, you become complicit with the status quo. And this complicity, he implies, would be the sacrifice of his independence of mind in favour of mindless submission to cruelty and prejudice.

Atticus's sister Alexandra's insistence that Scout shouldn't be allowed to play freely comes from the same place as her demand that Atticus stop defending black men: her wish to protect the status and reputation of the family before the gaze of white respectability. She recognises that play is dangerous, nurturing autonomy of thought and the urge to question and confront the existing order of things.

Scout's own route through the novel allows her both to perceive and to question this emotional and imaginative stagnation. The trial of Tom Robinson, in particular, makes visible the strict yet unmarked lines of demarcation between rich whites, poor whites and blacks that shape the shared and divided life of Maycomb.

In one of the novel's weirder exchanges, Scout and her summer playmate Dill discover that Dolphus Raymond, a disgraced aristocrat and supposed alcoholic, is actually drinking Coca-Cola out of a paper bag. Raymond tells the children he plays up the role of town drunk to give those townsfolk who don't like the way he lives—with a black woman and their mixed-race children—an easy explanation: "folks can say Dolphus Raymond's in the clutches of whiskey—that's why he won't change his ways. He can't help himself . . ."

Raymond's insight is that where the paths of thinking are so narrow, a different way of living or seeing is quite literally unimaginable without an alibi like alcoholism.

His pantomime drunkenness is a sop to his fellow citizens' inability to imagine the very possibility that anyone would think or feel differently from themselves. It is a play-acting of the most constricted and uncreative kind, geared not towards changing reality but towards maintaining appearances, however corrupt and dishonest.

What is transmitted to Scout by her father, on the other hand, is the capacity to question, to approach the world with curiosity and free from the crushing weight of presumption and prejudice. Only in this way can her imaginative life survive.

The same goes for the rest of us. The spirit of play, as Alice reminded us, is our most reliable companion through the endless frustrations and confusions we'll encounter at every stage of our lives. A life genuinely alive with creativity and desire is possible only if we can continue to allow ourselves to come out to play.

2

Childhood Part 2: Schooling

I spent a good deal of Year 4 in tears.

Year 3 hadn't exactly been great but I'd muddled through, buoyed by low parental expectations and the merciful presence of three other kids vying with me for the honour of last place in class. This was based on the meticulous calculation of annually accumulated marks and announced by the headmaster before the entire school with all the good-natured humour of a serial killer. Although I came a solid last in Term 1, the end of the year had witnessed my triumphant leapfrog of a full four places. I was going up in the world.

Mrs. E, my Year 3 teacher, had always seemed to find more occasion for amusement than concern in my erratic classroom performance. I imagine my labelling of the laboratory instrument as a "Bunce 'n' Burner" might have elevated me instantly to the heights of staff-room legend.

But Year 4 changed all that. The moment Miss H set eyes on me, her brow seemed to knot with exasperation that soon became audible in the commands and rhetorical questions she directed at me—"Sit *down*," "Speak *up*," "Where is your *head*?"

The faces in the corridors and hall and gym quickly lost any hint of the genial tolerance I'd been used to.

A spreading impatience turned me into fair game for teachers and pupils alike. My surname's first vowel could no longer be pronounced without being subjected to torturous sing-song elongation (*"Coooooooohen!"*); my every word and action seemed to trigger an automatic eye roll.

I began to bring home regular reports in which Miss H castigated me for being "too much of a baby." "He needs to take a deep breath and think," she once wrote, "before bursting into tears because he 'can't do it.'" Those scare quotes were the ultimate humiliation.

Unlike her sappy colleagues or my credulous parents, she wasn't falling for my sensitive space-cadet shtick. Ruthlessly unsentimental, she made no secret of finding everything about me, from my short stature and emotional fragility to my need to be told everything at least twice, entirely infuriating.

Her point, impressive in its firmness and consistency, was that we were at *school* now. We had lessons, homework, sport, each requiring a state of alertness, a spirit of basic self-management and responsibility. "This is pathetic! You are *eight*, not *four*!" she berated me before an uproarious class, after I presented her with "homework" consisting of two sentences lifted from the first page of a Ladybird book on the Norman Conquest. She groaned as the tears sprang unbidden to my eyes. "Sit down," she sighed, resolutely unmoved.

*

Alice, Bunny and Scout showed us how integral imaginative life is to the complicated and often treacherous process of becoming oneself. Free play opens and expands the child's imaginative life, just as the restriction of play contracts and constrains it. But there comes a time when the physical and mental energies invested in play are rerouted into the accumulation of worldly knowledge and social know-how.

Psychoanalysis tells us that there is a place in our unconscious mind in which we hold stubbornly to a kind of radical narcissism; it's a kind of indestructible residue of our infantile self, impervious to change or reason. It insists that the world is mine, you just live in it. It doesn't want to know about compromise, responsibility, or measure or anything other than its own gratification. School is a fundamental assault on this region of the mind—a necessary one from the perspective of social and even personal development, but no less wounding for all that.

In the course of this chapter, we'll be following fictional school pupils who endure emotional and physical abuse, deprivation and manipulation. I'm all too aware that, set alongside them, my own experiences of an impatient teacher seem less than remarkable. The material for a searing misery memoir isn't quite there.

The fact is, Miss H was onto something and knew it, and she probably knew I knew it. But she had a fatal lack of curiosity as to why a child of eight might act like he was four. She was telling me to grow up but, to borrow the insight of my friend's daughter, *I was a child*. And unlike most of my classmates, I had no relish and much dread at the prospect of being ushered systematically into grown-up values and behaviours.

Erikson sees the school-age phase of development as the emergence of what he calls "a sense of industry." It is characterised by a new preference in the child for "reality, practicality and logic" as against the previous inclination towards "play and fantasy." I find this formulation as problematic as it is useful; placing play in a binary relation to reality suggests that in order to grow up healthily, one must forsake the airy regions of the imagination and learn how to make and remake the world outside us.

Erikson observed that the school-age child "may still rather be the baby at home than the big child in school." Miss H, on the other hand, evidently found any such reluctance to embrace maturity unthinkable other than as evidence of a child's wilful perversity.

I sometimes wonder whether Miss H was infuriated by my implicit demand for special treatment. I certainly resented her forcing on me the hard realisation that life would make no exceptions for me. But sometimes, as our first novel reminds us, this blow is inflicted long before a child goes to school.

i "The strangest sense of freedom": Jane Eyre

Risks to current security and well-being of JE, ten, are of great concern. On her own account, adoptive mother prevents her from interacting with her biological children, keeping her in near-total isolation. Also, strong suggestions of emotional and physical abuse from the eldest of the children, tolerated and even encouraged by mother and household staff. Much discussion of sending her "to school"; we have some concerns that intended institution is likely to exacerbate JE's feelings of emotional and material deprivation. Nonetheless, preference is to leave R household. We were surprised to find that despite neglect and cruelty, presentation was far from passive or lethargic. Ferocious in condemnation of R family and own defence. Resilience and defiance point to good prospects for adult life.

The opening of Jane Eyre's autobiographical narrative plunges us into an atmosphere of unrelieved lovelessness and hostility. Growing up in the household of her late uncle Reed, it seems Jane has never known herself other than as an object of resentment and disdain. She is subjected to regular physical assault from her cousin and to enforced isolation and emotional abuse from her aunt.

We might imagine that a child who endures an early life of this kind would internalise the hatred she's received and so become morose and passive in the face of her oppressors. But, in Jane's case, nothing could be further from the truth. She repeatedly risks further punishment with defiant blows and words of her own. Where does she find these resources of inner strength and conviction?

Although she may lack conscious memory of it, Jane came into the world loved and wanted. Rejected by her family for marrying a clergyman they felt was beneath her, her mother was the more determined to make a family of her own; baby Jane's arrival was joyously received. After both her parents succumbed to typhus in her early infancy, Jane was adopted by her uncle, Jane's mother having been "a great favourite with him." As his own death approached, Uncle Reed asked his wife to raise Jane alongside their own children.

Mrs. Reed's resentment at this commitment ended the chain of loving care and began a regime of unrelenting hostility and neglect. But the love of Jane's earliest carers had made its imprint on her mind and implanted in her a belief in her right to life and selfhood.

So when Mr. Brocklehurst, supervisor of Lowood Institution, the school to which Jane will shortly be sent away, visits the Reed home and joins her aunt in excoriating her wickedness and deceit, Jane doesn't assent meekly. After Brocklehurst leaves, she confronts her aunt, accusing her of "miserable cruelty," pitilessness and deceit.

It's not just Jane's words that induce in me, even now, the child's thrill in witnessing righteous resistance to adult injustice, but the description of her state of feeling in letting loose on her aunt:

> Ere I had finished this reply, my soul began to expand, to exult, with the strangest sense of freedom, of triumph, I ever felt. It seemed as if an invisible bond had

burst, and that I had struggled out into unhoped-for liberty.

Perhaps this passage has such an electric effect on me because it puts me in touch with the same feelings of limitless power that possessed me when I'd imagine felling a bullying classmate or teacher with a single blow of the fist or tongue or both. The embarrassing truth is that it took quite a few years to adjust to a reality in which I wasn't universally loved. The unsentimental candour of Charlotte Brontë's description lies in how far it goes beyond the simple expression of righteous protest; Jane here is a beast of unshackled rage and vengeance, screaming at her aunt in "a savage, high voice."

What Jane brings to Lowood, then, is a ferocious sense of self. The school's response is to pour cold, brackish water on this inner fire. The Lowood section of *Jane Eyre* (1847) gives us a heightened and dramatic account of the taming of the "savage" ego inflicted by school. Isn't this taming what most of us undergo at school, though mercifully not by the same means?

Jane is worn down largely by the sheer violence and deprivation inflicted by the school. Teachers, routines and material conditions all conspire to break the pride and self-love of its pupils in the name of their "spiritual edification." Lowood pupils are malnourished, fed woefully inadequate portions of burnt or otherwise inedible food. Polluted cooking and drinking water expose them to illness, while the dormitories freeze in winter.

Alongside this lack of basic necessities runs a regime of harshness and humiliation. Brocklehurst publicly orders the shearing of girls' hair, preaching a mission "to mortify in these girls the lusts of the flesh; to teach them to clothe themselves with shame-facedness and sobriety, not with braided hair and costly apparel"—even as his own luxuriantly long-haired daughters appear in the room clad in "velvet, silk and furs."

During the same visit, Brocklehurst shames Jane in front of her peers, placing her on a stool before them and drawing on Mrs. Reed's reports of her wickedness to condemn her as "not a member of the true flock, but evidently an interloper and an alien," enjoining pupils to "avoid her company, exclude her from your sports and shut her out from your converse" and teachers to "weigh well her words, scrutinise her actions, punish her body to save her soul."

Shortly after this vicious diatribe, a desolate Jane is comforted by her older friend Helen Burns, and declares her preference to die rather than be consigned to a loveless life:

> "to gain some real affection from you, or Miss Temple, or any other whom I truly love, I would willingly submit to have the bone of my arm broken, or to let a bull toss me, or to stand behind a kicking horse, and let it dash its hoof at my chest—"

Helen's response shows us the more subtle and perhaps more effective means of taming Jane's fiery selfhood. She interrupts, saying, "Hush, Jane! . . . you think too much of the love of human beings: you are too impulsive, too vehement." We can see her point. But then again, I hear so much more of myself in Jane's desperation to be loved than in Helen's appeal to quiet endurance.

Based on Brontë's eldest sister, Maria, who suffered a brutal school regime and slow death by consumption with the same stoic grace, Helen has a far more profound effect than the school's torturers on Jane's pride and self-regard. Perpetually victimised by the sadistic Miss Scatcherd, Helen absorbs the blows against her with unsettling equanimity. Miss Scatcherd is fully justified in all her harsh corrective measures against her, insists Helen, for "when I should be listening to Miss Scatcherd and collecting all she says with assiduity, often I lose the very sound of her voice: I fall into a sort of dream."

Although Helen presents Jane with a model of Christian humility and self-abasement, one could say that she's simply learned to manage the hatred and hostility directed against her by internalising them. Dreaminess in class is not just a simple expression of character, but betrays a prideful over-investment in her inner life, becoming an offence against humility and ultimately to God.

It cannot be a coincidence that Jane, who never really surrenders her self-love, survives the plague of tuberculosis that kills Helen. The vulnerability of Helen's physical defences is surely a symbolic analogue, if not a direct consequence, of her threadbare psychic defences. Put another way, we are more prone to life-threatening illness if we don't consider our lives worthy of preservation.

For all that she loves Helen and learns through her to curb her emotional responses, Jane steadfastly resists her ultimate lesson, continuing to place the highest value on her mortal life and on the love of others. Years later, facing her death from hunger and cold after fleeing from Rochester's house, she clings tenaciously to life, preferring to beg at the door of the Riverses' house than to submit meekly to the judgement of her Maker, as Helen had done years previously.

Nor is she willing to rest content within the narrow tramlines of a "respectable" life. Jane's lust for life fills her with an overwhelming desire for the new and unknown. During her years as a teacher at Lowood, she can assume Miss Temple's qualities of serenity and grace; but the "motive" for maintaining this state of tranquillity dissolves once Miss Temple leaves the school to be married.

Jane's unassuming humility, in other words, lasts only for as long as it's useful to her. Deprived of any motive to stay at Lowood once Miss Temple has left, her "old emotions" return with a vengeance: "I tired of the routine of eight years in one afternoon. I desired liberty; for liberty I gasped; for liberty I uttered a prayer." Jane's psyche is attuned far more acutely to the excitations of life than to the repressive dictates of Calvinist virtue.

One of the most poignant manifestations of this interior aliveness is her awareness of how she's perceived physically. Every direct or overheard judgement of her plainness is dutifully recorded, a narcissistic wound she works through by staring it straight in the face. She is not, she confesses, without vanity; when Bessie, a former servant in the Reed household, tells the eighteen-year-old Jane that she looks as she would have expected—"you were no beauty as a child"—she responds with a smile at Bessie's candour, but is not thereby "indifferent to its import; at eighteen most people wish to please, and the conviction that they have not an exterior likely to second that desire brings anything but gratification."

This painful awareness of her modest share of physical beauty only heightens her yearning to desire and be desired in return. That Jane's self-love and hunger for the world survive Lowood's regime of hardship and shame must have something to do with that deep-rooted intimacy with her loved infant self. That security means that the constant pressure of conformity is unable to touch that kernel of narcissism in us, which is so liable to run away with itself and yet so necessary if we're to live humanely.

There are surely lessons here for our own age. Social media and the use of self-display as the central currency of our culture have dragged narcissism into our everyday language and conversation. It is an accusation we throw at others (while never seeming to suspect it in ourselves) with alarming frequency these days.

Psychoanalysis and Brontë both remind us that narcissism is too complex and rich a phenomenon to be merely a casual insult. To be sure, there are pathological and damaging forms of narcissism, and we don't have to look far to find them. But Jane's remarkable story of survival and determination underlines the urge to the preservation, nurturing and, yes, the love of one's self as an essential feature of a healthy and satisfying inner life.

Let's return for a moment to Jane's wild avowal of desperation to be loved. When a child declares she'd rather be kicked in the chest by a horse than be deprived of affection, what is she really saying?

We can dismiss her as childishly histrionic, but in so doing we miss the precise judgement concealed inside the words. The French psychoanalysts César and Sára Botella have argued that our deepest unconscious fear—more so than even violence or physical pain—is total neglect, the void of any human presence in our lives.

In *King Lear*, we're presented with the parallel tragedies of Gloucester and Lear. Each suffers unimaginable humiliations and cruelties. Following Edmund's plot against him, Gloucester has his beard plucked and his eyes gouged out. Lear descends into madness, wandering the heath naked, betrayed and abandoned by everyone in whom he'd placed his trust. Shakespeare leaves us in no doubt as to whose agony is more profound.

Were they asked to analyse the fundamental difference between these two horrifying ordeals, the Botellas might point out that the physical torments undergone by Gloucester are experientially "full"; they overwhelm and saturate body and mind alike. In contrast, Lear's experience of total abandonment is one of radical emptiness, depriving him of the minimal conditions to continue life. It is the feeling of having nothing and no one, without or within, to help sustain our ongoing existence. This is surely the distinction implicit in Jane's preference for the horse's kick. She would rather be full of a pain she can feel than stripped of the basic conditions for feeling anything.

Lowood is a boarding school, to which Jane is sent away as an unwanted child. It's worth recalling that Brontë is writing not only out of personal experience, but in the broader context of the nineteenth century, in which boarding school would increasingly be recognised as a place of abuse and danger. Whether catering, like Lowood, for the orphaned poor or for the children of the very rich, boarding schools became notorious breeding grounds for the unregulated cruelty of teachers and fellow pupils, as well as malnourishment, disease and neglect, resulting in alarming numbers of pupil suicides.

While the worst excesses of physical punishment and emotional abuse seem largely to have disappeared from today's boarding schools, many children continue to be sent there from early childhood. In 2011, the British Jungian psychotherapist Joy Schaverien coined the term "Boarding School Syndrome" to describe the cluster of psychological symptoms common to many adults schooled away from home as children.

Schaverien found a peculiar vulnerability to anxiety in adults who had been sent to boarding school. In ordinary circumstances, the home provides a more or less sound container for the routine anxieties of childhood by recognising and adapting itself to a child's needs as she grows. The child intuits the presence of this container for her difficult feelings, sensing that these are being seen, heard and understood.

In boarding school, as Schaverien notes, the opposite happens: children are forced into a regime, sometimes more and sometimes less benign, of compliance with an impersonal system of rules and practices. They do not perceive themselves as having a central presence in another adult's mind. Lacking the privacy and solitude that might be afforded by their home, they have very little space and time to play in solitude and develop their imaginative lives.

Bryn, a handsome and athletic man in his late twenties, was working with modest success as an actor when he first came to see me. At the time, he was in the middle of a long run in a supporting role in a West End play, his first steady and reliably paid job after nearly a decade of ducking and diving.

The problem he brought to me is hardly uncommon in his profession. He suffered from terrible performance anxiety; the hours before each show were coloured by terror so debilitating that merely describing it to me brought him to tears. So vivid was his reconstruction of the experience, I wondered aloud if he were suffering a kind of stage fright right now. He thought for a moment, then said, "Well, yes. I've been terrified all morning about what you're going to make of me. I could easily imagine you laughing me off, telling me you've no desire to spend your time listening to a neurotic fool."

I soon realised that he was always expecting some version of this response, especially when the person responding was someone whose help he needed. The prelude to a performance was always made that much worse by Bryn's unwillingness to share his anxiety with anyone, inside or outside the cast, for fear of receiving only dismissive laughter in return. His working life had become an unending, sweat-drenched ordeal exacerbated by his having to bear it alone.

He was plagued by fantasies of unravelling before an audience full of family members, with his parents conspicuous in the middle of the front row. He would see the look of poorly disguised disappointment on his mother's face; his father's head turned away from the stage, no doubt willing himself to be somewhere, anywhere else.

"Those images of your parents sound like they're very familiar," I said.

He paused—not, I think, because he was contemplating how to respond, but because he knew and was a little nervous about what he was going to tell me. He swallowed, then launched in.

"When my parents drove me to school at the beginning of each term, there was always some time spent milling about outside, talking to teachers, other parents. It was during that time that my dread really reached fever pitch. I desperately didn't want them to leave, but equally desperately wanted them to leave—so I could at least say the worst moment was done with. I'd stand paralysed, not talking to anyone, just watching them making clipped small talk with all these equally stiff toff parents.

"Then, when the time was approaching, I'd ask my mother, 'But where's Daddy?,' and just asking the question would make me cry. She'd always say, 'You know your father, darling. He's wandered off. He can't bear to see you upset.' Mummy was obviously made of sterner stuff. She'd look at me falling apart and just look a bit, well, fed up."

"Your father turns away, your mother looks disappointed," I said. "Just like your theatrical nightmares."

"I know. I didn't want to make the link, because it feels like I'm accusing them of traumatising me," he mumbled inaudibly, then trailed off, staring into his lap.

In our subsequent work together, we realised that Bryn had spent most of his life anxiously anticipating the withdrawal of those he loved and needed. He was under permanent compulsion to prove himself worthy of continued care and attention, yet always unsure how to achieve them. At times he would try to be charming and funny and clever, at others to be quiet and demure and unassuming. Not knowing who he needed to be at any one moment, he could never feel secure in who he was.

Life changed markedly for the better when Bryn got into drama. "The teacher took to me. He would talk up the elegance of my voice and movement to the other boys. Suddenly, instead of hovering needily on the edge of one or other gang of boys, I was in demand among all of them. Mr. Overton would have me and a few of the other boys to tea in his rooms. The feeling of being chosen by him, special to him, felt like a kind of ecstasy. I spent most of my school career trying to please him."

In fact, Bryn was beginning to suspect he'd spent most of his adult career trying to please him, the one adult who'd made him feel like the centre of attention. Acting had got him friends, confidence, purpose. "Except the further school receded into the past, the more acting started to feel precarious and unreliable as a way not just of making a living but of feeling good about myself." For years it had done the opposite, leaving him doubting all the times that he'd done enough to gain the approval he craved.

As he came to understand how being sent away, displaced from the centre of an external and internal home, had come to shape his life's path, Bryn began to overcome the terrible fright that had dogged his acting life. The fantasy of failing and flailing and losing the love and esteem he yearned for ceased to exert such an iron grip over his mind, to the point he could shrug it off. If he tripped or fluffed his lines, or spoke them a little flatly, it might damage his reputation temporarily, lower his profession's opinion of him. What it wouldn't do, he realised, was cause anyone who mattered to stop loving him.

Acting became easier once he was no longer persecuted by this fantasy of love's loss. But it also became less necessary. He no longer felt he had to cling to it as the sole means of ensuring that he was cared about. Almost exactly three years after he'd first come to see me, Bryn announced with a smile that he was quitting acting.

I was the younger of two boys, Erikson's "baby at home." I was well schooled in the dark arts of sibling rivalry, the unending struggle to secure the status of most lovable child. It often involved playing up my perceived smallness and vulnerability, ensuring that my brother was always caught in the role of aggressor and provocateur.

My intimate knowledge of our differences shored me up for the war at home. Knowing our respective advantages and deficits gave me the chance to outmanoeuvre my brother, to make myself look good and him look bad. I was skilled at contriving scenarios in which I'd be found by one or other parent cowering in terror under the blows of the older, bigger boy.

Unsurprisingly, these skills proved not to be transferable to school. Lacking the same intimacy with the twenty-three other kids in my class, each competing for the same attention and praise, each starting from roughly the same position as me, I quickly lost all sense of how to retain my place as favourite. I hated the anonymity of the classroom, the demand it imposed on all its members to comply with its routines and rules. Everything was happening too fast. I felt like I was being press-ganged into premature conformity to an alien regime.

In this sense, school is where a fundamental problem of life starts to come into focus. Life in the classroom and playground impresses the need to renounce one's imagined specialness. We are admired for amusing our friends and impressing our teachers, not for keeping ourselves apart. School introduces us to the discipline of the group, the necessary subordination of the one to the many.

Freud saw this conflict as a tragic one, for it admits of no definitive resolution and consigns us to live in the state of permanent *Unbehagen*—"discomfort," or "discontents" as Freud's translator James Strachey has it. In the memory of my helplessly tearful self, I see a distilled image of that discomfort: the pain of being caught between my own need for love and security, and the impersonal demand to comply with the ways and rules of the group. There is simply no way of adjudicating these claims that would leave everyone happy.

At school, you're just one among many. Society, wrote the great American essayist Ralph Waldo

Emerson, "loves not realities and creators, but names and customs," and school can often seem like the medium through which this conformity is cultivated and enforced. To make matters more painful still, we are pressed upon by at least two systems of man-made laws, rules and customs at school: the adult system of reward and punishment for academic attainment and behavioural compliance, and the children's far more complex system of peer regard.

We can gain the good opinion of fellow pupils by being models of industry, ability and achievement, or of slackness, clowning and indifference. The good opinion of our teachers can make us the object of loving admiration or of contemptuous disdain. School thus induces in us a constant background anxiety about who we're supposed to be and how we're supposed to be acting at any given moment.

This anxiety is amplified by the way a particular role or identity is assigned to us from early on in our school career, which can then make us feel compelled to live inside its constrictive terms: the class clown isn't meant to make a serious or thoughtful contribution to class discussion; the quiet, bookish type isn't expected to crack outrageous jokes. It takes courage and imagination to break out of the prisons of character that school builds around each of us.

Which brings us to our next book—one of the most painfully vivid renditions I know of how this anxiety feels from the inside.

ii "Something really unfair": Paddy Clarke

PC, ten, referred for anxiety. No signs of material deprivation, though four young children must be strain on household budget. Settled at school, part of gang (age-appropriate) of local boys with whom he "gets up to mischief and stuff." Some concerns about bullying, oblique allusions to aggressive "ceremonies" conducted by friend and gang's leader. Rather withheld, mistrustful of adults? Steady questioning did yield a sense of concern for parents; wondered why "Da didn't like Ma any more." Also, younger brother. Emotional confusion here: "I need to look after him now. I really hate him." Seemed to be fighting back tears as he said this. Second consultation arranged with view to more regular sessions. Large potential for acting out as adolescence approaches, must be monitored.

Jane Eyre's tenacious hold on her own self-worth helps her survive and thrive. Through abuse, hunger and humiliation, she maintains the unshakeable conviction in herself as worth loving and looking after.

But not everyone is assured of such conviction. One could grow up, for example, as the eldest of four siblings, one's place at the centre of parental attention repeatedly displaced by the newest arrival. One could grow up in the shadow of a volatile and unhappy marriage, with a father coiled in alcoholically fuelled resentment and a mother in a permanent state of distracted fear. One could grow up in a school and neighbourhood in which survival depends on one's superior endowment of strength and ruthlessness, where classroom lessons and play are each conditioned by expectations of casual violence and danger.

These experiences would likely induce a state of fundamental insecurity in any child. They certainly do so in the case of Paddy Clarke, narrator and protagonist of Roddy Doyle's *Paddy Clarke Ha Ha Ha* (1993). Paddy's front of rambunctious bravado belies his constant, anxious gauging of the moods and motives of the adults and children around him.

In the fictionalised, late 1960s Northside Dublin suburb of Barrytown, primary school is as charged with casual aggression as the streets in which Paddy and his friends play, wreaking havoc and destruction. Within the first few pages, they have burned off his younger brother Sinbad's lips by forcing a capsule filled with lighter fuel into his mouth and lighting a match to it, as well as set fire to a local building site.

Far from being a bastion of learning and good order, school is home to a different kind of lawlessness, a place of indiscriminate and unthinking verbal and physical aggression meted out by teachers to pupils and by pupils to one another.

Take Mr. Henderson, or Henno, the class teacher who cheerily confuses discipline with sadism. In an early classroom scene, the hapless Ian McEvoy has fallen asleep at his desk as Henno tests the boys' spellings. Sitting next to Ian is Kevin, to whom Paddy is an ambivalent and anxious best friend. "Will I wake him up?" Kevin asks Henno.

—No, said Henno.

Henno put his finger to his lips; we were to be quiet. We giggled and shushed. Henno walked carefully down to Ian McEvoy's side of the desk; we watched him. He didn't look like he was joking.

—Mis-ter McEvoy!

It wasn't funny; we couldn't laugh. I felt the rush of air when Henno's hand swept through and smacked Ian McEvoy's neck. Ian McEvoy shot up and gasped. He groaned. I couldn't see him. I could see the side of Kevin's face. It was white; his bottom lip was out further than his top one.

Perhaps it's personal experience that makes this vignette so unbearable to me. It isn't so much the smack that stirs my memories—I was on the receiving end of spontaneous physical punishment only a couple of times in my school career and these flashes of cruelty got under my skin far less than the teacher's pleasure in inviting kids to laugh at the humiliation of one of their own. It's the finger to the lips that distresses me most; I remember similar gestures—eye rolls at a "stupid" answer, gratuitously sarcastic barbs played for my maximal embarrassment before my peers.

The atmosphere for Paddy at home is equally volatile and unpredictable. He is an invisible witness to his parents' long and rancorous rows, which increasingly end with his father's violence against his mother.

Understood in this context, Paddy's anxious shifts between bravado and cowardice, loyalty and disloyalty (especially towards his brother Sinbad) are confused survival strategies, consequences of the continuous pressure of split-second decisions to maintain his precarious advantage among those who matter: his mercurial father, ruthless friends and hard-nosed teachers.

Paddy makes these crucial decisions about whether to stay loyal to a friend or appease an enemy, be kind or ruthless, be brave or cautious, with only the barest understanding of why the children and adults around him, not to mention Paddy himself, act the way they do.

In one scene early on, he is told by his mother that Ian McEvoy's mother only works at the Cadbury's factory because she has to. Paddy's bald gloss on this information is "I didn't understand." But not understanding doesn't stop him picking a squabble with Ian the next day:

—Your ma only works in Cadbury's because she has to!

He didn't know what I meant. I didn't either, not really.

—Because she has to! Because she has to!

I gave him a shove. He shoved me back.

Unwittingly assuming his mother's snobbish pride at being comfortable enough not to have to take a factory job, Paddy has no idea of the minefield of class and status hierarchies he's wandered into. Where the currency of social life is bullying and intimidation, the question of how to stay on top is at once imperative and entirely puzzling. Paddy is constantly forced to fight for causes he doesn't remotely understand.

Daily life becomes exhausting when a secret and not very effective gauge of others' moods and wishes is permanently whirring at the back of your mind. The minutest interaction becomes an occasion for anxious calculation, most painfully and poignantly where Sinbad is involved. Paddy's predicament is that he can reach his achingly sad, silent and vulnerable younger brother only by hurting him. Little brothers, he reflects, are mere props for their big brothers' power and status:

> When the brothers were together, . . . it was easy to see them the way we saw them; little, jokes, sad, nice. They were our friends because we hated them; it was good to have them around. I was cleaner than them, brainier than them. I was better than them.

The Darwinian politics of the group require that little brothers are reduced to generic caricature, embodiments of inferiority and weakness. When circumstances at home and school conspire to make him see Sinbad as a separate person with real experiences and feelings,

Paddy's brash superiority gives way to confusion and vulnerability.

Paddy is confronted with Sinbad's vulnerability late in the book, when Henno strides over to Paddy's desk and thrusts an open copybook under his eyes, the ink running wet down the page. He looks up, sees his brother crying beside Henno and realises the book has been streaked with Sinbad's tears. "Look at that," Henno orders Paddy. "Isn't it disgraceful?"

> I didn't say.
> All that was wrong was the tears. They'd ruined the writing, nothing else. Sinbad's writing wasn't bad. It was big and the lines of his letters swerved a bit like rivers because he wrote very slowly. Some of the turns missed the copy line but not by much. It was just the tears.

Paddy's focus here is not on Henno's gratuitous humiliation of his brother, or the unexplained tears, but on the handwriting itself. It is not only the streaks that make Sinbad's emotional defencelessness visible, but the letters' size and shape and positioning, the slowness and tentativeness of their composition. Unable to understand the meaning or motive for this display of adult power and cruelty, Paddy clings to the one thing he can really know. Sinbad's letters provide an island of clarity in a sea of perplexity. He notes, "It was a new feeling: something really unfair was happening, something nearly mad. He'd only cried."

Henno's shaming of Sinbad continues unabated as he directs Paddy to show the copybook to their mother "the minute you get home. Let her see what a specimen she has on her hands." Paddy must consent on pain of being punished himself, while trying surreptitiously to convey his new sense of solidarity with Sinbad: "I wanted to look at Sinbad, to let him know . . ."

"I'm not going to show the copy to Ma," he tells his brother. But Sinbad is silent, and Paddy is left at this moment, and for a long time after, unable to reach his withdrawn and lonely brother.

Paddy's predicament is comic and tragic for the same reason: he is trying to navigate states of feeling in himself and others that he can make no sense of. This explains why his attempt at breaking free of Kevin's influence at the end of the novel is so disastrous. When he starts a playground fight with Kevin and tries to form an alliance with a tough newcomer to the school, his strategic calculations inevitably go awry, leaving him ostracised and isolated.

Perhaps it's inevitable that Paddy's social ostracism should coincide with his father's departure from the family home. The boy whose mind has been working overtime for his entire eleventh year on the desperate task of fitting in, being liked and cultivating special status at home and at school finds himself fatherless and friendless:

—Paddy Clarke—
Paddy Clarke—

77

Has no da.
Ha ha ha!
I didn't listen to them. They were only kids.

Paddy Clarke has, in a strange way, finally got his wish to be special. He is "the man of the house now" and can look down on his chanting tormentors as being "only kids." But few lines could make him sound more like a kid, as confused and anxious as ever.

Given that I don't see children in my practice, I'm often amazed by the volume of detail I hear daily about school life. This is partly because many of my patients are parents, and because we are living in a place and at a time when children's educational attainment is one of the great sources of social anxiety and competition.

Though sound enough, this explanation doesn't do justice to the intensity and passion with which many parents in the consulting room talk about this issue. There is the endless and exhausting deliberation over the criteria for choosing the right school; then, once the child is placed, concerns that discipline is too harsh or too soft, that their child is being pushed too hard or not hard enough, that she's being persecuted by teachers or bullied by pupils, that he's too solitary or overly social, that there's too much religious education or not enough sport or music or computing.

The child in this scenario starts to sound like a rare and delicate hothouse orchid, forever vulnerable to the minutest shifts in temperature, light, quality of soil and water.

Marina, a full-time mother of four children, would spend whole sessions relating the knotty dramas of their school days. The fury with which she invested these stories was peculiarly gripping. I would catch myself clutching the arms of my chair as she told me about the swimming teacher who "shouted at Will for splashing when he'd just been standing there quietly in the shallow end! And then shouted at him again, just for saying it wasn't him, it was Alexis, *which was true!*"

When Marina finished these stories, tears invariably sprang to her eyes; the expression she wore could only be compared to a grief-stricken child's. She seemed caught in total identification with her son, feeling her way into his sense of hurt and injustice until it became hers. I sometimes found it difficult to keep the proper distance from her stories, to remind myself that they were about the ordinary frustrations of a child at school.

Nor is Marina unusual. Craig regularly took up the role of crusader for his only child, Mia, railing against teachers who failed to compensate for her severe dyslexia, against pupils who mocked her stammer in the playground. With Craig I found the adrenal rush of anger and aggression rip through me as he denounced the "clueless prick of an English teacher" who had told her the previous day that her handwriting was messy, even the "prissy little princess" who called her "M-M-M-Mia."

I wondered at my internal cheering as he muttered darkly that the nine-year-old child was "right at the top of my shit list."

Other parents have the opposite effect, arousing feelings of fierce irritation in me. Jill spoke with pride of the huge improvement in her two sons' school marks since she introduced the two hours of twice-weekly tutoring, which they had to fit in alongside lessons in cello and clarinet and Italian. She detailed the long discussions she had with their individual teachers, asking numerous questions and taking copious notes on how best to steer them through the various syllabuses. When I remarked on how closely she was involved in her children's lives, she bristled, picking up on some implied criticism it was hard for me to deny. "I get it," she said. "I'm one of those nightmare pushy mothers. Forgive me for wanting my kids to have the best start in life. It's tough out there, in case you hadn't noticed."

What is it that drives a parent to such intense emotional identification and practical involvement with their kids' schooling? Why does school, where children are supposed to gain some autonomy and independence, become the occasion for parents to become more adhesive and intrusive than ever?

Perhaps this is because their children have become surrogates for themselves, the vicarious means through which they can right the wrongs and repair the disappointments of their own childhoods. A famous passage from Freud's famous 1914 essay, "On Narcissism," casts some light on this universal tendency of ours:

> If we look at the attitude of affectionate parents towards their children, we have to recognise that it is a revival and reproduction of their own narcissism, which they have long since abandoned ... The child shall have a better time than his parents; he shall not be subject to the necessities which they have recognised as paramount in life. Illness, death, renunciation of enjoyment, restrictions on his own will, shall not touch him; the laws of nature and of society shall be abrogated in his favour ... Parental love, which is so moving and at bottom so childish, is nothing but the parents' narcissism born again, which, transformed into object-love, unmistakably reveals its former nature.

I never fail to be struck by the gentle wit and beauty of these insights. Freud takes what we might well think of as some of our worst tendencies—meddling in the lives of our children, claiming every kind of exception for them, indulging the most self-indulgent, sentimental fantasies of their futures—and allows us to see them as expressions of the most tender and vulnerable dimension of our humanity.

In loving their children so fiercely, Marina, Craig, Jill and most other parents are loving their lost childhood selves. But this isn't evidence of some alarming pathology; it is one of the many ways our child selves continue to haunt our adult ones. All the times we were scorned and mocked and neglected are relived through our children. All our dreams of triumph and recognition and admiration are continued through our children.

The unconscious fantasy of parenting is that we will rewrite the unhappy script of our own childhoods, excising all the pain, lifting all the restrictions, bringing untold joy, love and satisfaction to these new versions of the child in us. Our child, in short, will be special in ways that eluded us.

But perhaps we should be careful what we wish for. How might we feel if this dream for our children was made reality? What if some charismatic adult mentor— a teacher, say—were to mark them off from the crowd and grant them the special status of being the crème de la crème?

iii "Leading out": Sandy Stranger

SS, ten, presents as an intelligent girl caught up in unusually complicated peer relationships, specifically with a "set" of girls who function under informal guidance of a charismatic and influential teacher. From interview, we infer continued pursuit of a range of pastoral and social interactions with Miss B that stretch well beyond normal boundaries of school activity, curricular or extracurricular. Among consequences of this unusual arrangement is notably low opinion of relations with parents, other teachers and pupils outside "set." SS seemed at various points during assessment to be lost in reverie, at others to be excessively concerned with minutiae of Miss B's professional and romantic life. SS presents with level of gravity and social wariness that should be cause for great concern in a child her age. Notably humourless throughout the assessment bar one outburst of laughter that seemed entirely unrelated to previous discussion. When questioned as to what was so funny, replied, "Sexual intercourse."

My patient Bryn's stories of tea with Mr. Overton bring to mind the most joyful episode in the Lowood section of *Jane Eyre*, when Jane and Helen are fleetingly rescued from the hell of cold and malnourishment to enjoy a fire, seedcake and a teacher's loving interest in Miss Temple's rooms.

The pleasure induced by this scene, at least in me, might seem out of proportion to its contents. But more than the cake and the warmth, the scene's quality has to do with the atmosphere of loving care conjured by Miss Temple's deep interest in her pupils. Her invitation has in it the faintest suspicion of special treatment, of lightly pushing the envelope of propriety.

Being picked out by a revered teacher for membership of some elite group, especially an informal and unofficial one, is bound to stir feelings of gratitude and triumph. The teacher who cultivates such a group needs to be a skilled navigator of that hazy boundary between serious attention and inappropriately differential treatment.

When I entered sixth form, I found the eclectic reading I'd done in poetry and fiction to avoid O-level revision belatedly rewarded by two charismatic English teachers, who had opposite but complementary styles. The intense curiosity possessed by a few of us about literature and other arts was suddenly and thrillingly noticed and nurtured.

On Friday afternoons the A-level syllabus would be suspended, leaving us free to explore tantalising new territories. Soft-spoken, deadpan Mr. D would sit before a horseshoe of boys reading melancholy lyrics by Cavafy, Roethke and Miłosz, strange names that conjured the magic of sounds and truths I'd only dreamed of. Urbane, expansive Mr. B played us Debussy, showed us Diaghilev, Vanessa Bell, Paul Klee and Apollinaire, bringing us face to face with the possibilities of madness and risk and shock.

In common with the lessons of Miss Jean Brodie, the content was less important than the intimation of places and experiences far beyond the confines of our comfortable homes and classrooms. Unlike Miss Brodie, the English masters kept the cultivation of their most eager pupils on the right side of favouritism. There was no crossing into social intimacy or intrigue, much as I might have secretly wished it. But those afternoons gave me an unmistakable sensation of triumph, of initiation into some exclusive fellowship of the worldly.

Perhaps this explains why, on discovering Muriel Spark a few years later, *The Prime of Miss Jean Brodie* (1961) had such immediate resonance for me. Miss Brodie's quest is to gather to herself a "set" of girls she can infuse with her educational ideas and values.

In practice, what this means is that the girls receive an eclectic mass of instruction distinctly perpendicular to the "authorized curriculum" and deemed by the headmistress to be "useless to the school as a school." This philosophy is aimed at drawing out the singular soul of each girl, in defiance of the conformity of the notion of "team spirit" Miss Brodie disdains as vulgar, along with the spiritually barren curriculum which has "no thoughts of anyone's personalities apart from their specialty in life."

But a paradox underlies this philosophy: the aspiration to realise each girl's unique character involves a long and intricate process of manipulation. The growth and development of each pupil are filtered through the single, narrow channel of Miss Brodie's personality. Perhaps this explains why every one of the art master Mr. Lloyd's attempts to paint the girls in Miss Brodie's set ends up looking like Miss Brodie.

The girl who notices this insistent resemblance, and who is generally the most perspicacious about Miss Brodie's secret intentions, is Sandy Stranger. Sandy is initially carried along with the rest of the girls on the wave of their teacher's special attention. Anticipating the eventual unfolding of real events, the ten-year-old Sandy's reveries insert her into the most fraught scenes of classic romantic novels—including *Jane Eyre*—where she acts out the role of facilitator to Miss Brodie's grand passions.

Despite her youth, Sandy can see that the magnetic effect of Miss Brodie on the young girls derives from what the novel calls "sex." This is a psychic as much as a physical force, the broad waters of desire and fantasy in which Miss Brodie and her set of girls swim. In a 1923 article called "The Role of the School in the Libidinal Development of the Child," Melanie Klein built on Freud's insight that schooling draws on children's sexual energies, seeking to "sublimate" or channel these into the pursuit of knowledge. As children, our excited discoveries of the body's different regions are redirected by our educators into the accumulation of different bodies of knowledge.

Klein's point is that harnessing these energies in the service of learning can be both motivating and inhibiting. Powered by libido, the child can make large inroads into the mysteries of the world around her. But children also know that curiosity can be dangerous; they are aware there are regions of knowledge, conveniently encapsulated in the single word "sex," blocked off to them, and this prohibition of access can be as frightening as it is fascinating. Children imagine that discovering truths meant to be hidden from them will provoke severe punishment. The links Klein draws between the progress and inhibition of learning on the one hand and sexual curiosity on the other can be confirmed by anyone who's observed the play of children and the excitable and outlandish ways they imagine adult sexual life. The children of the Brodie set certainly bear out this observation.

Ten-year-old Sandy and her best friend, Jenny, speculate earnestly on the "sexual intercourse" of parents. "He must have committed sex with his wife," remarks Sandy of new parent Mr. Lloyd, before whispering, "Can you *see* it happening?" Over the years that follow, this excited fixation on the horrors and fascinations of the sexual body will spread into group-wide fantasies of the passions of Miss Brodie.

Miss Brodie's educational project makes explicit the links between sexual and intellectual curiosity that for most of us remain unconscious. In other words, her "leading out" of her girls is also a seduction, involving the same confusion that ensues whenever children are pulled into the erotic lives of adults.

The Brodie girls, in Spark's subtly strange language, are each "famous" for something—"sex" (Rose Stanley), stupidity (Mary Macgregor), athleticism (Eunice Gardiner), rage (Monica Douglas), vowel sounds (Sandy). What Sandy comes to see is that these markers of character don't really make for separate, fully differentiated individuals, but function instead as the components of a single body:

> Sandy looked back at her companions, and understood them as a body with Miss Brodie for the head. She perceived herself, the absent Jenny, the ever-blamed

Mary, Rose, Eunice, and Monica, all in a frightening little moment, in unified compliance to the destiny of Miss Brodie, as if God had willed them to birth for that purpose.

It's worth remembering that the book is set in the early 1930s. The colour of this passage takes on a darkly political hue when Sandy discerns, as the girls walk through Edinburgh, a disconcerting resemblance to the marching fascisti of Mussolini lustily extolled by Miss Brodie: "It occurred to Sandy . . . that the Brodie set was Miss Brodie's fascisti, not to the naked eye, marching along, but all knit together for her need and in another way, marching along."

Both forms of unity involve a kind of sublimated eroticism, in which the being at the head is invested with the desire and longing of those he rules over. The comparisons are, at one level, absurdly overblown; Miss Brodie is no god or demagogue. And yet she exerts the same unquestioned power over her subjects, binding them together with the same string of desire, or "sex."

Sandy turns out to be the one girl to see the dangerous implications of this little set-up, to realise that the pleasure of the girls' special status is also a subtle abuse. This is partly because she's the most perceptive and ruthless of the set, but also because when Miss Brodie's extravagant romantic plotting crosses the line between fantasy and reality, it is Sandy who lands in the middle of it.

Like Emma Bovary, Miss Brodie confuses her life with a romantic novel. Unlike Emma Bovary, she is fully conscious of so doing, and tries to railroad her life and the people around her into the tramlines of an implausible love story. Faced with her passion for the married art master Mr. Lloyd, Miss Brodie chooses the histrionic path of tragic renunciation. Her love will instead be lived vicariously through Rose Stanley, whom she sends to Mr. Lloyd as a model, grooming her for an affair with the man she cannot have.

Psychoanalysis teaches us that the problem with trying to manipulate the flows and channels of sexual energy is that they will always slip our grasp. Trapped in the plot of a cheap romantic novel, Miss Brodie assumes that Mr. Lloyd will gravitate sexually towards Rose because she's the prettiest of the girls. The novel reminds us that desire is not so simple.

In his studio, Mr. Lloyd suggests to Sandy that he paint the Brodie set's group portrait, wondering aloud how it might turn out. Sandy, who is already beginning to strain against the stifling nature of the group, turns to him "in her new manner of sudden irritability and said, 'We'd look like one big Miss Brodie, I suppose.'" Lloyd laughs delightedly at Sandy's caustic insinuations about his real feelings for Miss Brodie, "Whereupon he kissed her long and wetly. He said in his hoarse voice, 'That'll teach you to look at an artist like that.'"

Lloyd's arousal at this moment is provoked by the "insolence" of Sandy's stare, conveying how sharply she's attuned to the perversity of a pupil being offered up as a sexual surrogate for the teacher. This complicity is evidently much more exciting to Lloyd than mere prettiness. It's worth recalling that Sandy is fourteen years old, a reminder of the chasm between Miss Brodie's contrived melodrama and the ugly reality.

Miss Brodie's vision of education as a leading out of the soul turns out to be a much darker project of emotional control. Sandy exposes the hidden links between Miss Brodie's gushing admiration for Mussolini and Hitler (whom Miss Brodie will concede, after the war, "*was rather naughty*") and the ways she exploits the curiosity and longing of vulnerable young girls to coerce them into unquestioning conformity. It is her understanding of the weave of sex and politics in Miss Brodie's methods that both motivates and enables Sandy to help Miss Mackay finally oust her troublesome staff member from the school. Sandy can see that Miss Brodie's sexual intrigues are too elusive and clandestine to pin down and use as evidence; but the fact that she speaks openly for the fascist enemy is not.

But this conclusion is no simple triumph of justice and sanity. It signals not just the collapse of Miss Brodie's experiments but the full restoration of grey normality and the standardisation of learning. For Sandy herself it will lead to her entrance into a nunnery—pledging herself to the ultimate state of "unified compliance" and the renunciation of sex.

The Prime of Miss Jean Brodie won't let us forget that education, so ripe with possibilities for breaking open our imaginative and intellectual lives, is equally rich in the potential to damage us.

Miss Brodie's recruitment of pupils to her private cause is both unfair and ethically dubious, not least because it's also very exciting. What ten-year-old wouldn't want to be chosen to join a covert rebel alliance against their school and its stuffy, rule-bound leaders? It is a very special place to be, and therefore a perilous one.

Any process in which one set of people is tasked with cultivating the growth and development of another is fraught with all kinds of risks. One of these parties is, by definition, not fully formed, and therefore suggestible and vulnerable to abuse and exploitation. The charismatic teacher who enlivens lessons and inspires self-discovery might be the same teacher who indoctrinates and manipulates the young people in her charge. The evolution of safeguarding practices in schools and other educational, medical and pastoral settings reflects a recognition of this basic truth: to be placed in the care of another is also to be put at risk of their abuse or neglect.

This is something no one who experiences psychotherapy, from either side of the couch, can fail to be aware of. From its very inception, Freud noticed how the set-up of the process was apt to provoke the strongest and most unsettling feelings. As early as 1895, in his first published account of psychotherapeutic technique, he writes of a female patient who recalled her wish that a man she'd been interested in "might boldly take the initiative and give her a kiss," after which, "at the end of a session, a similar wish came up in her about me."

During this process, known as "transference," past objects of the patient's love, hate and desire come to be represented in the image of the analyst—this new significant other who offers to attend to our deepest needs and wishes.

Almost as soon as modern psychotherapy came into being, it was recognised as a crucible of intense vulnerability and danger. To hand your mind's development, cultivation and healing over to someone else is the most basic gesture of trust, and for that very reason open to abuse and exploitation.

Psychotherapy brings into sharp focus a fundamental truth of the human condition, that we are born *helpless*. Lacking the means to secure our own care and growth, we find ourselves consigned to the care of others—parents at first, but then all kinds of surrogates: other family members or friends, nannies, childminders, teachers, sports coaches, music tutors, mentors.

These figures, and our parents especially, assume an ambiguous place in our inner lives; if all goes well, they become the people who facilitate our independence and enable us to take charge of at least some portion of ourselves and the world around us. But they also reside in us as images of our original helplessness and our continued vulnerability to others. Put very simply, our carers can hit us as well as hold us. For the very reasons they can make us feel safe, they can also make us feel frightened.

The overlaps between psychotherapy and teaching are worth mentioning because they touch on one of the most familiar, important and dangerous impulses in our inner life: the wish to be special.

School is where we spend a lot of time chasing this dream by being crowned the smartest, toughest, prettiest, sportiest or most popular among our peers, an exception to all rules. And it is where most of us discover we're all too *un*exceptional, where the demands and expectations to perform tasks and follow rules like everyone else spoil our narcissistic fantasy of being unlike anyone else.

This need not be such bad news. For one thing, how would it be possible to live locked inside the cell of our dreamed-of specialness? School draws us, sometimes reluctantly, sometimes eagerly, out of that cell, ushering us into a world of common norms, aspirations and fears. The experience of inhabiting that shared world helps us to imagine ourselves otherwise. And without that capacity, how would an enterprise like writing or reading fiction, or practising psychotherapy, or parenting or being a friend or lover or colleague, or any other process that involves attuning ourselves to the thoughts and feelings of others, be possible?

Jane, Paddy and Sandy, each in their different ways, suffer being displaced from their dreamed-of position at the centre of the world. This is no doubt a great, perhaps traumatic disappointment; but it's also what makes it possible for them to tell us their stories, and for us to enjoy them.

3

Adolescence Part 1: Rebellion

A glorious early spring afternoon, 1987. I was seated at the large mahogany dining table of my friend Adam's north-west London home. Of the fifteen or so guests celebrating his father's birthday, Adam, his little sister and I were the only ones under forty-five. We both knew his parents had encouraged him to invite me because I was a "good boy," a steady presence likely to keep in check their son's regular and full-throated denunciations of Thatcher, capitalism, colonial oppression—and their invited guests.

I'd been at this same table a few weeks previously, when Adam had responded to a retired stockbroker's passing comment that he "didn't think much of the Labour these days" by promising that, when the time came, he would "personally oversee the dispensation of revolutionary justice" against the old man. "That's not very nice, Adam," his father, Peter, had responded with a nervous smile. "No," Adam replied, "revolution isn't very 'nice,' Peter, but then neither is the parasitic expropriation of workers' labour power." "Mmm, I shouldn't imagine so," the broker said, nodding agreeably, apparently unruffled by the prospect of summary execution. With a broad, clench-toothed smile, Adam's mother turned to the old

man and said, "Adam's a big fan of the workers!"
"Well . . . why not? Why *not*!" the old man replied with
an indulgent smile of his own, as Adam closed his eyes
tightly and snarled in despair.

My unstated role today was to prevent any similar
exchanges from marring the celebrations. And I seemed
to have done a decent enough job of keeping him distracted with talk of foreign films, recent post-punk
releases and his new girlfriend, who, he complained with
an incongruously gormless grin, was "as much a deluded
bourgeois reformist as you." "It's a shame that the iron
logic of revolution will not spare her," I started to say,
when the doorbell rang and his mother sprang up and
said, "Gosh! Who on earth could that be?"

The voice at the door was so loud that the table fell silent,
fixing all ears on his words. "Good afternoon, madam.
Is Mr. . . . Adam W— available?" "Oh," she said, "it's for
Adam!," but instead of walking to the door with his usual
brisk importance, my friend, the sudden and exclusive
focus of the assembled guests, seemed to root himself
nervously to the spot. "Sorry, who should I say . . ." we
heard, then, "Lewis Kramer, madam. North London
Branch Secretary, Communist Party of Great Britain."
I half-anticipated that Adam would raise a clenched fist
and proclaim the coming of the revolution. Instead, head
bowed, he walked hesitantly out of the room, looking a
bit like the intended victim of one of his own executions.

If I were casting around for a good image of personal hell, I could do a lot worse than Peter's face in

that moment, blushing excruciatingly under the gaze of the table's silent guests. Caught between the indelicacy of talking about what was happening at the front door and the clumsiness of talking about anything else, we all just sat there, eyes glued to our dirty plates, lips clamped rigidly shut. The atmosphere was pregnant with a strange compound of horror and comedy as the exchange between Adam and Branch Secretary Kramer carried resoundingly down the corridor.

"I see," Kramer was saying. "So . . . you're a little way off full PARTY membership, but we'd be pleased to receive and ACCEPT—following all due process, of course—your application to the YOUNG COMMUNIST LEAGUE."

"Right. I could join the . . . the Young Communist League."

"Indeed. SUBJECT to the relevant committee approvals processes. AND subscription payments, of course. Ha ha ha!"

A silence, broken by Kramer after half a minute: "Was there anything more you wanted to ask me, Mr. W—?"

Adam paused. In a low, uncharacteristically childlike tone, he asked, "Does it matter that I'm at private school?" A stifled half-laugh, half-raspberry finally escaped my clamped lips.

"Not at ALL, Mr. W—, not at all! The Party welcomes its members from ALL classes and economic strata. We don't discriminate!"

"No," someone at the table murmured, "I imagine you don't."

Within a few weeks, Adam had discovered Trotsky and binned the Young Communists form. We remained good friends over the years that followed, even as he baited me for my squeamishness towards revolutionary violence, gangster rap and hallucinogenics, while I eye-rolled his every new sectarian denouncement and allegiance and was eventually prohibited from any mention of the Judaean People's Front.

In the previous chapter, we saw how Jane, Paddy and Sandy each played out a different version of the drama we all experience of trying to manage the impossible tension between the wish to stand out and the demand to fit in. But each of these options implies a goal of acceptance and approval by some hierarchy or other—of adults, peers or both. They exclude the more radical option of standing outside the norms and values of the world, of saying no to everyone and everything. This is the stance of rebellion, and it defines our image of adolescence in life and literature alike.

When I recall my adolescent self, I don't see a fiery naysayer. Any hint of political, emotional or hedonistic excess and a shaming self-consciousness would overtake me, my eye reversing into selfie mode and confronting me with a living record of my own ridiculousness.

But what I do remember is an utter fatigue, even disgust, at the different and sometimes contradictory kinds of conformity demanded of me. Parents, teachers and friends all seemed to want me to be or do something different—gentle and tough, serious and flippant, dedicated to schoolwork and yet coolly indifferent to it. And sometimes the only response that made sense was the internal scream of "sod them all." I didn't want to care about doing well or being cool, approval or disapproval. I just wanted to get out from under the burden of the world's expectations, to be free of that permanent prickly, judging gaze on the back of my neck.

Perhaps our conception of adolescent rebellion has been too restricted by folklore and pop culture cliché. We think of adolescent rebels smoking, swearing, snarling with contempt, of their mocking the hypocrisy and conformism of their parents' society, of their precocious cynicism and wide-eyed idealism, their defiantly ugly hair and clothes and music. In imagining rebellion, our minds reflexively think of wilful opposition to order and authority, whether in the form of delinquency or moral self-righteousness or both.

But not all adolescents externalise their hostile feelings in such obvious ways. As we're about to see, rebellion wears many masks.

i "I've no idea": Portia Quayne

PQ, sixteen, presents as detached and reticent, beneath which one senses high degree of fear and confusion. Within two-year span, lost first father, then mother. Now living in London with half-brother, twenty years her senior, and his wife. Father's first wife "banished" him from house following affair with patient's mother. Patient has led peripatetic existence from birth, shuttled between cheap European hotels, very little contact with other children. Some concern as to whether new guardians can comprehend the scale of traumatic loss and disruptive change suffered by their new charge, and implications for emotional health and stability.

Portia Quayne, the confused protagonist of Elizabeth Bowen's *The Death of the Heart* (1938), may seem a distinctly odd exemplar of adolescent rebellion. For most of the novel, she is almost pathologically non-confrontational. In fact, she is so acquiescent in the face of the casual hostility and manipulation of almost everyone around her that we feel pulled between pity for her and exasperation with her. Why doesn't she stand up for herself? Why does she let the world walk all over her?

Questions like this alert us to how much more readily we identify with the strong than the weak. The spectacle of another's defencelessness has a shaming effect on us, putting us in touch with our own feelings of confusion and inadequacy. When we witness it, we feel the need to assure ourselves that in the face of verbal or physical attack we'd give as good as we got. Characters like Portia are unsettling in this regard, as they remind us that we're just as likely to freeze in terror and self-doubt.

In which case, why try to claim her for the rebels? Seemingly defined at every turn by her chronic inability to know what to think, say or do, it's hard to imagine anyone less resembling a rebel, from the outside at least.

But from the inside? Aren't the moral and emotional certainties of adolescent protest and scorn a cover story for the same insecurities and inadequacies that are so glaringly evident in Portia? The difference is that most of us grow up among other kids, and manage to absorb enough of the unwritten rules of peer interaction to maintain some semblance of self-confidence.

Psychoanalysis places great emphasis on this sense of security as an essential element in our humanity. It reminds us that we begin entirely dependent on the care of others, and that this dependence, at least in the modern West, persists into at least the heart of adolescence if not well beyond. And it's in adolescence that our fundamental ambivalence about this state of affairs comes to the surface.

The adolescent is frequently pulled between wanting and rejecting the love and reassurance she enjoyed as a child; between cuddling up to her mother and telling her to just *leave me alone*, I'm not a *kid, all right*! On the one hand, we want to hold on to our dependence and the comforts it brings; on the other, we desperately want rid of it, to be spared the reminder that we remain so much in need, materially and emotionally.

Rebellion tends to look and sound like the triumph of separation over dependence, of self-assertion over compliance. But it often has the effect of establishing a new regime of compliance. Use the right slang, listen to the right music, get the right haircut, hold the right opinions and you'll be OK, more or less. In adolescence, the habits and conventions of the world around us are a kind of protective armour against our own fragility and uncertainty as much as against the malice of others.

This is surely why adolescent rebellion can seem hard to distinguish from the most rigid conformism, especially as consumer culture becomes ever more adept at appropriating and monetising it. Rebellion in this sense means being in the know—worldly, streetwise, nobody's fool. It creates an implicit line between the clued-up in-crowd and the clueless losers.

All of which leads me to wonder if there is anything all that rebellious about rebellion as we conventionally understand it; if the properly radical stance for the would-be rebel might be not knowingness but innocence.

At sixteen, Portia has never known an in-crowd to be part of—or excluded from. The child of her genteel middle-aged father's extramarital affair with the bohemian Irene, she has spent her first sixteen years in the cheap European hotels to which her father was banished once his first wife discovered the affair.

When the novel opens, Portia's mother has recently died, and she is living with her older half-brother, the withdrawn, depressive Thomas, and his elegant, caustic wife, Anna, in Regent's Park. Beyond Anna's erratic attentions, Portia's solitude is alleviated only by Lilian, a self-satisfied classmate from their West End finishing school, and Matchett, the Quaynes' self-righteous housekeeper. This atmosphere of irritable neglect, indifference and false friendship seals her vulnerability to the attentions of Eddie.

Having spent her childhood wandering the cities and resorts of Europe, with neither formal education nor social life, Portia has no resources with which to make sense of the new world she now inhabits. Her predicament reminds us that an ordinary childhood involves learning to read far more than books; it means reading faces, gestures, tones, expressions verbal and non-verbal—the subtlest as well as the most obvious social and emotional signs.

If you spend time around children and adolescents, you'll notice how skilled they tend to be as readers in this sense, regardless of their more formal levels of attainment in book learning. From a semitone's shift in vocal pitch or the position of an eyebrow they can discern the subtlest variegations in sincerity, irony, coolness or pretension. Social media and consumer culture, for all their undoubted ills, are very effective educators in the intricacies of sign systems.

The social codes of the English upper middle class of the 1930s would have been no less difficult to decipher than today's, especially to an unschooled outsider plunged abruptly into its centre. This partly explains the despair Portia feels on arriving in London. Her sense of being cast adrift in an incomprehensible world is only exacerbated by the impression that everyone else seems to know exactly what they're saying and doing.

As she's known only the company of her earnest, kindly parents all her life, people suddenly appear to her as an insoluble puzzle: "every look, every movement, every object had a quite political seriousness for her: nothing was not weighed down by significance." And nowhere is she more alive to this than in her new home:

> In her home life (her new home life) with its puzzles, she saw dissimulation always on guard; she asked herself humbly for what reason people said what they did not mean and did not say what they meant.

It's difficult to imagine how strange and frightening an atmosphere so heavy in irony and ambiguity would be to someone who knows nothing of those qualities. What happens to a person when they lose their confidence in their capacity to read their environment?

Ellen didn't immediately give me the impression of being severely depressed or traumatised. On the contrary, though her story was painful, I was struck during our first meeting by the intense, lively intelligence and caustic humour she brought to its telling. It was only as we were winding up the session that I started to glimpse a much darker state of mind: her voice lowered, her sentences tailed off, her pauses lengthened ominously, her frank, open gaze turned evasive.

Over the years of work that followed, I learned to recognise these abrupt shifts of mood as integral to who she was, or rather to who she'd become. It was as though she was being shuttled willy-nilly across two sides of an internal split at her very core. One side was inhabited by the cheerful, highly capable paediatrician who fronted her working and social lives; the other by what seemed like an excruciatingly shy child, poor in words, understanding and resourcefulness.

The defining period of Ellen's childhood in Toronto saw her father leave her mother for a family friend. This unremarkable episode of marital breakdown and betrayal was rendered catastrophic with her mother's contraction of a terminal cancer, about which she was told in only the vaguest terms.

At the age of eight, soon after her mother's diagnosis, she and her younger brother were taken by her father and his new partner to live thousands of miles away from their mother in Vancouver. She had only a hasty and confused goodbye with her mother, who assured her they'd see each other very soon. A few months later, her father accompanied his children to her funeral. Neither she nor her brother cried: "My dad told me I looked pretty and everything would be fine. I'm really not sure I had a clue what was going on."

As she grew up, this bewilderment became the basis for a kind of secret self. In adolescence, while her brother went into a tailspin of truancy and drugs to the soundtrack of explosive rows with his stepmother, Ellen carefully maintained an exterior of exaggerated normalcy: top grades, easy sociability and compliance. But at night she'd often lie awake, staring into the blackness, gripped by a terrible, wordless dread.

Ellen came to me because this split was no longer sustainable. Days on autopilot at work were being followed by evenings spent alone staring blankly at screens or pages. She might just about have been convincing others in her role as a hardy, cheerful grafter, but she was no longer convincing herself. For all the smiles and good sense, she was starting to fall apart.

What was more, she was beginning to confront a fact of her inner history she'd long been avoiding: she had only the most threadbare and insubstantial memories of her mother. She wondered if the reason why she spent so much time staring at and thinking about nothing was that she was scrabbling around inside the chambers of her mind searching for her and finding only emptiness.

In "Mourning and Melancholia" (1917), one of his most famous essays, Freud asks how it is that an experience of grief intensifies to the point that it never seems to end, to achieve what he called "working through." The problem for this "melancholic" mode of mourning, writes Freud, is that the mourner "knows *whom* he has lost but not *what* he has lost in him." In Ellen's case, this seemed literally true: the essence of her sadness lay in knowing her mother's identity but having almost no sense of her as a person.

Having such a void at her heart was making her seem weird to herself, and increasingly, she reckoned, to everyone else. She would turn around to friends at social gatherings and make unsettling, mirthless quips; to someone who asked what she was doing tomorrow, she replied she'd "probably just lie in bed and find new ways to despise myself." It might have been all right if people knew her as a nihilistic joker, but nothing could have been further from the truth: "I used to be the kind of person other people saw as always knowing what to say or do, and now I feel like the exact opposite."

The fabric of Ellen's life was perforated by a hole that seemed to be expanding. Her familiar vitality and curiosity were being swallowed up by the blank depression at her centre, as though her mother's absence had become more real to her than the presence of anything or anyone else. She was feeling like a stranger in her own life. The traumatic incomprehension of the child she once was had returned to make a claim on her adult self.

This is what brings Portia to mind when I think of Ellen, notwithstanding how different they are. They are children whose orphan status deprives them of a life's map and compass, leaving them to stumble confusedly through the world, unsure if they can trust themselves to understand what anything or anyone else means.

Portia's big question—why don't people say what they mean and mean what they say?—is a fundamental one for all human relationships, and therefore for psychoanalysis.

In fact, psychoanalysis starts from this gap between saying and meaning. What it calls the unconscious is the elusive presence in us of the thoughts, feelings, desires and anxieties that are concealed to ourselves as well as everyone else.

Having an unconscious means we can never be sure what we're doing or saying, or even what we're thinking or feeling. Dreams and so-called Freudian "slips" show us that our minds teem with impulses and ideas which escape the notice of our conscious selves. But unconscious motives also guide our everyday ways of being and relating. Which of us hasn't at some point been perplexed by our own behaviour, wondered at an inexplicable outburst of rage or tears or laughter, or at the sabotage of a cherished ambition or desire?

The fact that we perpetually elude our own understanding is what makes us so endlessly infuriating and so fascinating. If I could identify the single most frustrating question people in the consulting room ask about themselves, it would almost certainly be: "Why can't I be more straightforward?" Variations on this question include "Why do I spoil the things I most enjoy?" and "Why do I hurt or run from the person I most care about?"

The adult world as Bowen portrays it is one in which this ordinary human perversity has become an entrenched and unquestioned fact of life. None of the adults around Portia expect themselves or anyone else to behave responsibly or reliably; in fact, her assumption that they would is treated again and again as a piece of abject naivety. What

makes them seem so cynical is not that they take their
internal contradictions as a given, but that they show so
little curiosity about them, and so little desire to understand or manage them. It's in this sense that Portia is a
rebel despite herself; not a moody insurrectionist against
the old order, but a child who shows up the dishonesty
and cruelty of adult society simply by retaining her own
innocence. The first imperative of the gilded world of
Portia's adoptive guardians and their circle is to keep up
appearances, however at odds they may be with the truth.

During her summer stay on the Kent coast, Portia
falls in with the social circle around her hostess's adult
children, Daphne and Dickie. However, no sooner does
Eddie comes to visit her than he makes an easy conquest
of Daphne. In a darkened cinema, Dickie's cigarette
lighter momentarily illuminates Eddie holding and
stroking Daphne's hand right under Portia's eye.

The next day, Portia responds to Eddie's casual
betrayal with her customary guileless bewilderment—
why, if you're here with me, were you holding hands with
her? He swats the question away like an irksome fly: "You
and I know each other, and you know how silly I am. But
if it really upset you, of course it was awful of me. You
really mustn't be hurt, or I shall wish I was dead."

Unappeased, Portia continues to probe his behaviour.
Why does he seem to talk and feel completely differently from one moment to the next? Increasingly rattled
and shamed by her insistent, artless questions, he tells
her not to exasperate him: "How can I keep on feeling

something I once felt when there are so many things one can feel?" Her reply is the more heartbreaking for being framed as a kind of troubling logical conundrum: "But I don't see how you can say you are serious if there's no one thing you keep feeling the whole time."

The poignancy of Portia's confusion shades into dark comedy when she goes on to confront Daphne about the hand-holding incident and is met with breathless outrage. Daphne expects her young house guest to comply with social codes and draw a discreet veil over what she saw in the cinema. Portia's open reference to the incident is a scandal that in Daphne's mind far exceeds her own duplicity and scheming. If she hadn't liked what Eddie was doing, Portia mildly reproaches, "You could always have struggled."

> Daphne gave up. "You're completely bats," she said. "You'd better go and lie down. You don't even understand a single thing. Standing about there, not looking like anything. You know, really, if you'll excuse my saying so, a person might almost take you for a natural. Have you got *no* ideas?"
>
> "I've no idea," said Portia, in a dazed way.

On reading this scene, it's hard not to feel pity for Portia and a corresponding disgust for Daphne. It's also hard not to laugh; the incongruity between Daphne's nastiness and Portia's impassivity is irresistibly funny. But are we laughing at Portia or with her? Surely both—we laugh at the poor ingénue with no inkling of other people's capacity to manipulate and deceive; but we also laugh with her because, as we see from Daphne's rage, nothing is liable to wind up a schemer more than someone who can't or won't play the game. The blood sports of social and sexual competition require all participants to be fully conversant with the rules. A "natural"—an old-fashioned equivalent for an idiot—confounds the entire system; how can you play a game with someone who not only doesn't know how to play, but doesn't even know it's a game?

We can imagine a witty comeback to Daphne's catty parting swipe, "Have you got *no* ideas?" But surely none could be more exasperating than Portia's, "I've no idea." What does her response even mean? "Indeed no, I have no ideas," or "I don't have any idea whether I have any ideas"? Does *she* even know which it is? The exchange shows us that elusive and rather hilarious point when dull-wittedness and genius meet.

Intuiting the hypocrisy of adult life and the crookedness of its rules, Portia quietly declines to play along. "Inwardly innocent people," writes Bowen's narrator in one of her wonderfully oblique philosophical interventions, "exist alone . . . The system of our affections is too corrupt for them."

The innocent as unwitting lone wolf, refusing the compromises and deceits of the world around her; what could be more rebellious than that?

*

But wait—is there really such a thing as an innocent? From the point of view of a psychoanalyst, the answer would have to be no, at least if by "innocent" we mean "pure of heart" or "guileless." The basic premise of psychoanalysis is that in unconscious life there is no innocence, that no human psyche is free of narcissism, envy, cruelty, voraciousness, lust or any of the other great vices of our race.

What we mean by innocence in the case of someone like Portia is not that she has no "bad" feelings, but that they are inaccessible to her or that she knows very little of them. When others are abusive or mocking, she seems not to notice, as though such attitudes were simply absent from her emotional repertoire. But one way of reading Bowen's novel is as a subtle exploration of innocence as a kind of life strategy, an unconsciously sly way of getting what we want. It's hard to believe that Portia doesn't register on some level how her stance of innocence both frustrates and seduces others, or how strangely effective it is as a means of getting attention and interest.

Portia, as we've seen, differs from most of us in having grown up without the siblings or peers who would have led her astray, initiating her into the ways of manipulation and duplicity and rivalry. Although she was born of a "shameful" adulterous union, as well as being hapless and ineffectual, her parents were also relentlessly kind. Added to which they're now dead. In other words, they don't make very promising targets for rebellion.

So how is she to discharge those nastily oppositional impulses, or even to feel them? Perhaps by winding others up with her apparent incomprehension.

Not understanding a single thing is a form of oblique, concealed rebellion against hypocrisy and dishonesty. Direct and open rebellion can occur only when the rebel is clear about who and what she's rebelling against.

ii "A holy son": Johnny Grimes

JG, fourteen, seemed taciturn and serious-minded. Living in tiny, barely habitable apartment with mother, stepfather and half-brother. Stepfather prominent in part of one of the many small evangelical congregations in the locality (Harlem). Close with mother, but enquiry into relationship with stepfather hints at serious strain. Highly intelligent, giving a strong impression of intense but heavily restrained anger. Though not explicitly stated, strong indications stepfather violent towards him.

Rebellion is shaped by the contexts in which we live and relate to others. Portia is parachuted abruptly into a world of high status and privilege whose arcane and deceptive codes of behaviour leave her feeling both confused and excluded. By contrast, Johnny Grimes, protagonist of *Go Tell It on the Mountain*, James Baldwin's debut novel of 1953, has grown up in a community and family shaped by poverty and racism, both of which sow the seeds of his painfully suppressed rage and resentment.

Violence, sex, delinquency, political dissent—these are a few of the many ways to provoke, reject and alienate the parental order. Think of Adam's visit from the local Communist Party. It's doubtful that any of the people round the table felt threatened or horri-fied, or even much concerned, by his political beliefs. What made the scene so excruciating was the implied attack on his father's authority and his mother's care, on the entire system of codes and values governing the family.

Over the three years he'd been seeing me weekly, Carl would talk about his father only to warn me he wouldn't talk about him—"Well, not like *that* anyway," he would say, as though we both knew what *that* was. "You've no idea how much he's given me, he's been such a major presence in my life. I'm not going to just start coming here and . . . well, you know," he would tail off. He'd then repeat warmed-over, impersonal praise he might have lifted from an admiring newspaper profile. Carl's father, now retired, had been a leading figure in cancer research, credited with discoveries in genetic transmission that had revolutionised approaches to treatment and saved innumerable lives.

"His contribution was extraordinary," he would tell me with more than a hint of agitation. "The man is a giant in the field. That's just beyond dispute."

More than once, I observed that he talked to me about his father as though correcting someone who had slighted him. It didn't seem to get us very far, but then neither did anything else. I found myself bamboozled and a little exasperated by the emerging pattern. He would allude to something his father had said or done in Carl's childhood—disparaging his science homework, or screaming wild invective at his mother—then leap to some bland generalisation: "But all fathers do that," or "That's what marriage is like." The trail of his father led only to the same brick wall of nervous reticence.

Now in his early thirties, Carl was formidably intelligent but struggling to get a handle on life. Seemingly promising relationships would collapse abruptly after a single, explosive row. He would quit jobs within weeks of starting them, filling the session that followed with withering denunciations of his ex-boss's stupidity.

Carl's stories, his tone of voice, his very physical presence were infused with a palpable anger. Anyone who came to be involved with him in any way would end up on the receiving end of his rage, and I was certainly no exception. When I suggested he might be struggling with his hostile feelings towards his father, he would tell me furiously that if he'd known I was in the "blame the parents" school of psychotherapy, he'd have taken his business elsewhere. Why was I forever sniffing around the supposed sins of his father? It was such a bloody cliché, he'd thought I was smarter than that.

It didn't require years of clinical experience to infer that Carl's aggressive idealisation of his father, and his brittleness in the face of even the mildest questioning of it, masked a barely contained rage against him. Nor was it hard to see how readily this rage was displaced onto every male authority figure he encountered. Every outburst against me, moreover, would be followed in the next session by a shamefaced and anxious apology, as though I'd been spending the time between cooking up some suitably cruel punishment for his impudence.

Why was it so difficult for Carl to voice his anger against his father? Often the very intensity of our feelings has an inhibiting effect on their expression. Somewhere in us lurks the suspicion that yielding to them will cause us to unravel, to become slaves to our own murderousness and depravity. Carl, as we'd eventually discover, wasn't frightened so much of shouting at his father as of killing him. What was he supposed to do with the horribly gratifying fantasy of watching the life drain out of his father's eyes and flailing limbs as he slowly strangled him? "And as I imagine it, I think to myself, 'Why don't you try saying something snarky now, old man!'" Carl's tenacious love of his father was his last line of defence against his homicidal rage.

What on earth could Carl, raised in an atmosphere of unquestioned prosperity and prestige, have in common with the stepson of a lay preacher in 1930s Harlem? Perhaps the disparities are so glaringly obvious as to mask the affinities. Both experienced their adolescence in the shadow of a tyrannical father whose revered public status concealed his private cruelty and pettiness. Both were internally riven by a tormenting question: how can I hate my father when the world around me tells me I must love him?

The state of our internal lives is always intimately bound up with the conditions of our external world. Poverty and abuse are the air Baldwin's characters breathe. But rather than make this an occasion for monotone protest, he uses it to explore the different ways it shapes human relationships—between lovers, parents and children, siblings and friends. The spectre of his humiliation by employers or the police, for example, can mean a father becomes more despotic at home, which in turn renders his sons increasingly desperate and resentful.

Violence has shaped Johnny's life since before he was born. His biological father, Richard, framed and beaten for a convenience store robbery by Southern police, killed himself within weeks of Johnny's conception. Meanwhile his adoptive father, Gabriel, grieves an unacknowledged son born of a brief affair, victim of a racist murder in the same town as Richard. Each, in other words, functions for the other as an unloved and unwanted replacement for the father or son they might really have loved. Failure and disappointment are written into their relationship from the first.

Johnny spends much of the novel trying to imagine ways to survive the mutual hatred between himself and his father. One of these is to cherish to himself his sense of his own intelligence. At five, we're told early on, the elderly white principal of his school singles out his lettering on the blackboard and tells him, "You're a very bright boy, John Grimes." This moment becomes a kind of talisman for Johnny, the source of an indestructible sense of self. This very pride "was his identity, and part, therefore, of that wickedness for which his father beat him and to which he clung in order to withstand his father."

The hellish knots of this dynamic are beautifully conveyed in this passage: Johnny survives his father's violence by clinging to the very quality of character which provokes it. It's a disturbingly astute encapsulation of how mutual hate comes to be nurtured and perpetuated: Johnny can only survive by loving what his father most hates in him, ensuring that he's hated all the more:

> His father's arm, rising and falling, might make him cry, and that voice might cause him to tremble; yet his father could never be entirely the victor, for John cherished something that his father could not reach. It was his hatred and his intelligence that he cherished, the one feeding the other.

Johnny's younger brother, Roy, is Gabriel's biological son, and far more openly contemptuous of him. But where Gabriel shows nothing but cruelty to taciturn Johnny, his anger with Roy is leavened by indulgent affection.

The difference in attitude, no doubt, is the difference between a reluctantly adopted and a natural son.

But it is also the difference between two kinds of rebellion. Roy's relationship to his father is the classically adolescent one of swaggering defiance. While it can provoke Gabriel to anger, it doesn't induce suspicion. Flaunting his distaste for his father's joyless, punitive way of parenting, Roy ensures that Gabriel doesn't need to guess at his son's feelings towards him. Johnny's outward display of compliance, on the other hand, masks a deeper and more passionate hatred, unmitigated by any sense of blood ties.

Gabriel's awareness that Johnny isn't his true kin and his jealousy of the dead man who fathered him prove fertile breeding ground for paranoia. He broods that Elizabeth, his wife, is in league with Johnny against him, silently but insidiously mocking him. She is "hardhearted, stiff-necked," he tells himself, invoking the famously severe Old Testament adjectives; and Johnny "was exactly like her, silent, watching, full of evil pride—they would be cast out, one day, into the outer darkness."

The harsh language of biblical retribution laid over the texture of everyday emotion induces in me a feeling of queasy foreboding, a sense that some terrible reckoning may be just around the corner. I had the same feeling listening to Carl talk, albeit in a rather less scriptural register, about his long-suppressed rage against his father.

There are many reasons to read *Go Tell It on the Mountain*, but perhaps none more compelling than the electric last chapter, "The Threshing Floor," which takes us moment by moment through Johnny's torturous passage to personal salvation. We witness him fall to the floor, possessed by some nameless terror, thrashing and screaming as he plunges into his own internal abyss, "a sickness in his bowels, a tightening in his loin-strings."

When Johnny emerges from this all-night inner journey, his fellow congregants are jubilant with praise: "The Lord done raised you up a holy son." The church sisters, his mother and his mentor Elisha all join in the rapturous celebration of Johnny's spiritual awakening. But the hostility between Johnny and Gabriel remains untouched by this infectious spread of holy fellow feeling.

In fact, Johnny's awakening seems only to deepen their mutual antipathy. They both appear to recognise the younger man's ascendancy in the church as an implicit provocation and challenge to the older man's place in the family and the community, less a gesture of reconciliation than a new and more subtle way of hating him. The phrase "holier than thou," with its connotations of concealed rivalry and aggression, never seemed more apt.

At the end of the novel, the family returns home after the long and draining night in church. As Gabriel climbs the stone steps into the entrance of the house, he stares at Johnny, "who blocked the way." Gabriel orders him upstairs, but Johnny lingers to say goodbye to Elisha and watch him leave. Then: "He turned to face his father— he found himself smiling, but his father did not smile."

There is a world of meaning in this almost imperceptible exchange of glances. Each of them seems to understand that the smile Johnny sends Gabriel's way, however conciliatory and appeasing it may appear to outsiders, is an implicit triumphal taunt, rebellion in the sinister guise of holy reverence.

"Hey, Johnny, what are you rebelling against?"
"What've you got?"

Everyone loves that famous comeback from Marlon Brando in *The Wild One*. It captures perfectly the spirit of dangerous, punky nihilism whose target is everything and nothing. But it also offers a smart and concentrated insight into the nature of youthful rebellion. Unlike the protester or the revolutionary, the rebel is not attacking this or that aspect of the existing order but order itself. More basically, he defies any discipline, restraint or restriction on his freedom to do what he wants.

In psychoanalytic terms, we could say that every rebellion stages a confrontation between the id, the mind's teeming reservoir of sexual and aggressive impulses, and the superego, the fearsome representative of the severe parent in us that seeks to curb and punish those impulses.

It's easy to see how neatly this model works in a context like 1950s America, when everyone from the state to the advertisers was perpetually enjoining the populace to political, moral and cultural compliance. A rebellious, insubordinate id and a draconian superego always have a mutually amplifying effect: the more you push at authority, the more it pushes back.

Freud tells us that in earliest infancy we are all id, a bubbling soup of primitive, anarchic energy. At a certain point in our development, this energy runs up against the roadblock of parental order and discipline. We manage this conflict by identifying a part of ourselves with this strict parent, internalising their authority. Our mind does this by diverting a portion of the id's energy to this parent within. In other words, the superego is made of the same stuff as the id, and so can be just as ferocious, tyrannical and irrational.

Freud paints a picture of the ego, the seat of reason and practical action, under siege from the competing claims of a voracious and destructive id (think exhibitionistic, tantrum-prone, unpredictable toddler) and a forbidding, dictatorial superego (think begowned, cane-wielding 1950s private school teacher). The two are perpetually upping the ante on one another.

The point here is that rebellion and order are inextricably bound up with one another. Rebellion needs the hard edges of power—school, church, state, military—to sharpen itself on. That conflict is first formed in the crucible of the family, where our force of will finds itself going into battle with the force of parental discipline.

In ordinary development, parents can give abundantly in all the good things—affection, praise, attention, treats—but can also take them away, imposing rules, limits, demands and sanctions. This duality makes them an object of both love and anxiety for their children. However, going back to my dealings with adults sent to boarding school as children, some of whom were as young as seven, it repeatedly struck me that they possessed a sense not only of abandonment and loss, but of a kind of emotional undernourishment.

The outsourcing of these dual functions of care to boarding school staff changes their very nature. Both reward and punishment lose their intense emotional charge: however fond or hostile a child feels towards a given member of staff, the bond between them is looser and thinner than that with their parents. As one patient put it to me, "Behaving badly meant something completely different at boarding school than at home. Not just because you got into worse trouble, but because the rules had nothing to do with love or hate. Praise meant I'd done well, not that I was loved; trouble meant I'd broken some rule, not that I'd disappointed or upset anyone."

That insight came after six years of therapy. Rob had first come to me after his wife complained he was incapable of intimacy. "I think that's a bit harsh," he added, which sounded to me like a wonderfully inadvertent illustration of what she was talking about. He would recount their arguments, lamenting her "irrational," "overemotional" responses. His thirteen-year-old daughter was "even worse," weeping uncontrollably over the most trivial things. Chuckling genially, he told me, "Last night she got terribly upset at dinner because some girl had told her that her hair was rubbish. Her mother's emoting with her and stroking her forearm, and all I could think to say was, 'I find it hard to believe you can get so upset about what some stupid girl says about your hair.' Well, that was a mistake. That really set her off. She's sobbing wildly, her mother's staring daggers at me. Bloody madhouse."

For a long time, Rob met all expressions of emotional life with the same irritable puzzlement: "If you have a problem, why not *do* something about it instead of bloody wallowing in it?" he asked. When I observed aloud that he spoke as though he couldn't understand why there were such things as feelings at all, he shot back reflexively, "Well, no, I don't think I can, really!," then stopped in his tracks, palpably disturbed at what he'd just said.

It was soon after this that he began talking about his experience at boarding school. Most of his young life had been spent away from home. During holidays, he and his younger brother were handed over to the care of nannies for much of the day. He would see his parents at breakfast, for a pleasant hour between his dinner and theirs, or perhaps for the odd outing to the theatre or church. "They were always kind enough, smiling and asking if we were enjoying ourselves."

At school, Rob was in the hands of responsible adults seeking to apply general rules fairly and consistently to all pupils; at home, he was looked after by domestic employees, with the occasional interval to enjoy his parents' detached congeniality. Deprived of the ordinary substance of daily family drama—anger, excitement, rivalry, disappointment, affection, sadness, hilarity—he had only the most minimal resources for developing a full inner life.

It wasn't that he felt nothing. On the contrary, he remembered feeling a full range of emotions, from intense ecstasy to abject misery; but these were wordless sensations felt within the cell of his own self, and they were never communicated to himself or anyone else. In his mind, they were odd internal eruptions he learned to put to one side, inconvenient intrusions into the hard work required to get on in life. Problems required solutions, not indulgent brooding.

It probably doesn't need saying that Rob never had a rebellious phase. Rebellion is the act not only of someone who perceives external injustice, but of someone for whom feelings matter, who cannot countenance the denial of the claims of their inner self. A rebel is someone listening for the stirrings of their unconscious desires as well as to their conscious judgements.

This isn't to say that Rob's story entirely excluded the possibility of a rebellion. Dissolute, unruly and antagonistic behaviour is hardly unknown at boarding school, or in emotionally barren upper-class homes. A different child might have been less compliant and more angry, less willing to submit to a regime of impersonal rules and emotional neglect, more apt to yield to the accumulating inner discontent and explode.

Rob's parents were from very similar families and had both been sent to boarding school from a young age themselves. This is worth noting not only for the obvious point that each generation dutifully followed this preferred child-rearing convention of their class. More than the external tradition of boarding school, what was transmitted down the generations was a radical restriction of emotional communication, a block on familial intimacy. Visible drama was vulgar and embarrassing; permanent sibling estrangements and filial disinheritances and marital infidelities were part of the family history, but alluded to only in passing whispers and eavesdropped exchanges that amplified the sense of their unspeakability.

For Rob's family, the suppression of painful stories and their associated feelings was more than a shared habit; it was a transgenerational inheritance, part of the shared unconscious life of its members. It conditioned his need to dismiss or trivialise feelings and concentrate on problem-solving. Rather than love, hate, yearn for or rage at his parents, why not accept them as the genial cameos they chose to be? Rob gives us a glimpse of a life lived as though the charge of family relationships and the ghosts of previous generations could simply be banished.

Life lived in this way becomes a matter of imitation rather than authentic experience, the performance of what Winnicott called a "false self," a self that complies with the imagined expectations of the adult world and its practical realities, cutting itself off from its own unconscious life. A self of this kind might resemble a clone, brought into the world as though from nowhere, unmarked by any family history, lacking in the bodily and emotional care (whether intimate or cold) of parents, or the fraught proximity of siblings.

iii "We had to behave like them": Ruth

R (no surname provided) appeared ordinary late adolescent, expressing many expected feelings and preoccupations: anxieties about boyfriends, rivalry and resentments towards female friends, suspicion of adult authority. Behind eagerness to fit in with peers, evident in veneer of bravado and "not caring," can be discerned profound insecurity and sadness. Has spent entire young life in residential care institutions, where reportedly prone to spinning elaborate, often nonsensical stories about secret practices and relationships of adults in charge. Repeated enquiries after R's family history yielded no information. Almost as though she had no parents, living or deceased.

Birthed in laboratories, raised in segregated boarding schools and sent as young adults to live in isolated shared housing communities, the characters at the centre of Kazuo Ishiguro's *Never Let Me Go* (2005), Kathy, Tommy and Ruth, experience a youth whose trials and sorrows seem much the same as ours. Like any children, they spin extravagant stories of the world around them; like any adolescents, they endure the insecurities, rivalries and longings provoked by intimate friendships and first loves.

But from the point of view of the society they serve, the minds and feelings of these young people are an unwanted encumbrance. Their one life purpose is to nurture internal organs, to be surgically harvested as they enter adulthood and donated to fatally ill citizens of the parallel, naturally born community.

Ishiguro sets the book not in some fantastical dystopia but in "England, late 1990s." There is little in the cultural or political atmosphere of the novel to suggest we are anywhere other than the familiar, liberal democratic society inhabited by its readers. The cloned children are not the victims of some totalitarian nightmare in the vein of *The Handmaid's Tale*'s Gilead or *Nineteen Eighty-Four*'s Oceania. Their lives are governed by dedicated and to all appearances decent teachers and carers, not prowling stormtroopers.

But this begs the question as to why they're so passive in the face of their fate. Why don't they rebel against the society that breeds them to die slowly and painfully, and believes that their lives have no value other than as bearers of internal organs?

The state that breeds the clones can hardly rule them through violence and intimidation—the clones will know that their value lies in their remaining alive and healthy. In any case, the state does not raise and kill them out of cruelty or hostility, but to provide a crucial service to its citizens. Clones offer a technocratic solution to the problem of disease: the most rational and efficient way to ensure their reliability as donors is to make their lives up to the point of donation as safe and comfortable as possible.

In other words, instead of securing clones' cooperation by force, the state gets them to identify with their own role in the process. Before becoming donors themselves, most clones spend a significant period as a "carer" for other donors. Instead of resisting their medical exploitation and homicide, they participate in it.

How does an entire section of the population come to be complicit in their own destruction? Born of genetic material in the laboratory rather than of a parental couple in a home, clones are deprived of human intimates from the outset. This doesn't mean that they're lacking in emotion; on the contrary, Kathy, Tommy and Ruth are all awash with it. What they lack is parents to receive and give meaningful shape to their feelings, objects on whom they can project their passions and rages.

In one of the novel's most wrenching scenes, Miss Lucy, the teacher at Hailsham boarding school who defiantly refuses to sustain the ongoing deception of the cloned children, overhears two of them talking about becoming actors in America. She abruptly addresses the assembled children and tries to set them straight:

> "Your lives are set out for you. You'll become adults, then before you're old, before you're even middle-aged, you'll start to donate your vital organs. That's what each

of you was created to do. You're not like the actors you watch on your videos, you're not even like me. You were brought into this world for a purpose, and your futures, all of them, have been decided. So you're not to talk that way any more . . . If you're to have decent lives, you have to know who you are and what lies ahead of you, every one of you."

But the reaction from the children to this searing, urgent dose of honesty is almost entirely blank. After she's stopped talking, Kathy tells us, "we were all pretty relieved." At no point do the Hailsham children seem to feel or even comprehend the intense rage that Miss Lucy feels on their behalf. Even once they're fully aware of the fate lying in store, they make no attempt to protest or rebel against it. They are inducted into their roles as carers and then donors, as though fulfilling an inexorable destiny.

Kathy's narration is tinged throughout with a tone of melancholic resignation, but Miss Lucy's anger seems oddly inaccessible to her. This restricted range of feeling is an effect of not being linked into the continuity of generations. Clones have no parents and cannot conceive children. Existing in isolation from past and future generations has profound consequences for sex above all.

For "people out there," notes Kathy, sex is intensely charged, an occasion for fighting and killing. The reason for this is obvious: "they could have babies from sex." "And even though, as we knew, it was completely impossible for any of us to have babies, out there, we had to behave like them. We had to respect the rules and treat sex as something pretty special." Later on, when the trio have left Hailsham and are living at the Cottages, Kathy notices how much the "veteran couples" in the complex conduct their relationships by means of imitation, specifically of American TV sitcoms: "the way they gestured to each other, sat together on sofas, even the way they argued and stormed out of rooms." This pale, desperate imitation of sexual intimacy is surely one of the most quietly devastating features of this parallel world.

The singular inner life that comes of being born naturally means that the cloned self is, in some senses, a false one, lacking the intimacy of ordinary child-rearing, the unconscious transmission of stories and secrets and mysteries from past to future generations, the presence or absence of siblings. The American-born British psychoanalyst Christopher Bollas points out that the mother, in her everyday routines of care, unconsciously transmits to her baby a style of being—vocal, gestural, expressive—which becomes the basis of the future child and adult's singular character. These forms of nurture, so universal we barely notice them, are not part of the clone's development. Without the resources to cultivate a true self, the clone can only form a self through imitation.

What makes the character of Ruth so haunting is that her capacity for petty manipulation, deceit and vindictiveness, as well as her deep vulnerability, render her indistinguishable from the "people out there." Throughout the story, she yearns to be different, to acquire those traits of character and behaviour that would make her "special" and mark her out from the clones, those things, as we would say, that make us human.

The stories Ruth spins, so strange to Kathy as a child, are an expression of this wish. The group of "special guardians" she recruits from among the Hailsham girls to protect Miss Geraldine from abduction by monsters in the nearby woods, like the pencil case she claims was given by her, are invented signs of Ruth's exceptionality. Ruth wants her schoolmates to imagine her as under Geraldine's protection, singled out for maternal care. These fantasies of specialness, comments Kathy, are common to all the Hailsham pupils, but Ruth takes them a step further.

This step involves an insistence on distinguishing herself from those around her. When Kathy confides in her about the overwhelming sexual urges she sometimes feels, Ruth, presumably imagining the truly human self to be above such animal desires, falsely denies ever feeling similarly.

In the central episode of the novel, a group from the Cottages track down Ruth's "original," "the actual model" from which she's cloned, indulging the fantasy that finding her would make a similar life available to Ruth (as though one could clone a person's life story along with their biological body).

It is Ruth, too, who latches on to the theory that a clone couple can be reprieved from donation if they are able to show that they are in love. This is her motive for remaining in a couple with Tommy and keeping him from Kathy. In a reparative gesture many years later, before she "completes" at her last donation, she enjoins Kathy and Tommy to visit "Madame," the head teacher at Hailsham, and discover if there's any truth to the theory; of course, there isn't. Having pushed against her fate for so much of her life, Ruth finally, like every other clone, submits to it, her illusions still intact. The fictional figure of Ruth casts poignant light on the likes of Rob, who resigned himself to a kind of emotional cloning.

To rebel against the existing order, a person must be able to locate themselves in a history that precedes them and a future that will survive them. This place in time is surely fundamental to our sense of selfhood. Perhaps rebellious impulses rear their head so powerfully in adolescence because it is at this time in our lives that we're most alive to the forces of the past (our family and the wider world which made us) and future (our hopes and desires). It's no coincidence that the current movement against climate change, a protest against the past and a radical claim on the future, is being spearheaded by teenagers.

4

Adolescence Part 2: First Love

How well do you remember those first stirrings of romantic love? Perhaps the question conjures a vivid image of her smile or his jacket, his shyness or her nose piercing. You might recall early meetings and declarations and kisses and serious discussions and the initial hints of his or her or your waning interest. When it comes to our earliest experiences of love, most of us retain snapshots and a vague narrative arc, which are gradually submerged in the soft-focus light of nostalgia as we get older and turn to other, perhaps more durable relationships.

But certain experiences don't readily lend themselves to a coherent narrative shape. In my fourteenth year, as I was shedding copious puppy fat but not the accompanying, equally copious self-doubt and anxiety, my mother took me to spend summer with her family in Canada. She'd recently separated from my father, and these weeks were intended as respite from the turbulence and sadness of the year just passed.

I spent most of the time sunk in sullen withdrawal, switching unpredictably into needy pleaser mode. But when we decamped for a few days to a wholesome holiday resort somewhere in rural Ontario, complete with swimming lake, ice rink and acres of surrounding woodland, I was plunged into full-blown moroseness. It wasn't the kind of place I felt like going to.

My sporting activity was awkward, a pale shadow of the vigorous North American kids swarming excitedly around me. Soon after arriving, I ventured for the first time onto the rink and was set steady—if near immobile with terror—by a manically encouraging female instructor. After half an hour of inching across the ice, I dared to lift my eyes from my feet. My body may have achieved a precarious equilibrium, but my insides were abruptly turned upside down.

She glided easily across the ice in a thick navy puffer jacket. Her long chestnut hair fell over her round face, affording glimpses of her large green eyes, dimpled cheeks and downturned mouth. A vise was tightening on my heart; my breathing, already curtailed by fear of falling, became alarmingly short as sweat coursed freely down my neck and cheeks. Within, I was a riot of chaos. Without, I was still as a corpse.

I'm not sure how I got off the ice or avoided drawing undue attention to myself for the hours and days that followed. I was a TV tuned to one channel, a mobile phone with only one contact, all other voices and faces and subjects a kind of undifferentiated perceptual sludge.

Nothing had prepared me for these sensations, nor did I have the language to make sense of them. Words like "attraction," "desire" or "longing" acquire meaning for us only through accumulated experience. While I knew these words and had read and heard enough stories to have some rudimentary sense of what they meant, they didn't occur to me at that moment, nor would they have been much help, any more than it helps to be told you have a contusion of the skull after being whacked over the head with an iron skillet. Verbal labels are not much use to a person in shock.

If ever I'd imagined falling for a stranger, the feeling evoked was of pure lightness and freedom. It conjured pictures of action men winning maidens with the same casual ease they felled dragons or terrorists—the direct opposite of the hell I was enduring now. This was happening not because of me but despite me.

Over the next couple of days, I continued to steal unreturned glances at her. One afternoon, I was loitering in the table tennis room, awaiting a willing partner for the one sport in which I wouldn't embarrass myself, when she walked in, flanked by her parents.

To my delight and terror, her father wondered aloud whether us kids wouldn't like to play a little game! Without a word or gesture of acknowledgement, we began a gentle rally. I tried to adapt my fluid strokes to her hesitant ones. After a couple of minutes, she laid her bat back on the table and muttered something to her father. Then they left, her father flashing me a faintly embarrassed smile. I didn't see her again before we left the resort the next day.

*

It occurs to me as I write this that I've never told that story before, either as an intimate confession or as a dinner party anecdote. But then, why would I? It isn't really a story at all, if by that word we mean the unfolding of a meaningful sequence of events. "I was at a holiday resort when I saw a pretty girl. I saw her a few more times and at one point played a warm-up table tennis rally with her at her dad's instigation. Then they left the room." If there's anything happening here, it's entirely imperceptible from the outside.

Anna Freud, pioneer of child psychoanalysis and daughter of Sigmund, observed that adults seem to have far clearer and more reliable memories of their adolescence than of their childhood. But this clarity, she adds, is superficial. What most of us retain as adults is choice facts, those moments and images we can assemble into a tidy montage. The intensity of the corresponding feelings of lust, need, vulnerability and pain is recalled much more hazily by most.

However, perhaps because for as long as I can remember I've paid a lot of attention (no doubt too much) to the minute ebbs and flows of my inner life, many of my adolescent memories invert this pattern. When the nameless girl in Ontario comes to mind, I feel those fleeting bodily sensations—the ticklishness in my lungs, the urgent swelling in my bladder—much more palpably than I see the ice rink or the hotel restaurant.

The capacity to remember in this way is often ascribed to dreamy, sensitive types, Proust and his madeleine being the most celebrated example. Being so alive to the play of our emotions is typically disparaged by parents and teachers as the sign of an unwillingness to face reality. This attitude encourages us to chuckle indulgently at the overblown dramas of adolescence—the promises of eternal devotion, the extravagant wish to die when we meet rejection. Looking down at our younger selves from the vantage point of midlife realism, we seem impossibly unworldly, silly and sweet.

We are embarrassed by our green and febrile adolescent selves, as we were once embarrassed by our buttoned-up parents. Where once we rolled our eyes at their emotional constipation, we now laugh at our past emotional incontinence.

Laughter is a very efficient way of belittling or dismissing what we secretly fear. If something is laughable, surely it can't be dangerous. But passions can be very dangerous, as we've learned all too painfully from the spread across the globe of fanaticisms of all stripes. We might object that a besotted adolescent and, say, a suicide bomber are hardly comparable, and in terms of their objectives and methods for fulfilling their passions, we'd be entirely correct. And yet the source of their drive and energy is the same.

In Portia, Johnny and Ruth, we discovered different ways of defying the hypocrisy, injustice and coldness of the adult world. Each of them put a spoke in the wheels of adult business as usual, forcing the men and women around them into a confrontation with their own unquestioned norms and values.

The first stirrings of love and passion force a different confrontation, with ourselves rather than with the world. D. H. Lawrence, from whom we'll hear more later, reminded us that first love feels nothing like the Hallmark cliché of songbirds chirping in a pastel sky. It is more like a violent and merciless invasion by some unknown alien force.

What struck me so helplessly on that ice rink was how the mind I thought was my own could suddenly and without warning be taken hostage by someone else. While I was far from being in charge of my sadness or anger or excitement, I at least had the feeling they belonged to me, that I could identify myself in them. Now I was being taken over by some outside force, overwhelmed by longing, abjectly miserable at the thought of her yet unable to think of anything else.

First love is a kind of rebellion turned inward, jamming up the circuits of ordinary functioning, forcing us against our will to ask ourselves what really matters to us. Had that nameless girl granted me a smile, taken my hand and led me into the woods for a long walk and silent communion of souls, I'd have gladly abandoned my family to hours or days or perhaps a lifetime of unhinged worry over my unexplained disappearance.

When passion reaches a certain threshold, it sweeps aside all other considerations, including the preservation of one's own and others' lives. This is one of the insights of perhaps the pre-eminent literary exploration of first love, *Romeo and Juliet*, where the sheer force of the couple's love tears through all laws and proprieties, toppling the precarious political balance of Verona and laying bare the hypocrisy and mendacity on which its "adult" society rests. No wonder the play has lent itself so well to adaptation to different contexts, from ruling classes to urban gangs. It shows us that wherever there's an order in place, passion can always come along and disrupt it.

i "Once passion is raging": Young Werther

W, artist, early twenties, of aristocratic stock with bohemian leanings. Recently moved to country, citing need for period of solitude. Initially presented as manically cheerful and idealistic, affirming love for nature and all humankind, eventually becoming infatuated with young local woman. Revelation of her prior engagement and unreciprocated feelings, however, has led to dramatic deterioration in mood, to point of severe suicidal risk . . .

If any work of literature has a competing claim for most celebrated portrait of first love, it would probably be Johann Wolfgang von Goethe's *The Sorrows of Young Werther*. First published in 1774, and then in a revised edition in 1787, it was written by Goethe over a frenzied few weeks at the age of twenty-four, quickly catapulting him to global literary celebrity. Over the decades that followed, Goethe's wondrously various and rich literary and philosophical output remained, to his continued regret, in Werther's shadow, as it does even today. The book draws on his infatuation with Charlotte Buff, who had rejected the burgeoning young writer for a high-ranking civil servant named Johann Kestner, and much of its fascination at the time lay in its tantalising disguise of real people and events.

It may not be Goethe's greatest book, but it is undoubtedly his most famous. And reading it, it's easy to see why. Few novels make more powerful use of the epistolary form so popular among European writers of the time; in confining us to Werther's side of a correspondence with his friend, it places us right inside the cage of his tormented heart and affords no escape. We don't simply watch his unravelling, we experience it from within.

Werther is a dangerous book, conveying the madness and violence that lurk at the edges of emotional life. And as is so often the case with dangerous books, reactions to it were divided between panic and parody. Just as we laugh at our own youthful emotional excesses, an entire culture laughed at *Werther*. In Germany, Goethe's contemporary Friedrich Nicolai earned his eternal enmity by publishing a satirical rewrite, *The Joys of Young Werther*, complete with bathetic happy ending, while in England William Thackeray's biting verse parody, "Sorrows of Werther," contained the immortal lines:

> So he sigh'd and pin'd and ogled,
> And his passion boil'd and bubbled,
> Till he blew his silly brains out,
> And no more was by it troubled.

Yes, these lines are funny. But then what more reliable way to diminish Werther's doomed passion than to make it laughable? The alternative is to inflate its danger, to play up its threat to the vulnerable youth of Europe and have it banned. This is what Leipzig city council did after hearing complaints that the novel encouraged suicide.

And according to many, the complaints were justified. In 1974, the American sociologist David Phillips coined the term "Werther effect" to describe the phenomenon of suicidal contagion. The reference was to an apparent spate of copycat suicides across Europe shortly after the publication of *Werther*, in which young men similarly devastated by unrequited love blew their silly brains out.

Modern cultural historians are divided over the question of how much this heavily publicised spike in suicide was based in fact and how much an early example of a sensationalist media confection. It's certainly the case that *Werther* quickly spawned a cult, the hero's trademark outfit of yellow pantaloons and blue jacket becoming the fashion statement of choice for bohemian young men everywhere.

Perhaps the accuracy of the claims about the Werther effect matter less than we think. Whether true or not, they alert us to the fact that literature can be an experience more than just diverting stories to read in the intervals between events in the real world. It hints that novels can be a matter of life and death, an urgent and risky encounter with ourselves and the world.

Werther is a prime example of the kind of book that, according to Franz Kafka, we don't simply admire, but *need*. "We need books," Kafka wrote, "that affect us like a disaster, that grieve us deeply . . . like a suicide. A book must be the axe for the frozen sea within us." Kafka's metaphor connotes both violence and liberation: caught up in the routines and habits of daily living, it is easier and safer to exist at the surface, to cut off from the pain and grief—as well as the joy and excitement—that come with having an inner life.

This numbness is the predicament many people bring at the start of psychotherapeutic work. We tend to imagine that people come to therapy in a state of great enervation and anxiety. While this is often the case, it's equally true that many people come complaining of the frozen sea within. They are aware of having once felt the sorrows and pleasures of life with great intensity and are unsure of why they're now so indifferent to them.

Graham, a genial and highly educated man in his early fifties, clearly matched this description. From early on in our sessions, he dwelt at length on his first adolescent experiences of love and desire. He told me of being bewitched by an exuberant, free-spirited girl he'd met aged eighteen at a summer school in Europe, of becoming hopelessly tongue-tied and self-conscious when he tried to speak to her.

This became a pattern stretching into his twenties. Often it would cause upset and confusion not only for him but for the young woman in question, whom he would initially approach with evident excitement and interest, then abruptly withdraw from her when "it all became a bit much." His seeming inability to extricate himself from this pattern induced mounting despair, humiliation and loneliness.

What struck and frequently irritated me about these forays into his youthful misadventures in love was that he would insistently chuckle his way through them. Eventually I wondered aloud why he seemed to find these distressing experiences of his so funny. "Weeelll," he said with the breezy worldliness of someone who's seen everything, "it's all just adolescent histrionics, isn't it?"

Graham was in some trouble at this point in his life. Unsure of what he wanted to do after university, he'd taken a succession of unfulfilling and poorly paid office jobs. He'd made a long-deferred decision to start a PhD in his early thirties, though his need to finance it through a demanding administrative job meant he was forty by the time he finished it. Competing with the glittering CVs of dynamic young women and men in their twenties for entry-level academic jobs proved unfruitful.

The result was that he remained in a dull administrative job, though now in a university, where the tedium was exacerbated by daily resentment and envy of the academic life he could only view from the outside. Beyond work he fell into a series of companionable but passionless relationships that invariably fizzled out after a few months or weeks. At one point, he said, shortly before he came to me, he "tried a man" for a while, which was all right, but wasn't the revelation he'd hoped for. "In fact," he laughed, "apart from the . . . *equipment*, it wasn't all that different in the end!"

"So now you're trying *this* man," I said, "hoping it might be different in the end, but doubtful as usual."

He laughed heartily and said nothing.

In the context of his current state of weary indifference, Graham's compulsively retold adolescent stories took on a poignant significance. They were his way of telling me that from the first stirrings of his desire, he'd known too much about love to risk it. Being in love, Freud suggested, involves "an impoverishment of the ego": all the energies we normally invest in caring for ourselves are poured instead into the object of our love. This accounts for one of the most enduring stereotypes of the lover: the pale, thin, wild-eyed lunatic, lost to themselves and the world.

That was never going to be Graham. In his barren emotional world, everyone, whether female or male, young or old, was equally pleasant initially and equally indifferent finally. He had approached the threshold of Werther's madness and pulled back, gradually numbing himself to the pain and chaos of feeling.

But lest we be too quick to pity him, let's turn back to *Werther*, because it may be that Graham had a point.

"Adolescent histrionics"—Graham's summary dismissal of his youthful infatuations—was also how the sorrows of the lovelorn Werther were viewed by many of Goethe's contemporaries. But in ridiculing Werther, many of these scoffers missed the point entirely. Their mockery was based on a lazy assumption that the book's perspective was the same as its hero's. This suggests that the book is an advocate for full-blown irrationality against good sense and self-regulation.

That, certainly, is what those furious contemporary denunciations implied: Werther loves another man's wife, so the book legitimises adultery; he sympathises with a murderer, so the book licenses murder; and of course, he makes a forceful case for suicide before killing himself, so the book endorses suicide. Reading *Werther*, the denouncers warned, would open the floodgates of madness and lawlessness.

What is missing from this literal-minded moralising are all the ways in which Goethe undermines his overwrought hero. Werther's letters are forever exposing him as a kind of emotional fundamentalist. It isn't enough for him to argue that hard graft and practical good sense are nothing without passion; he must insist that anyone who toils for a reason other than "because his own desire or needs lead him to do so, will always be a fool."

Like every fundamentalist, Werther thinks in rigid oppositions. In his mind, to make any concession to either social convention or self-interest is to kill off both the artist and the lover in oneself. Reason and feeling are destined to be at permanent war: "that jot of rational sense a man may possess is of little or no avail once passion is raging and the bounds of human nature are hemming him in."

Werther's total rejection of reason and balance is certainly powerful, even seductive; but the sheer militancy of his stance treads a very precarious line between emotional integrity and overblown posturing. The sense of the latter is amplified by his recourse to hoary old clichés, even in the throes of suicidal despair: "To lift the curtain and step behind it!—That is all! Why these doubts and hesitation? Because one does not know what lies beyond? and because one cannot return?" Sound familiar? Of course it does—it paraphrases arguably the most famous speech in the history of literature: the thought of dying "must give us pause," for it takes us to the border of "the undiscovered country, from whose bourn / No traveller returns." Even at this moment of rawest vulnerability, Werther is channelling Hamlet, speaking in a voice not his own.

All of this might lead us to wonder whether Graham isn't right after all. Perhaps desire, passion and all the other extremities of feeling provoked by love are just "adolescent histrionics" after all, a bad Hamlet impersonation. If Werther is embellishing and performing his emotions in this way, surely his love and suffering are more worked up than authentically felt?

But just thinking about our own experience of these emotions reminds us that this distinction between feeling and performing is too simplistic. After all, can we be so sure where one starts and the other stops? Does our use of wild overstatement to express our loving feelings signal that what we're saying is false, as in the title of a book by the American humorist Cynthia Heimel, *If You Can't Live Without Me, Why Aren't You Dead Yet?*

But perhaps the line is funny because it insists on taking literally what was clearly a piece of wild exaggeration. Telling someone we can't live without them doesn't actually oblige us to die should the relationship subsequently fail to work out. Nor, in fact, does it make us liars or drama queens. The classic defence in these circumstances, "I meant it at the time," might sound a bit weaselly, but it expresses a certain truth about the nature of feelings.

The intensity of feelings is tied to their volatility, their tendency to fall as violently as they rise. Adolescents know this better than most; what makes those years so frequently painful, and occasionally so joyous, is their turbulence. The body and mind in which we so recently felt at home are suddenly experienced as unpredictable strangers bent on persecuting us.

Anna Freud's point that we remember the isolated facts of our adolescence well enough, but not the accompanying emotions, starts to look like simple good sense. It is scary enough to have such raw and powerful feelings, but even more so to guess that we can't trust them, that we might just feel differently next month or week or day. Pulled perpetually between love and hate, fierce independence and childlike dependence, agony and ecstasy, the crucial sense of one's own and the world's continuity and reliability is laid waste.

Werther captures this predicament brilliantly. We can intuit from the letters that Charlotte, the object of Werther's obsessive love, can see what's attractive about his uncompromising ardour. But it's also what leads her to reject him in favour of his rival, the solid, dully dependable Albert—eleven years her senior and so safely distant from the mire of late adolescence in which Werther remains stuck. When Lotte first meets Werther, he is intoxicated with the joys of both nature and love; as she gently signals that her own love and loyalty are to Albert, he becomes a despairing, babbling wreck, unable to enjoy the familiar pleasures of rambling, art or society.

"His tranquil manner," Werther writes of Albert, "is in marked contrast to the turbulence of my own disposition, which I cannot hide." Lotte herself was never going to be a willing participant in some febrile romantic tragedy; one of the book's subtlest ironies is that she doesn't quite fit the mould of the woman men lose their minds over. She is cheerful, good-natured and sensible—a far better match for Albert than for Werther.

In other words, the novel offers the mildest hint that the Lotte seen by Werther is more his imaginative creation than the real, ordinary human being she is. This is one of the novel's more wry and universal insights: we are never more prone to distort another person as when we first fall in love. *Werther* teases us into asking what might have happened had Lotte responded to his advances: would he have enjoyed a lifetime's delirious fulfilment, or would he have been disappointed by her prosaic reality and shifted his attentions elsewhere? To invoke a popular saying, unfortunate but irresistible in this context, it seems very likely that Lotte dodged a bullet.

First love shows us the twin perils of our unbound feelings: they can reach a pitch forceful enough to overwhelm and even destroy us, and they can just as quickly drop off or turn around—love can abruptly become hate, joy turn unexpectedly to misery.

Graham intuited that being welcomed was ultimately more perilous than being rejected, that he was entirely unready to bear the burden of longing, and remained convinced for most of his life that this judgement was the right one.

As a young man, Graham had been so acutely attuned to the risks of love that he spent his whole life avoiding them. The same couldn't be said for Simone, a successful academic in her early forties. Twenty years before, Simone had fallen passionately in love with Kit, a fellow graduate student in a very different discipline, a few years older than her and "very brilliant." They had begun to make a life together, happily anticipating their shared future over pasta dinners in their tiny rented flat.

Until one afternoon that future evaporated in an instant. Arriving home from the library, she casually tapped the answerphone button for new messages as she walked briskly down the hallway. She heard his voice, half-noting an unfamiliar gravity in it: "It's me . . ." She was stopped in her tracks by the seemingly interminable pause. "I'm sorry, I can't do this." Walking absently into the bedroom, she stared into his empty wardrobe. He had left it open deliberately. Evidently he wanted to signal as clearly as possible that he was gone.

That he was leaving her was traumatic enough; but the real torment over the days and weeks that followed was his refusal to see or talk to her. Her every attempt to call him was met with a few vague and dismayingly stock phrases: "I don't know why, I just can't," "It's not working," and even, "It's not you, it's me" and a hurried goodbye.

A few weeks later she discovered he'd moved to a new city. He had managed to disappear from her life with an efficiency and speed so ruthless that she felt as though their entire relationship had been an extended hallucination.

Kit was the first man she'd loved, the first she'd felt anything much for at all, Simone told me. I was struck by the time and energy she'd invested in relating this story. After all, it had happened nearly two decades before. What about subsequent relationships? What about now?

But this was the point—there were no subsequent relationships, or at least none that had gone beyond three or four weeks. "I've tried," she said, "but I just can't seem to get interested." She looked down. "I can't seem to get past the feeling that my first love will turn out to be my last."

I discovered over the next few months that the spectre of disappearance had haunted Simone from early childhood. Her father, a mathematician, seemed both present and impossibly remote, a kind of fleshly phantom, stubbornly solid yet gossamer thin. The elder brother she'd worshipped as a child had joined an obscure Indian mystic commune soon after leaving university and severed contact with his family. Her mother's warmth and reliability provided an essential emotional counterweight, but it was hard to escape the conclusion that the men she and Simone loved were destined to absent themselves in one way or another.

Psychoanalysts since Freud have long been interested in the process of mourning, understood not only in the strict sense of bereavement, but as all forms of loss, including the love of a person, place or way of life. Freud first formulated the now commonplace idea that if we're to "move on" from a loss we must mourn it and let it go, as well as the corresponding notion that an unmourned loss has the effect of suspending us in a kind of emotional aspic, an interminable melancholy without relief.

According to the French psychoanalysts Nicolas Abraham and Maria Torok, there are certain losses that cannot be processed, that the ordinary work of grief fails to reach. In such cases, the lost person or entity behaves like an undigested foreign body, lodging inside the mourner's mind, where they are kept and preserved indefinitely. Abraham and Torok call this interior place of loss a "crypt."

It seems to me that Kit lodged inside a crypt in Simone's memory. She'd grieved his departure for a few weeks after he left, then determined to "pull herself together." She stopped talking about him to friends and family, and made it known she'd rather they didn't bring him up. Before coming to see me, she'd barely mentioned him in twenty years.

But she most certainly hadn't forgotten him. On the contrary, he was so deeply embedded in her that anyone else who tried to love her was fighting a losing battle. Objectively speaking, she was available. But psychologically speaking, she was promised to someone else, someone invisible and unnamed.

This basic story, in which a traumatically curtailed first love spoils all future romantic possibilities, is familiar to all of us, perhaps from personal acquaintance and certainly from the world of literary, dramatic and cinematic fiction. Think of Miss Havisham, rotting away in her wedding dress; or less ghoulishly, of Vladimir Petrovich, protagonist of *First Love*, Ivan Turgenev's great novella of 1860.

ii "A nice, good, clever child": Vladimir Petrovich

VP, taciturn, rather formal man of forty, unmarried with generous independent income. Initially hesitant to reveal the source of his current depression, he eventually spoke in a melancholic tone of having fallen in love at sixteen with a beautiful young woman of twenty-one. Enquiries on this point yielded little further elaboration, beyond ambiguous and confusing references to his father.

First Love is at least as much about the lifelong impact of first love as about the experience itself. Turgenev frames it as the long flashback of the "dark-haired, greying" protagonist at the age of forty, twenty-four years after the events he relates. From this vantage point of disappointed maturity, he vividly evokes the wide-eyed naivety of his sixteen-year-old self, "expectant and shy and wonderfully receptive and prepared for anything."

Turgenev catches brilliantly the vulnerability that comes with such receptivity. The boy who catches sight of the beautiful Princess Zinaida in the next-door garden isn't prepared for the bodily and emotional shock of love at first sight. The arousal of tenderness, lust, longing and awe brings both ecstasy and distress. When Vladimir's mother inadvertently fulfils his breathless wish to see her again by sending him next door to invite Zinaida's mother to call round, his response is tellingly split: "The unexpectedly rapid fulfilment of my secret desires both delighted and frightened me."

That confusion is amplified by the fact that the smitten boy in question is five years younger than his object of rapture, at an age when such a difference is a huge gulf in worldliness and personal development, one which Zinaida proves more than willing to exploit. Her burst of laughter the moment she catches him staring at her presages how his hopeless infatuation will again and again feed his humiliation.

It's no fun when your heart is in the hands of someone who holds all the cards, empowered to grant or withhold her favour according to her whim or self-interest. I can remember a few of my adolescent crushes being met with indifference or a warmly regretful non-reciprocity, but I never had to endure the peculiar mortification of having my interest received with the outright hilarity of a young woman approached by a love-struck boy.

I can also remember a fifteen-year-old boy in my circle at school, emboldened by a half-can of cheap lager at the annual disco, approaching an eighteen-year-old Upper Sixth girl he'd been mooning over for months. I watched from a distance with a few nervily amused mates, unsure whether we were willing him to triumph or crash.

With hindsight, of course, there was only one outcome. We had the rear view of his tentative walk-up, saw him fingering the back of his head, the side of his foot twisting awkwardly as he said something to her he had to repeat, his composure ebbing away in the face of her irritably puzzled "WHAAAAT?!" Then the laughter in her wide eyes, signalling unmistakably that she'd never heard anything so comically improbable, sending him back to us with a hardy smile of defeat. He may well have expected a roasting, but no one offered more than a muttered "Unlucky, mate." It was as though it had happened to the lot of us. And in a way it had. We were all feeling the pathetic incongruity between the furious hormonal drive thrusting us forward and the gawky unreadiness holding us back.

This is what Vladimir is made to feel on an epic scale by Zinaida, and not merely because of her oscillation between favour and disdain towards him. The ordinary humiliation of an unattainable love object is amplified by the growing awareness that her heart belongs to someone else, next to whom he is not much more than an endearing irrelevance.

"In your eyes I'm just a child," he protests to her, only to be told in response, "Well, yes, you are a child, but a nice, good, clever child, whom I love very much." Could a more brutal wound be imagined to adolescent male dignity and self-respect?

But it turns out Zinaida isn't just toying with her nice, good, clever child for sport. The resonances of the word "child" are far more shocking than the poor, piqued Vladimir can know at that moment. He will soon discover that the object of Zinaida's desolate pining is . . . his father. Vladimir isn't merely *a* child in the ordinary sense; he is *the* child of her lover—hence her constant shuttling between affection and cruelty; she doesn't know whether to love him as a stepson or to resent him as a rival claimant on her lover's heart. And more unsettling still, the older man makes her feel as much the hopelessly needy child as she makes Vladimir feel.

Vladimir discovers the identity of Zinaida's lover under tragicomic conditions. Having been informed maliciously by one of her spurned suitors that she and her lover have arranged a rendezvous in her garden under the cloak of night, he keeps watch there with a penknife and the steely resolve of a knight-errant, waiting to unmask his rival.

> "It's him! It's him at last!" raced through my heart and, trembling, I drew the penknife out of my pocket and with trembling fingers opened it . . . Red sparks whirled before my eyes, my hair stood up on end in fright and anger . . . The footsteps were coming directly towards me. I bent down and was ready to spring up at him . . . a man came into view . . . My God, it was my father!

It's tempting for a psychoanalyst to read this passage and cry "Aha!" with an upraised finger, especially when Vladimir goes on to remark, "The jealous Othello who had been ready to commit murder was suddenly turned into a schoolboy . . ." It isn't difficult to find support in this passage for Freud's most famous—and arguably most notorious—idea, the Oedipus complex.

But in spite of, or even perhaps because of, the easy fit, I'm unwilling to start pointing out the Oedipal motifs of primal father and castrated son in Turgenev's novella. Psychoanalysis isn't about triumphantly demonstrating how we all secretly want to kill our fathers and marry our mothers, but about showing us the intricate and singular ways in which our early relationships shape and inform our later ones, including our relationship to ourselves. In other words, it is about revealing the process, unique to each of us, of how we become who we are.

A psychoanalyst shouldn't look to literature for confirmation of what he already knows, but to be surprised, to discover new variations and twists in the infinite grammar of human relationships.

"I harboured no bad feelings towards my father. On the contrary, he seemed to grow in my eyes," Vladimir writes, while of his farewell kiss from Zinaida he remarks, "I greedily savoured all its sweetness. I knew it would never be repeated." Vladimir cannot summon the hate for his father and Zinaida that might have enabled him eventually to forgive them. Instead, he is left suspended between the two of them, frozen for life in the dual role of betrayed son and rejected lover.

This story of first love is also one of last love, of love as a kind of self-consuming force, burning itself out for ever in one terrible, unrepeatable conflagration.

But does that mean *First Love* is unremittingly bleak? Perhaps, but there may be the smallest chink of light. At the beginning of the story, the forty-year-old Vladimir is sitting with two friends reminiscing over first loves. He agrees to tell his story on the condition that he be allowed to write rather than speak it; this, he says, is the only way he'll get the story right, the very story we go on to read.

Why does this matter? Because Vladimir has buried this story within him. Telling it is a kind of belated act of self-healing, a way of taking an axe to the frozen sea within. Until she'd come to see me, Simone told me, she'd never revealed to anyone the extent to which Kit had damaged her ability to love.

In the last year of our work together, having told the story many times in many different ways, she met a man. She didn't know if they could last the course and dared not speculate; but for the first time in twenty years, she could finally bear to love someone, and to be loved in return.

iii "Well it doesn't really matter now": Frances

F, female undergraduate and aspiring writer, exceptionally intelligent and high-achieving, but burdened by feelings of chronically low self-worth and occasional urge to self-harm. Only child of very troubled marriage, which mother seems to have tried hard to normalise. Father alcoholic, unemployed. Entangled in complex, possibly damaging relationships with older married man and closest female friend, formerly a lover . . .

The books we've discussed so far in this chapter, written in the late eighteenth and late nineteenth centuries, respectively, seem to take for granted certain basic premises about first love. In the stories they tell, love is directed towards one person of the opposite sex to whom we remain devoted for the rest of our lives. Of course, this isn't to suggest there haven't always been deviations from heterosexual monogamy throughout the course of history; only that they haven't always been licensed by culture and law (or, indeed, literature).

In the twenty-first-century West, we are forming relationships under very different conditions. The ongoing feminist and sexual liberation struggles since the 1960s have left us far less constrained by societal, cultural and legal limits on the quantity, sexual orientation and gender identity of those we choose to love.

This is more than a cultural change. There is always an emotional correlate to the external conditions under which we love. It isn't a coincidence that the dominant note of both *The Sorrows of Young Werther* and *First Love* is a kind of delirious certainty. Werther and Vladimir don't come to love Lotte or Zinaida by way of steady, thoughtful contemplation of their virtues and attractions; on the contrary, their love is something they simply *know* instantly, body and soul, without having to think about or question it.

In the first of his *Three Essays on the Theory of Sexuality*, Freud makes a very useful distinction between the object of sexual drive and the drive itself. In our modern culture of love, he writes in 1910, we "emphasise the object": that is, our conception of love is bound up with the person we love. "The erotic life of antiquity" differed from ours in this regard. Where Freud's society found sex distasteful and could sanction it only within the tightly bounded space of a nuclear family, the ancients "glorified the drive and were prepared on its account to honour even an inferior object."

Perhaps in our own day the pendulum is swinging back towards the ancient model. For example, the increasingly vocal proponents of polyamory, for whom the love of one person is no barrier to the love of others, are clearly keen to promote the instinct over the object of love. If love is a good, why not spread it as widely and generously as possible, rather than concentrate it exclusively in one person?

But one doesn't have to sign up to such structured experiments to sense that the waning of the expectation of a sole lifelong love has cleared a space in us all. Even those of us who are still invested in the strange project of a long-term relationship are liable to puzzle over love's possible shapes and sizes, and to question and doubt what it is we want from it.

Frances, the complex, spiky narrator of Sally Rooney's *Conversations with Friends* (2017), is immersed in this ether of doubt as she wanders the treacherous landscapes of love and sex. Her Dublin is a wired global city of big banks and coffee chains and trust fund kids, a far cry from the shuttered repression of the city of James Joyce's *Dubliners.*

But much as we shouldn't understate the place of historical change in determining the ways we love, perhaps we should be equally wary of overstating it. If *Conversations* shows us how our post-liberation age has transformed the conduct of love, it also reminds us how much stays the same. Confusion, anxiety and volatility are as present for Frances as they were for Werther.

Freud's comments about the ancients help us recall that the mobility and unpredictability of sexual desire have always been a fundamental force in human life. Recall that Lotte sees the impassioned certainty of Werther's love for her as a form of dangerous instability, in unfavourable contrast to the reliable Albert. When Werther defends the young farmer boy who murders his widowed mistress when she rejects his love, he puts flesh on Lotte's doubts, demonstrating how easily and dangerously unbound desire gets out of all control, turning around itself to the point where the tenderness of one moment becomes the fatal violence of the next.

Rooney's novels turn on a similar problem: the weird and unsettling proximity of love to cruelty. In the relationships she portrays, tenderness and intimacy serve again and again as a virtual cue for the infliction of some casually brutal hurt—rejection, belittlement, wilful misunderstanding.

In novels, as in life, we find that the inner self is annoyingly uncongenial to the maintenance of a steady state. It is divided, pulled in different directions by different impulses—it wants safety and risk, consistency and change, to say yes and to say no. Perhaps this is why the people accused of being boring are also often the most reliable and straightforward: their alleged boringness lies in their willingness to keep a distance from the constant agitations of their inner lives; a capacity to live closer to the surface, where changes are a little more amenable to our control.

We don't tend to brood over or question a decision that is purely practical—what time you'll catch the train to work, or which restaurant you'll book. Only when that decision becomes coloured emotionally (are you happy in your job? who are you meeting at the restaurant?) do we start to doubt ourselves, to feel the anxiety of uncertainty.

In other words, it's our strongest and most undeniable feelings that tend to provoke the greatest confusion in us. When we fall in love, we at first enjoy being carried on the wave of exhilaration; but we may soon feel frightened or even scandalised by the way the reassuring habits and pleasures of our life previously—enjoying food, spending time alone, doing a good day's work—have been so ruthlessly upended. "What is happening to me?" we might ask ourselves. "Who have I become?" It's easy to imagine hating and resenting the very person we love for this power they have over us.

It can also cause us to question whether sexual love is the right basis for a lasting relationship. One of the reasons *Conversations with Friends* is so intriguing is that it's deliberately ambiguous as to which of Frances's two key relationships is her authentic first love: is it the older married man, Nick, with whom she experiences such ecstatic erotic transport; or her ex-girlfriend, now best friend, Bobbi, with whom she enjoys a more reassuring bond of shared experience and mutual understanding?

To complicate matters, both sets of feelings are liable to swift reversal: Frances periodically switches into cold hostility towards Nick and scratchy rivalry with Bobbi. Instead of hitting her with the lightning bolt of total certainty, love immerses her in a cloud of confusion.

Conversations is filled with exchanges in those wired modes of communication—email, text, instant messaging—we use to ensure a constant flow of contact with our network of family, friends and colleagues, and which so often foster ambiguity and misunderstanding, a predicament that resonates with my experience in the consulting room.

By now, it's impossible to count how many sessions have been filled from first to last with tearful and angry reconstructions of textual shouting matches. Carl would enter the room urgently, barely pausing to look at me as he settled onto the couch, all the while casting a theatrically wild-eyed stare at the phone he was clutching. He would scroll through interminable arguments with his girlfriend, appealing to me to adjudicate between his *obviously* unimpeachable rationality and her *obviously* unhinged craziness. There was Dara, who would melancholically recall every text or email from the women she dated, however innocuous, as evidence of their indifference or contempt towards her.

Conversations is expertly attuned to how disembodied textual communication amplifies the already rich potential in every relationship for doublespeak and misreading. In an instant-messaging exchange, her married lover, Nick, suggests their limited opportunities for seeing each other make the affair difficult to justify. Frances transcribes the messages that follow:

> me: I can't believe you're breaking up with me over
>   instant messenger
> me: I thought you were going to leave your wife so we
>   could run away together
> Nick: you don't need to be defensive
> me: how do you know what I need
> me: maybe I'm actually really upset
> Nick: are you
> Nick: I never have any idea what you feel about any-
>   thing
> me: well it doesn't really matter now does it

Frances shows herself here to be a highly skilled verbal contortionist. Coming after a single week of illicit sex and shared meals at Nick's marital home, her remark about leaving his wife comes across to Nick, and to us, as a piece of flagrant sarcasm. But when he calls out her defensive flippancy, she asks him how he knows she isn't "actually really upset," then brazenly ducks the question when he asks whether she is.

It's tempting to blame the medium for all the confusion sown by the messages. Perhaps Nick's confusion over Frances's real feelings would never have arisen had the conversation occurred face to face. The expression in her eyes, her tone of voice or her bodily gestures might have revealed what the fleshless words concealed.

But this is to assume that as long as we can see and hear them, people are easy enough to read. The basic premise of psychoanalysis is that they're not, and *Conversations* seems to bear this out. Frances is constantly using her face and voice to dissemble and mask her real feelings, to create false impressions of herself.

This was equally true for Carl and Dara. While they both seemed to mine their lovers' text messages for every last grain of potential misinterpretation, this was only an extension of the way they conducted their relationships in person. Texts and emails only bolstered their sense of themselves as victims of perpetual misunderstanding; but in its absence, they'd have found other proofs. Fearful of the rawness of direct emotional contact, they took refuge in contriving ambiguities and confusions that would ensure they never got too close.

From the very beginning of the novel, Frances lets us know just how much energy she invests in not giving herself away. We meet her in the back of a taxi with Bobbi and Nick's wife, Melissa, "already preparing compliments and certain facial expressions to make myself seem charming." As she gets more tired and drunk, she finds it increasingly difficult "to arrange my face in a way that would convey my sense of humour."

A little later, as she watches Nick buttoning a shirt on stage as Brick in *Cat on a Hot Tin Roof,* she "felt a sting of self-consciousness, as if the audience had all turned at this moment to observe my reaction." In each of these moments, Frances can only access her inner self by way of a long-winded detour through the eyes of others: on glimpsing Nick's muscled torso, she feels not her eye on him, but their eyes on her on him.

Falling in love for the first time is very difficult for a character like this. Those feelings of overwhelming surprise and delirious surrender we found in Werther and Vladimir can't circulate so freely around Frances's body and soul. The exception, perhaps, is in bed with Nick, where the sheer force of her pleasure wears down her defences and allows her to enjoy bodily and emotional intimacy with a directness and intensity missing from the rest of her life.

Frances's obfuscations of her own feelings deceive herself as much as they do others. Her dissembling is less manipulative than anxious, a function of her basic mistrust in her own instincts: she hears messages from her interior but is unsure whether she can credit them.

In passing recollections of childhood, Frances shows us that the source of her mistrust comes from parents unable to model love for her; right up to their bitter divorce, their marriage was a long exercise in evading all contact. That same evasiveness seeps into their relationship to their daughter, to whom they each seem unable to show the love they feel. These withholding tendencies come to shape Frances's conception of herself as "emotionally cold," too distant from herself to know how or what she feels.

First love for someone with that history is liable to be shot through with wariness and doubt. A child who can never feel sure she's loved is also someone unschooled in the knowledge of their own desire. Stripped to its bare bones, Frances's predicament is that she doesn't know what she wants, or how to go about finding out.

Rooney is roughly the same age as her protagonist, which has led many of her readers to characterise *Conversations* as a generational novel, a portrait of love in the millennial era, showing how a new sexual openness and fluidity have transformed our relationships.

Novelistic depictions of love are inevitably shaped by prevailing norms of courtship and forms of sexual identity. But this is no more or less true of *Conversations* than it is of *The Sorrows of Young Werther* or *First Love*; the portrayals of love in those novels, after all, are equally conditioned by the historical conventions of romantic feeling and expression. But we don't think of them as merely "generational" novels. On the contrary, we read them because they reach to us across history, telling us in the language of their own times about emotional experiences as resonant and real now as then.

We can't know whether *Conversations* will be read a century or two from now. But it belongs alongside the two earlier novels because, like them, it explores deep and strange truths about love—its volatility and turbulence, its violent and sudden fluctuations between joy and pain, affection and rage, the internal struggle it provokes between independence and dependence. Frances's unstable movement between sexualities is only one way in which this fundamental confusion at the heart of love manifests itself.

But what is the source of this confusion? We're given a clue towards the end of the novel when Frances, physically and emotionally hollowed out, slips into Dublin's Thomas Street church, where she asks herself who, if anyone, she really loves:

> I love my fellow human beings. Or do I? Do I love Bobbi, after she tore up my story like that and left me alone? Do I love Nick, even if he doesn't want to fuck me any more? Do I love Melissa?
> Did I ever? Do I love my mother and father?

"Do I love my mother and father?" Frances traces her history of love all the way back to her real and indelible first loves—at least according to psychoanalysis. Sometimes, despite best efforts, a shadow of doubt is cast on that first love, which the next first love will find hard to escape. Werther seems to have gleaned more about love from overblown poetry and drama than from his parents; Vladimir's model of a man's love is his father's cruelty and entitlement. The adult can't plunge safely into love's seas if she hasn't been taught to swim in them as a child. And even then it's all too easy to sink.

5

Adulthood Part 1: Ambition

It began as a discussion about his future. I was talking with my eldest son about interests, aspirations, career paths. I had quickly assumed the role of parental sage, but some subtle tightening at the corner of his mouth told me I was missing the point. Elbow on the table, fingers distractedly rubbing the back of his head, he paused a while, with an uneasy, patient half-smile.

"The thing is," he sighed, "talking about the future assumes there's going to be one."

Recalling this remark and the shudder it induced in me, I'm aware of that reflexive impulse to protect him from all harm and disappointment, and how easily it shades into a childish aversion to any hint of anxiety or sadness in him. I wanted the two of us to leapfrog blithely over these hints of fear and vulnerability, to land softly in some safe zone where his happiness and security and the fulfilment of all his dreams would be permanently proofed against the changing conditions of life. For all the hours I spend each day making myself available to the difficult feelings of others, I sometimes feel as though I'm barely able to endure a moment of my own children's.

I wanted to erase that sentence of his, along with all its intimations of a future depleted of hope, excitement and possibility. I knew the external reasons for his gloom towards the future: the physical and imaginative shackles of Brexit, living costs that punish any aspiration to work for the public good, a labour market shrunk by automation and AI. And looming over all of these, the black cloud of climate change. Dismal stuff for sure, but also generalised and impersonal. This was *his* future we were talking about, not the world's. Why confuse the two?

As I opened my mouth to respond, I could practically hear the crank of my own rusty defences. "But surely as long as you're alive you have to assume there'll be a future?"

"But why can't I just turn the question round on you?" he said. "Doesn't it occur to you that what's happening in the world right now means you can't just assume there'll be a future?"

I paused, struggling for words. "I do know what you mean. But I'm not sure what happens to me where climate change is concerned. It's like it's too big somehow, too abstract to perceive as a daily reality."

He smiled again, failing to conceal the irritation on his face. "I know it's kind of a thing among your generation, but I get frustrated when I hear that. I guess at my age it must have seemed abstract to you, some distant possibility that could never touch you personally. Whereas there are times when I honestly can't think of anything that feels *less* abstract. Sometimes I'm out and as I look at people walking the streets, drinking coffee, shopping, I find myself wondering, isn't it all a bit weird, this normality? I want to scream at everyone to do something, including myself, because I know I'm one of those people, oblivious to the tidal wave about to flood the streets. But maybe you're right. You can't spend your life in this fog of doom. There are good things to get excited about. But then I'm reminded of how precarious it all is and I feel this jolt of despair."

His words opened a silence that amplified my painful sense of inadequacy. What to offer? A hug, a kindly assurance, a reassuring homily? At the edge of planetary extinction, paternal comfort seemed to have met its limit. All I knew was the very thing you *never* want to know where your child is concerned: that he was scared, and that I couldn't make it better.

"At the climate protest the other day, I listened to this girl give a speech," he continued. "She was talking about how she'd tweeted about the action and hardly any of her classmates replied. But two girls did, to say it was OK, they weren't worrying about climate change any more. They'd already decided they wouldn't have kids, so they didn't have to feel so stressed about the future."

The story was a grenade thrown into my power of speech. I stammered, "But that's . . . I mean. That's just. Terrible."

"Yeah. And I don't want you to think I'm ready to just give up like that. I don't accept what those girls imply, that my generation can only run down the clock before we all expire. But I can't pretend I don't know what they mean, or that I don't feel the same way sometimes. When you really look the threat in the face, talking about hopes, ambitions, just the idea of a personal future seems unreal, pointless even."

At moments like this, parental love feels like the worst affliction. I'm pretty sure I'd have preferred the fiercest blast of rage or contempt to this gentle intimation of total despair. Anything—mindless hedonism, wilful ignorance, bored indifference—seemed easier to bear than this terrible question of whether, and for how long, life would be worth living.

Lighten up, I tried to tell myself. After all, whatever the dangers, they're no different for him than for anyone else; at least he faces them rich in the advantages of love, education and prosperity. But this too is scant consolation; if you knew the planet was going to explode in ten minutes, it's not the countless billions you'd grieve for, but the few faces of those nearest to you.

In Freud's "On Narcissism," he discusses the wildly inflated dreams parents have for their children. These, he suggests, are really the parents' forgotten childhood fantasies of becoming a hero, a prince or a queen—now channelled vicariously into their children. Childhood dreams are expressions of the sorest, "most touchy" point in the narcissistic system: "the immortality of the ego." To be a knight or warrior princess is a kind of child's code for living for ever. Growing up forces us to renounce that wish; having a child gives us a second shot. "Parental love," writes Freud, "which is so moving and at bottom so childish, is nothing but the parents' narcissism born again."

Our children, in other words, become the vehicle through which we keep alive our dreams of immortality. Even as our conscious minds try to see our kids as clearly and realistically as possible, our unconscious insists on their matchless beauty and brilliance. No teacher could ever appreciate them enough, no employer could ever deserve them enough, no suitor could ever be worthy of them. Everyone dies, yes, but our child is not everyone.

This may help explain why we have so much difficulty in taking seriously the facts of climate change; the prospect of our extinction violates that primitive belief in our children as the perpetuation of ourselves far beyond the puny confines of our individual lifespan. For many of us, the idea that every last trace of us will disappear from the world is unendurable. Nor is it so different for non-parents, for whom the same unconscious fantasies of immortality, and the same horror of permanent erasure, can be channelled into creative, social and institutional achievements that they hope will outlive them.

Portia, Johnny and Ruth showed us that rebellion, more than just a struggle against the wrongs of the past, is the struggle to preserve and build a future. Like rebellion, ambition requires the assurance of a future in order to be meaningful. We could say rebellion and ambition are negative and positive sides of the same coin.

In psychoanalytic terms, rebellion represents the killing of the father who stands in the way of our desires and refuses our demands—"The King Is Dead!"; ambition expresses the wish to occupy his place and so extend and expand his presence in the world—"Long Live the King!"

But perhaps this is too simplistic, for just as rebellion can be a way of tacitly affirming life, ambition can be a way of unwittingly destroying it. After all, what is environmental catastrophe if not the unintended consequence of our ambitions for the world, our wishes to increase material prosperity, to shorten local and global distances, to heat and light and shelter and feed exponentially increasing numbers of people? In achieving these seemingly laudable aims, have we not exploited, enslaved and destroyed innumerable human beings, species and natural resources?

As we're about to see, this strange ambiguity at the heart of collective ambition is equally visible at the level of our individual lives. The ancient Greek concept of hubris describes the human vulnerability to overreaching, to becoming blindly arrogant and venal in pursuit of our desires. Few characters match this description better than Julien Sorel, protagonist of Stendhal's great novel of ambition, *The Red and the Black* (1830).

i "This desert of egotism": Julien Sorel

JS, twenty, proved difficult to reach on account of open contempt for assessor. Son of a peasant carpenter (some doubts about biological paternity), whom he alleges abused him for his delicacy and love of learning. Broke down suddenly recalling recent secret affairs with two women, before reverting to previous mode of aggressive bravado, boasting to assessor of their "noble rank" and "coveted beauty." Ended interview in distinctly persecutory mode, muttering obscurely of conspiracies against him, threatening lethal violence against "her" (name withheld). Unwillingness to engage makes it difficult to assess risk to self or others.

We first meet Julien sitting on a roof beam at his father's sawmill, supposedly supervising the woodcutting process but in fact oblivious to anything other than the book he's reading, until his infuriated peasant father sends it flying out of his hands with two violent blows.

The "slight young man of eighteen or nineteen" is held in contempt by his father and brothers for his delicacy and resented for his learning and haughtiness. The book he is so enthralled by is *The Memorial of Saint Helena*, a record by Emmanuel, comte de las Cases of conversations with his exiled master, the Emperor Napoleon. De las Cases's hagiography, attesting to Napoleon's charisma, wisdom and ingenuity, is the tribute of a fanatical devotee.

It is one of the three works, we're told, by which Julien lives, and for which "he would have died." Napoleon is the inflated model for his own secret ambitions to greatness. Early in the novel, we see Julien contemplate a sparrowhawk from the elevation of a great rock in the woods outside his home town of Verrières, where he's been appointed tutor to the mayor's children. In the bird's strength and isolation, he sees Napoleon's destiny and wonders, "would it one day be his?"

Since his earliest childhood, Julien has been possessed by visions of Bonaparte, once "an obscure and penniless lieutenant," who, by sheer force of will, "had made himself master of the world." But unlike his inspiration, he has grown up in an atmosphere not of revolutionary hope but one of corruption and paranoid reaction. In 1830, the height of the French Restoration, a shrewd, ambitious young man of peasant stock understands that the path to a great fortune no longer runs, as in his hero's day, through military talent; instead, "it is necessary to be a priest."

Julien's first mentor, the Abbé Chélan, discerns in his young protégé "a sombre flame in the depths of your being, which doesn't speak to me of the moderation and perfect abnegation of worldly advantage necessary to a priest." And Julien can only agree; this flame, he notes, "it's my ambition to make my fortune."

What exactly is wrong with Julien's desire to make his fortune? In a discussion of the history of the concept of happiness in American political life, the philosopher Hannah Arendt offers some rich clues. She points to the second US president John Adams's idea of "the passion for distinction" as the most "essential and remarkable" of human faculties. The desire to distinguish oneself in life, which Adams called "emulation," is a great virtue when channelled in the service of public happiness. Recalling Freud, we might say that our unconscious belief in the immortality of our own ego has its positive side.

But when the desire for distinction serves the aims of personal power, it becomes a vice, which Adams called "ambition." This kind of ambition, Arendt argues, became endemic in America when Thomas Jefferson's ambiguous concept of "the pursuit of happiness," enshrined in the Declaration of Independence, came to be equated with private gain rather than public good. For Arendt, this privatisation of happiness, in Adams's terms the triumph of ambition over emulation, came to corrupt the national soul of America.

The consequence of this spreading materialism was that the new nation, founded in the highest spiritual ideals, came increasingly to resemble the corrupt old Europe from which it emerged—the very Europe Stendhal mercilessly skewers in his novels. The uncoupling of ambition from any wider political or spiritual ideals is the great theme of *The Red and the Black*. And Stendhal's wonderfully dyspeptic autobiography, *The Life of Henry Brulard* (deemed too shockingly candid by his literary executor, it wasn't published till fifty years after his death), reveals this to be as much a theme of his life as of his novels.

In his memoir, Stendhal's father, Chérubin Beyle, emerges as an opportunistic hypocrite and snob, a petty, shrewd provincial obsessed with buying and selling land, a pious Ultra (the contemporary French term for royalist reactionary) with a "timid, rancorous, unfriendly" character. The child Henry, bereaved of his beloved mother, longs to escape from the shuttered confines of his father's home, where he is deprived of the company of other children and reproved for laughing.

Chérubin's desire for his son to inherit his lawyer's position is evidence for the latter that "he didn't love me as an individual, but as a son who would carry on his family." His father sees his son merely as a means to uphold the family's status, not as a separate person seeking his own fulfilment. To his father, the continuation of the family line means the immortality of his own ego.

Stendhal portrays his passion for mathematics, the ultimate expression of pure, disinterested intellect, as his ticket out of the suffocating small-town atmosphere of Grenoble. Not for him, a petty life of sordid money-grubbing. But scratch the surface and it seems his motives aren't so pure. Henry's resentment derives in large part from the fact that his father lost much of the fortune he'd made during the Empire period in reckless speculations, depriving the young Henry of the generous inheritance he'd been banking on.

Add the textbook Oedipal rivalry with his father for his mother's heart ("I loathed my father when he came and interrupted our kissing"), intensified by her early death, and Stendhal's contemptuous attacks on his father start to look a little suspicious. Is he so free of the self-interest and vindictiveness for which he condemns his father? The more he tries to differentiate himself from his father, the more he resembles him. He disdains his father's petty snobbery while aligning himself with his mother's aristocratic Italian genealogy and dismissing his father's Dauphinois family as provincial peasants. And he is far from free of the interest in money and status he claims to find so vulgar in his father.

Isn't this pull between moral conviction and materialistic desire all too recognisable to most of us? Following John Adams, we all want to believe, especially when we're young, that our ambitions are rooted in the noblest motives—to help our fellow human beings, to increase worldly happiness. But Arendt reminds us that in our competitive individualistic societies, where we're encouraged to see the pursuit of our own happiness as isolated from the pursuit of a common happiness, private ambition is liable to cut itself off from public good.

Julien's worship of Napoleon illustrates this point nicely. He is inspired by Napoleon's fame and power, not by the sweeping liberal reforms that gave birth to the modern state, or by any other of his achievements as a military leader and statesman. Politics, as portrayed in *The Red and the Black*, has little to do with the advancement of public happiness and everything to do with cynical expediency.

Living as tutor to the children in the household of the Ultra mayor, Monsieur de Rênal, Julien keeps a portrait of Napoleon hidden in a box under his bed. When the mayor and a valet set about replacing the house's mattresses, Julien panics at the prospect of the portrait's discovery. The public disclosure of his admiration for the "usurper" Napoleon would kill his career in the church of French Restoration society before it's had a chance to begin.

All Julien's feelings, including love and desire, are filtered through the same calculus of self-interest. His initial passion for Madame de Rênal "derived from the joy of possessing so noble and so beautiful a woman" rather than any tender feeling for the lady herself. In the second part of the novel, after graduating from the Besançon seminary, he is appointed secretary to the Marquis de la Mole, Paris diplomat and royalist. He soon sets about conquering the heart of Mathilde, his boss's haughty and beautiful daughter.

With this second great romantic triumph, we see even more baldly how thoroughly Julien's passion is fuelled by his ambition and egotism. It isn't that he's incapable of love; more that his love of anyone else becomes just another way of loving himself, a vehicle for his bottomless narcissism. Stendhal lets us eavesdrop on his self-aggrandising thoughts during his comically stopstart seduction of Mathilde. In a particularly excruciating passage, he contemplates his great generosity in deigning to "take pity on a family of this rank!"

Having received a bold letter of declaration from Mathilde herself, he considers leaving Paris without responding and leaving her to languish in suspense. The thought of himself, penniless and without rank, disdaining the "offered pleasure" of a celebrated young woman of the nobility, sends him into private ecstasies: "A clear spring sent to quench my thirst in this burning desert of mediocrity that I cross so painfully! By God, not so stupid; each for himself in this desert of egotism that men call life."

In this version of life, love is just another front in a war of all against all, another way of promoting one's own interests at the expense of everyone else's. The egotist's way of loving is oddly miserable, because it alienates the lover from his own emotions; rather than feeling the intensity of his infatuation for his beloved, he sees her only through the lens of others' admiration and envy. Winning Mathilde means boasting not only "the most brilliant young woman in high society . . . but also the divine gratification of seeing the Marquis de Croisenois, son of a duke, and who will be a duke himself, sacrificed to me." Victory over the young marquis is infinitely more gratifying than the love of Mathilde.

Julien's ultimate problem, though, is his difficulty in sustaining this stance of ruthless ambition. At a certain point, the force of his passion penetrates his carapace of pure egotism. Julien is pulled between steel and fire, between the single-minded accumulation of fame, power and riches and the spontaneous eruptions of his heart. Cold calculation wars in his mind with reckless action.

Julien cannot manage the coexistence of these opposing impulses. Assailed by the urgings of his head on one side and his heart on the other, he explodes when Madame de Rênal threatens his anticipated marriage to Mathilde, culminating in the violent crime that undoes him.

The Red and the Black reminds us that ambition can literally be deadly. Julien's shooting of his former lover is a prime instance of how ambition can turn against itself to become pure self-destruction. Anticipating the sabotage of a glittering marriage that would have outdone his wildest dreams of worldly success, Julien blindly follows the impulse that will lay waste to everything.

It's hard not to see in Julien's career a powerful iteration of the most puzzling and disturbing story the human species has to tell: its tendency to wreck itself at the very moment it imagines it has secured its future.

Ambition can be a feature of almost any stage of the life cycle. But it's on the cusp of adulthood that this basic and unsettling ambiguity at its heart is revealed, for it's here that ambitious young men and women first feel the pull between the paths of love, justice and human solidarity on the one hand and of power, greed and self-interest on the other.

Most of us come to steer an uneasy course between the two, living sufficiently ordinary and unobjectionable lives to ensure that we aren't fully identified with one path or the other. But for the three characters discussed here, there is something irresolvable and finally debilitating about the pursuit of their desires.

That ambition tends to harbour this destructive element within itself casts some light on my experience during an Extinction Rebellion protest, some four days into their action across central London in 2019.

The protesters were occupying Marble Arch, from which all traffic had been diverted, bringing the area to a standstill. Despite the density of this temporary population—attested by row upon orderly row of nylon tents, the fetid odour emanating from the compost toilet and the general air of congenial busyness—without the reliable punctuation of car horns and rumbling diesel engines, the atmosphere was anomalously quiet. Tired, unwashed bodies reclined against walls, a few danced languidly to poorly played prog rock guitar solos, while others hungrily scraped wooden forks across paper plates of dhal and shredded lettuce.

On a small makeshift stage near the entrance to Hyde Park, the organisers were introducing a series of speakers, each of them putting forward an idea for sustainable living. A young man, skinny and private-school handsome, stepped up to the mic, pulled out his phone and began to read off it, his speech interrupted every few seconds by his scrolling thumbs. He was discussing the principle of subsidiarity, an important and worthy topic, but hardly rousing. His delivery was slow, his voice low and flat, he stumbled over his words.

I quickly became irritable. It was a nice initiative, to create a space amid the urgency of political protest for the presentation of serious ideas and concepts, but bringing them alive required fluency and charisma, not the bungling niceness of some hapless posh boy. I scanned the audience scattered across the verge opposite, expecting to find my reaction confirmed. But the expressions on these faces betrayed no impatience or disdain, only courteous, attentive interest.

It occurred to me that placing a low premium on the speaker's performance shifts attention from the style of speech to its content. He certainly couldn't be accused of verbal seduction, of working up his audience with silky phrasing and punchy slogans. In Plato's *Gorgias* dialogue, Socrates warns against the demagoguery and collective delusion whipped up by skilled rhetoricians; well, there was no danger of that here. For all the self-evident flaws of his speaking style, it was clear that he was much more interested in sharing an idea than in winning followers. Where I'd been grouchily impatient, I found myself oddly and deeply moved.

This scene might tell us something about the way some so-called Gen Z–ers think about ambition today, audible too in my son's words. It's not so much about a pious renunciation of personal ambition, more a sense of its inadequacy, even irrelevance, to the needs of the moment. The spectre of tsunamis and forest fires makes a mockery of any dreams of the ego's immortality. In the disarmingly gentle receptivity of that crowd, I intuited something like a need to channel their personal ambitions into a world beyond and bigger than themselves. Time will tell whether this is a fleeting impression of the moment or the harbinger of real change.

*

I don't want to sound naive. Ways of being that have been entrenched in the human soul for millennia don't evaporate in the course of a single generation. I doubt there are many people, regardless of age or class background or any other variable, not excluding that large crowd of protesters, who haven't indulged fantasies of fame and riches, or some other path to securing their immortality.

The consulting room has taught me how tenacious a hold on us these fantasies can have. Patients will often trace them back to early childhood, to the image they saw reflected in their parents' eyes that they were destined to be special, great, exceptional.

I'm struck especially by how much daily misery finds its roots in those parental messages. Sunil, the elder of two sons, couldn't recall a day in his childhood when he wasn't explicitly reminded of his superiority—to his brother, Viv, to his peers and to the rest of the world. This incessant praise was often hard to distinguish from a reproach, or at least a warning: "My mother would drive me to school and lock gazes with me in the rearview mirror. 'Don't you forget,' she'd say to me, 'how much smarter you are than those other donkeys, Sunil!' Any test or competition and she'd remind me I was the best, and everyone needed to know it. Poor little Viv, he'd just sit there staring out the window, like he wasn't hearing any of it."

But the thing about poor little Viv is that he was doing just fine these days, with his thriving and lucrative dental practice and big, noisy family. Viv had no idea what to make of his brother seeing a shrink: "He's a lovely guy, my little brother, but not the deepest, you know? Like, Mum and Dad introduce him to this girl and he didn't seem even to question their choice. Five minutes later she's popping out the kids. When he couldn't get into med school, Dad told him to do dentistry, and a few years on, there he is, root canals and crowns up the wazoo."

For Sunil, Viv's broad smile, now so straight and white, perfectly captured his blindly compliant character, and his apparent lack of any independence of thought or desire. "He's so desperate to please!" That might be the case, but his desperation was certainly paying off. It was amazing how he'd become their parents' cast-iron favourite, while they never seemed to know what to say to Sunil.

Sunil was an economist specialising in public finance, a professor at a London institution with enough private consultancy work to ensure his own finances were more than sound. The institution was prestigious, which made me wonder aloud why he kept disparaging it. "I suppose it's got a decent enough reputation, but it's hardly the LSE, or Harvard."

This measurement of achievement against some punishing ideal of the "best" was Sunil's habitual, not to say obsessive, way of seeing himself. He was stuck at a middling institution, had written some well-regarded articles, got on the radio every so often, but his ambition to reframe the conversation around public-sector finance had never been realised. "I never seem to get the time I need to write that definitive book, and now it's looking to me like someone else has got there first. The students or the admin always get in the way. You know, thinking on this scale requires a vast amount of reading and processing of ideas. Being like my brother, frantically ploughing through the appointments schedule, is not an option. Serious thinking takes the time it takes."

And he was single too, having passed through more unsatisfying relationships over the last decade than he'd care to count off, none of which had ended well or lasted more than a couple of years. "Maybe I'm too demanding, at least that's what countless people have told me," he said, his tone betraying his umbrage at the implication that he thought too highly of himself. "Apparently you're not supposed to have standards these days. Wanting a woman to be beautiful makes you superficial, wanting her to be smart makes you an intellectual snob, wanting her to be charming makes you a vain boor. Well, forgive me for having standards!"

But scratch the surface of Sunil's "standards" and they revealed a curious tendency to being set a notch above the thing or person to whom they were being applied. One previous girlfriend "lacked that edge of refinement that makes the difference between attractive and really beautiful"; another was "really very sweet but hearing her trying to hold her own at these high-powered dinner parties just made me wince." And it was by no means women alone that fell foul of these standards. His own publications and lectures, his home, his salary and his social group were all slightly below par, spoiled not by being bad but by not being quite the best—which was somehow worse.

What was the origin of these mysterious, punishing standards if not the daily onslaught of praise bordering on worship he had heard in his parents' voices and saw in their adoring eyes? Sunil's fatally misplaced act of loyalty to his parents was to take them at their word, to swallow their hype. He was deeply bitter about the wordless disappointment that seemed to radiate from their smiles and chatter these days, as well as the total and seemingly permanent reversal of the boyhood hierarchy between his brother and himself.

I can't pretend it was easy to warm to Sunil. His casual arrogance and implacable sense of superiority made me grimace inwardly. But my antipathy was balanced by the thought that he wasn't unjustified in his bitterness. From his own perspective, he was the victim of a cruel deception by his parents, who had implanted in him the conviction that he was destined for greatness. His scrupulous fidelity to that message had been rewarded by their, and his own, perpetual disappointment.

And yet the one thing that Sunil resisted, as though his life depended on it, was any suggestion that his ideals might be self-defeating or wrong-headed. "Piketty showed you can write a best-selling, massively influential book on economics. George Clooney showed you can marry a woman who's as brilliant as she is beautiful. Why shouldn't those be the standards to aim for? Who said it's better to settle for mediocrity?"

Sunil's scorn for any notional second best found its deepest and most painful expression in his seemingly incurable longing for Jasmin, the girlfriend he'd met at Cambridge and who still represented for him the pinnacle of human perfection. He'd talk about the spell of her dark eyes and infectious smile, her matchless wit and the clarity and elegance of her mind with such vivid immediacy that it was all too easy to lose sight of the fact that he hadn't seen her in person for more than thirty years.

He had been with Jasmin a little more than a year when she threw him over for "some inbred rowing captain." For months he was disconsolate, letting his hair grow long and unkempt, wandering the Cambridge streets mournfully in the same threadbare tweed jacket, reducing all human contact to his weekly tutorials. "I left university with a starred first and one friend."

A few years ago, he had stumbled across her photo in an article about a new wave of female entrepreneurs and was startled by the shudder of grief and desire it induced in him. From this point on, he would spend a sleepless night at his desk every few weeks, nursing a tumbler of whisky and staring glassily for hours at a low-resolution photograph of her smiling face on his laptop.

During the morning sessions that followed nights like this, he would lie on my couch, clamping his eyes shut, scratching his stubble and rubbing his temples, his silence interspersed with groans. "What if I found her?" he asked me one morning. "I'm serious. What if I got in touch? Since she finished with me, my life has been one long, slow puncture, all the drive and ambition gradually seeping out of me day by day. I feel like she's my best hope of pumping the air back in."

"I wonder who you're really looking at when you stare at that picture," I replied. "Is it her, or yourself? This young woman whose loss you've never got over, isn't she just you in disguise?"

"Are you saying I secretly want to be a girl, Prof?" he wisecracked mirthlessly. "Because you're barking up the wrong tree there."

"I'm saying you've convinced yourself she was the key to the perfect life you were destined to have and were somehow cheated of. That's why you can't let go of her."

A long silence followed. I was surprised to see a thin stream of tears running down his left temple, the first he'd shed in six years of analysis. Fighting full-blown sobs, he said, "I feel like she's my last chance to be that magical being, boy genius, superhero I used to think I was. I used to think you'd help me bring that boy to life, but you haven't, Prof. I hate to say it, but you haven't. So maybe she will! Maybe she'll show me how to live . . ."

ii "Bound to get ahead": Jay Gatsby

Handsome and luxuriously dressed (handmade shirt especially opulent), JG, thirty-one, spoke to assessor in peculiar and disconcerting accents of a languid aristocrat, addressing her throughout as "old sport." Rather obfuscated in response to questions about childhood but claims of high birth seem exaggerated at very least. A follow-up risk assessment is recommended, given the patient's hints of involvement with professional criminal elements. Underlying flamboyant presentation, long-standing and entrenched melancholia clearly detectable. Asked about instances of low mood, he alluded to a romantic disappointment some five years ago, from which he has evidently been unable to move on. Allusions to nightly vigils staring across lake at marital home of the young woman in question—safeguarding issues?

I'm going to pause before disclosing my response to Sunil and consider another man who spent years staring into some spot in the middle distance, fantasising about the woman who would complete him and give meaning to all he did.

Jay Gatsby's spot isn't an image on a screen, but a green light at the end of a dock. The dock belongs to the East Egg mansion across the water, where the unimaginably wealthy, old-money Buchanans live in mutual, perversely companionable hatred. By the time we reach the oft-quoted final paragraphs of F. Scott Fitzgerald's celebrated 1925 novel, we've come to understand that Gatsby has amassed his own colossal, ill-gotten fortune and settled in the opulent mansion across the water solely in order to win back the love of his life, Daisy Fay of Louisville, Kentucky.

The green light is the promise of Daisy herself, "so close that he could hardly fail to grasp it." Gatsby's fantasy is that winning Daisy will transform him at a stroke from vulgarly ostentatious hoodlum to gallant knight and saviour. The dreamed-of future with Daisy will redeem his sordid past, bathing his criminal deeds in the noble light of love.

What Gatsby never realised, in the elegiac words of his narrator, Nick Carraway, is that this dream "was already behind him." He doesn't see that he's already lost what he's trying to find; this, Carraway concludes, is what we all do in one way or another. We chase after the green light of the "orgastic future," and when it eludes us, we simply "stretch out our arms further."

Carraway's suggestion is that there is almost always more to ambition than sheer material accumulation. The truly ambitious individual may have one eye on the next million, the next promotion, the next burst of public adulation, but the other eye is fixed on a more elusive point in the distance. In Gatsby's case, this is the green light on the dock, signifying Daisy. Or perhaps we should say "Daisy," because whether Gatsby really loves and yearns for the specific real-world person who goes by that name seems doubtful at least.

Gatsby is surely more in love with his idea of Daisy than the flesh-and-blood version. We might argue that he's no different in this regard from every other man or woman who falls in love, from Werther to Dorothea Brooke, that we all project our own needs and fantasies onto the objects of our desire. But Gatsby takes this human tendency a step further. His version of Daisy isn't merely an idealised gloss on the real one. She plays the role in his mind that for others might be played by God or Truth or some other ultimate metaphysical principle.

Just as, for the devout but downtrodden individual, God might give meaning and coherence to a life plagued by suffering and sorrow, Daisy's love, in his mind at least, promises to shape Gatsby's lonely, chaotic life into a harmonious whole.

Even those new to the novel are likely to twig quite quickly that Daisy will do nothing of the kind. For all her charm and beauty, she turns out to be shallowly acquisitive, cowardly and destructive. This may be why Gatsby's obsessive quest to win her back has such a resonance in our own age of blind materialism and aspiration.

It might also help explain why I've placed this discussion of *The Great Gatsby* under the heading of "Ambition" rather than, say, "First Love." As in John Adams's distinction between emulation in the name of a higher good and ambition in the name of self-interest, Gatsby seems to believe that he's pursuing the former and that his criminally acquired bootlegging fortune will be redeemed by the purity of his love for Daisy.

But in a world corrupted by money and greed, higher and lower forms of ambition are bound to become confused. Is it really Daisy that he sees in that distant green light? Isn't it rather some elusive, ultimately ridiculous hope of transforming his worldly life into one of exemplary beauty? But instead of ending his life in old age, a silver-haired Daisy at his side, he's found floating face down in his crimson-tinged swimming pool, a spectacle for rubbernecking boys.

So how and why did Gatsby's life end so sordidly? As Julien Sorel has already shown us, and as the growing power and influence of today's tiny billionaire class are making all too plain, the pursuit of a fortune is a dangerous beast. In 1930, five years after Fitzgerald published *The Great Gatsby*, the British economist John Maynard Keynes, in his essay "Economic Possibilities for Our Grandchildren," looked forward to a world in which the pursuit of excess wealth for its own sake would be "recognised for what it is, a somewhat disgusting morbidity, one of those semi-criminal, semi-pathological propensities which one hands over with a shudder to the specialists in mental disease."

Ninety years later, with more than half the world's wealth concentrated in the hands of the richest 1 per cent, and much of that wealth itself controlled by a tiny number of billionaires,* it seems depressingly safe to confirm that Keynes was a tad optimistic on this

---

* In 2017, *Forbes* magazine reported that the three richest billionaires in the US own more than the entire bottom half of the country's population.

point. Far from being a quaint relic of an unequal past, obscene ostentation has become one of the iconic features of our age.

Fitzgerald mercilessly exposes the deleterious psychological and moral effects of this kind of wealth on those who possess it. Freed from even the minutest burden of necessity by his vast unearned wealth, Tom Buchanan's life has become a random and empty parade of polo matches, extramarital sex and blowhard bigotry. Carraway notices his "cruel body," a cauldron of compressed brutality, shockingly and gratuitously unleashed at the slightest hint of frustration—invariably against women. Tom's viciousness looks like the effect of a seething mass of energy lacking any outlet for its meaningful employment. Few characters could evoke more precisely the "disgusting morbidity" of which Keynes speaks.

Tom and Daisy are, in their friend Jordan Baker's famous phrase, "careless people." But aren't people who never have to consider the cost of anything, who can buy their way into any pleasure and out of any trouble, bound to be careless? Able to acquire anything they please, the Buchanans are never forced to consider what really matters to them, a privation that takes on the dubious guise of a privilege.

Born James Gatz into a life of poverty, Gatsby is very different in this regard. Having nothing endows him with an equally dubious advantage, namely the painful itch of aspiration. We get a glimpse of how deeply this itch has taken root in him near the end of the novel, when Gatsby's estranged father arrives at the house for his son's funeral.

Henry C. Gatz swells with pride as he surveys the infinite distance his son has traversed between the anonymous North Dakotan town of his birth and this enormous mansion in which he died. He carries two mementos with him: a cracked and dirty photograph of the same house, sent to him by "Jimmy" and "more real to him now than the house itself," and "a ragged old copy of a book called *Hopalong Cassidy*" Jimmy "had when he was a boy."

On the flyleaf of the book is a series of handwritten lines under the heading SCHEDULE, itemising Gatsby's tough boyhood regime of early rising, exercise, study, work, sport, elocution and poise. Contemporary American readers are likely to have recognised these disciplines as corrupted versions of Benjamin Franklin's notes for self-improvement in his famous diaries. But Gatsby's routine is directed not, as in Franklin, towards the cultivation of civic virtue but of personal gain.

For Mr. Gatz, the notes are living proof of the juicy fruits of determined ambition. Without a trace of irony, he tells Carraway that "Jimmy was bound to get ahead. He always had some resolves like this or something."

Gatsby's father either fails or doesn't want to notice that his son's "resolves" have culminated in his violent death. He doesn't allow the fact that his first visit to his son's house is for his funeral to get in the way of the illusion that he lived the exemplary American dream, rising from rags to riches through sheer will and hard work.

In the version he tells Carraway, Gatsby took leave of his "shiftless and unsuccessful" farmer parents at sixteen, scraping a living as a clam-digger and salmon-fisher along the shores of Lake Superior, while spinning in the "constant, turbulent riot" of his heart "grotesque and fantastic conceits" of "a universe of ineffable gaudiness." Into the shallows of these shores, the yacht of elderly multi-millionaire copper trader Dan Cody dropped anchor.

For young James Gatz, Cody's yacht "represented all the beauty and glamour in the world." In the moments he rows over to it in order to warn Cody of a dangerous wind on the way, he invents and becomes Jay Gatsby, a Platonic ideal of a rich man of leisure to which "he was faithful to the end." Finding him "quick and extravagantly ambitious," Cody offers him a berth that becomes a five-year apprenticeship in ruthlessness and acquisition until the older man's suspicious death.

When, as a soldier on leave, he meets Daisy Fay— "gleaming like silver, safe and proud above the hot struggles of the poor"—she falls seamlessly into his Platonic conception of the Great Gatsby, soon to become the fabulous enigma of West Egg.

For all that she embodies his ideal, Gatsby is surprisingly clear-eyed about Daisy. When Carraway tries to specify the quality of her voice, Gatsby abruptly says, "Her voice is full of money." He knows, in other words, that Daisy's bewitching charm is an effect of her overbearing entitlement, her unquestioned status as "the king's daughter, the golden girl." Gatsby knows who Daisy really is, but chooses not to, just as he knows and chooses not to know the truth about himself.

My patient Sunil knew too, even as he stared mournfully at the perfection he'd lost for good, that he was only staring at another human being, no less confused and flawed than anyone else.

So when Sunil cried out that Jasmin might finally show him how to live, I replied, "Why are you so convinced that you don't already know?"

iii "I don't really know": Esther Greenwood

EG, nineteen, unusually tall, somewhat gawky young woman boasting highly impressive record of academic and creative achievement, currently one of twelve female students taking part in hotly competed month-long internship scheme in New York. Appeared reticent and sullen at start of assessment, responding to questions either in terse and rather disdainful expressions of irony or not at all. Most pronounced harshness was reserved for herself, however, as she decried inconsistency of her feelings for young medical student she had been involved with, difficulty in forming friendships and general feeling of deep confusion as to who she is. Despondency became so pronounced as to induce the assessor to ask whether she had thoughts of ending her life. Did not respond, though tears came to her eyes.

Julien Sorel and Jay Gatsby remind us that even fulfilled ambitions can end in irremediable disappointment. They are both young men of humble origin whose exceptional drive, talent and sense of purpose bring them abundant social cachet and riches. Yet both men's lives end violently, chasing some impossible object of desire that can only elude them. Madame de Rênal and Daisy Buchanan are the illusory remedies they seek for the incurable malaise of their lives.

Ambition certainly yields Sorel and Gatsby a great deal; it's just that none of these rewards turn out to be what they wanted. But perhaps this reveals an unsettling truth about ambition: that there's something unavoidably tormenting about it. Speaking of the sexual drive, which he saw as the ultimate channel of all human desire, Freud wrote that there was something in its very nature that "is unfavourable to the realisation of complete satisfaction." Because we never really know what we want, the pangs of desire and aspiration can never really attain the satisfaction they seek.

For Esther Greenwood, ambition is at the heart of the disquiet that ultimately leads her to seek to end her own life, a compulsion all the more poignant when cast in the retrospective shadow of her creator's own suicide. For Esther, the pressures and expectations stirred up by her ambitions turn out to be so debilitating that she unravels long before she can realise any of them. In contrast to the two male characters, it is the possibility of success rather than actual success that undoes her.

The Bell Jar takes place in 1953, during "the summer they electrocuted the Rosenbergs." We are in New York, where Esther has won a month's internship at a fashion magazine. This is the New York of *Mad Men*, the glittering epicentre of an emerging consumer culture. It is the cradle of what the German sociologist Byung-Chul Han would call "the achievement society" sixty years later.

An achievement society, as Han describes it, is one that projects individual success, acquisition and status as its supreme ideals; these are the psychological drivers of a consumer society. In a more traditional industrial society, the prime imperative is production rather than consumption—hard work, discipline and dedication. In psychoanalytic terms, an industrial society is driven by the superego, the internal figure that seeks to induce guilt in us for our insufficient levels of conscientiousness.

The superego's motto is "You must!" In a consumer society, this forbidding voice is not the most effective in ensuring our compliance. Consumerism is more motivated by what Freud called our "ego-ideal," the inner voice created by the unconscious belief, originally transmitted to us in infancy by our parents, that we are, or at least can be, perfect. Its motto is not so much "You must!" as "You can!," the great slogan of the era of positive thinking and maximised potential.

The ego-ideal is less harsh schoolmaster than wildly encouraging personal trainer. It speaks to us as an ally rather than an object of disdain, seeking only that we be the best we can be. This means that while it can spur ambition and impel creativity, it also induces feelings of shame and inadequacy at falling short of the self we "know" we can be.

Across more than a decade of practising psychoanalysis, I've been increasingly struck by the prevalence of this tendency. Men and women describe a perpetually enervated state of mind caused by the nagging sense that they've not achieved enough and that they're always a step behind where they should be. In Han's words, "The feeling of having achieved a goal never occurs." Any sense of contentment quickly gives way to guilt at their own complacency, as though the feeling that life is good, or at least good enough, were the gateway to decadence and decline.

My patient Sofia felt she was forever running the same punishing mental treadmill, resisting any sense of satisfaction in favour of the "magically transformative event" she told herself was just around the corner. No job, no man, no home could remotely match the perfection of the ideal she was chasing.

There was Jim, whose intensity of ambition proved an obstacle to doing anything for any sustained period. He was a promising novelist who could never quite finish a novel, a prospective landscape gardener who'd never completed his training, an aspiring chef fearful of the time and money any restaurant would swallow up. Shuttling anxiously between these options, he would get caught up in first one then another grandiose fantasy of the possibilities: he could be as seminal as Philip Roth or Margaret Atwood, he could win commissions for five acres of Hyde Park, his restaurant would rival the Fat Duck. The stages between obscurity and fame had to be leapfrogged somehow; he had no interest in a novel that sold a few hundred copies and got a couple of nice reviews, or to mow suburban lawns or chop parsley for some big-name chef who'd yell obscenities at him.

Fixated on what she hadn't achieved, Sofia could take no pride or pleasure in what she had achieved. Caught between competing fantasies of being great, Jim could not reconcile himself to being merely good. Perhaps nothing in the consulting room amazes me more insistently than the way this quest for greatness can deprive people of an ordinarily good life.

Things can be worse still: indecision, and the indefinite suspension of life that it causes, can signify the deepest misery, as Sylvia Plath's *The Bell Jar* (1963) shows us.

It is a novel of two unnervingly distinct halves. The second half describes the descent of the imaginary bell jar over Esther's patch of the world, an airless glass dome that interposes between her and everyone else, consigning her to a state of alienation and bewilderment, causing a desire to end her own life that results in successive admissions to two psychiatric facilities.

In spite or because of its occasional flashes of pitch-black humour, the novel's second half is unremittingly grim, drawing us into suffocating proximity to Esther's suicidal despair.

The book's narrative arc is now sufficiently well known that even new readers will have an idea of the dark places into which it eventually leads. This wasn't the case for me when I first read it. At seventeen, I was dutifully obeying the female friend who told me I had to read it. Knowing almost nothing of the book or of Plath gave me the peculiar advantage of being able to experience just how inadequately (though this inadequacy is deliberate and artful) the first half prepares us for the second.

Split off from the second half, Esther's misadventures in New York—the drunken Southern belle, the assorted creeps, the food poisoning, the excruciating chats with a disappointed boss—make for twistedly entertaining exercises in the comedy of embarrassment, anticipating the likes of *Girls* or *Fleabag* ("I noticed, in the routine way you notice the colour of somebody's eyes, that Doreen's breasts had popped out of her dress and were swinging out slightly like full brown melons"). I didn't have the sense I was witnessing the stirrings of a suicidal breakdown.

But read the first part in the retrospective light of the second and the hints of unravelling become clearer. What might have seemed the ordinary discontents of late-adolescent confusion starts to look more like the gradual opening of a terrifying internal void. Esther's sense of her own being is so thin and precarious that any path or identity she could choose looks to be as arbitrary and meaningless as all others.

The same bell jar that separates Esther from the world also separates her from herself. Rather than inhabit herself, she looks at herself askance, as though at someone she barely knows. Nothing about herself can be felt as natural or taken for granted; her very existence is a tormenting puzzle. She has a life, but no sense of what she's supposed to do with it, or why it's worth doing anything with it at all.

This malaise is inescapably bound up with being a young middle-class white woman in the 1950s, for whom independence is only a brief and indulgent prelude to a life of stultifying domestic servitude and sexual conformity. But Esther responds with more than indignant protest. Being a woman feels to her like a kind of existential deficit, as though her life were fundamentally unnecessary. This in turn induces a feeling of radical inadequacy, of lacking a sufficiently dense sense of self to know how to live, or even whether to live at all.

"I was supposed to be having the time of my life," Esther says at the start of the novel in reference to her time in New York. "I was supposed to be the envy of thousands of other college girls just like me all over America." The problem is that she can see no intrinsic link between the glamorous young intern she's meant to be and the person she is. She may appear the poised master of her own destiny, "steering New York like her own private car," but her experience of the office and parties and bars is one of passive inertia, "like a numb trolley-bus."

When Jay Cee, editor of *Ladies' Day*, asks her what she wants to do, Esther hears herself say, "I don't really know." There's a wryly comic side to this cluelessness, in the sharp self-awareness with which she views her own haplessness: "I tried to imagine what it would be like if I were Ee Gee, the famous editor, in an office full of potted rubber plants and African violets my secretary had to water each morning."

But the humour masks the depths of anxiety and misery lurking in this state of indecision. The many possible paths Esther imagines for herself can only cancel each other out, for none of them line up with even the most cursory sense of her own identity or desires. Contemplating the year ahead, she determines to complete her thesis on *Finnegans Wake*, then to become an apprentice potter, then to work as a waitress in Germany, until "plan after plan started leaping through my head, like a family of scatty rabbits."

The image is so brilliantly apposite because proliferating baby rabbits look and behave interchangeably. Like rabbits, Esther's plans appear to harbour many possible futures, but each turns out to be as arbitrary as the last. The same is true of the broader prospect of her life. Esther envisions her life as a green fig tree abundant with fruit, each signifying a different future: a home and children, a career as an editor, world travel, a succession of exotic lovers, "an Olympic lady crew champion, and beyond and above those figs were many more figs I couldn't quite make out." Esther continues:

I saw myself sitting in the crotch of this fig-tree, starving to death, just because I couldn't make up my mind which of the figs I would choose. I wanted each and every one of them, but choosing one meant losing all the rest, and, as I sat there, unable to decide, the figs began to wrinkle and go black, and, one by one, they plopped to the ground at my feet.

The extended metaphor is deliberately overwrought, and seems calculated to render Esther ridiculous, a victim to what might be dismissed these days as "first-world problems." What is incorrect as well as unhelpful about such a judgement is the inference that the complaint is merely an inability to decide between an array of enviable options, as though it really were a matter of not being able to choose between being a magazine editor or an Olympic rower.

This is no more true of Esther than it is of Sunil or Sofia or Jim. In all these cases, indecision is a consequence not of having too many good options, but of a hole at the heart of their own selfhood that makes any choice seem meaningless. The surface comic effect of Esther's fig tree metaphor obscures the real despair at its heart: to someone unable to reach for one or other fig, their abundance feels less like a surfeit of life than an intimation of death.

John Adams's idea of a personal aspiration rooted in the "emulation" of the best in the service of the common good should be heard as more than mere piety. It's an attempt to sketch out an ideal relationship between who we are and what we do. This may be an ideal worth rediscovering in the age of reality TV personalities, YouTube influencers and social media stars, in which money, fame, status and all the other fruits of ambition are rapidly becoming their own end, disconnected from any necessary link to the person who pursues them.

The conversation with my son helped me grapple with the fundamental stakes of this problem, to see that ambition requires at least two conditions if it is to be properly meaningful: a sense that we are substantial enough to be able to know and trust our own desires, and our own judgement about what matters; and a belief that the world itself is a going concern, with a future that would justify what we invest in it.

For Julien Sorel, ambition was cut off from the quest for either personal integrity or public good. For Gatsby, ambition was a means to attaining some transcendent but ultimately illusory redemption. And for Esther Greenwood, the very impossibility of ambition, of feeling any intrinsic connection between who she is and how she might live in the world, was the basis for suicidal depression.

Our tendency to want more than we have is the sharpest of doubled-edged knives. Without it, we wouldn't be able to hope for sublime creative achievement, or deep and enduring love, or the extension of justice and human rights. But the reign of consumer culture, with its emphasis on material accumulation and status, has turned this tendency into a source of constant frustration and unhappiness. Perhaps the existential threat facing humanity offers us an opportunity to resolve this dilemma, a chance to uncouple our ambitions from an empty notion of success and to reconnect them to our sense of who we are and of what the world needs from us.

6

Adulthood Part 2: Marriage

My last first date took place in 1992, sometime between the elections of John Major and Bill Clinton. I called her landline to ask her out. This was the dark age before email, texting and social media. In the absence of any online footprint, she consulted a mutual acquaintance, who told her I was all right if she didn't mind a bit of self-importance and intellectual pretension.

Not unlike George Eliot's Dorothea Brooke, the first of this chapter's protagonists, my date married the man she'd been warned against. I'd like to believe hers wasn't quite so catastrophic a choice, though if my most impressive boast is being a better catch than the Rev. Edward Casaubon, a strong contender in a crowded field for the most undesirable husband in all world literature, I'm probably in trouble.

Today few of us can access the kinds of organic social networks that helped the young men and women of George Eliot's provincial English towns find their future mate. Millions turn instead to the virtual networks of internet dating.

I remember when those TV ads first appeared, promising true and lasting love through an app, peddling dubious claims of attractive members in limitless supply and the most reliably "scientific" methods of matching them up; a young woman's face lighting up in wonder the moment she sees her date, the moonish smiles of the newly forming couple as the restaurant staff clear up busily around them.

I am admittedly lacking in first-hand experience in this area, but I make up for it handsomely in second-hand reports from my consulting room. Practising psychotherapy has provided me with a deep well of tales from the jungle of internet dating. If the TV glow of love-struck men and women forms one half of a mental diptych, the other half is formed of these stories of creepy first texts and obscene photo messages, outdated profile pictures, poorly feigned conversational interest and perfunctory fumbles on sofas.

On one panel, TV's shiny ideal; on the other, life's grim reality. Don't these contrasting images reveal our split thinking about love and relationships? In fact, once we look for it, we find all our stories about marriage betray this same divided conception. In Jane Austen, for example, the stories of romantic enchantment in the foreground (Elizabeth and Darcy, Fanny and Edmund) always unfold against the background of a series of established marriages (Mr. and Mrs. Bennet, Sir Thomas and Lady Bertram) in which love has long since given way to weariness, resentment, cynical self-interest and mutual indifference. Similar contrasts have been observable in TV sitcoms since the 1970s.

In imagining long-term loving relationships, our culture finds it difficult to resist these extremes of sentimentality and cynicism. No wonder marriage is in so much trouble if we can only seesaw between the soft-focus romance of the honeymoon and the humdrum disappointment of what comes after. This might account for why popular counsel these days often suggests that we should enter marriage with more "realistic" expectations.

But the problem with this prescription is that making a lifelong commitment to one other person isn't especially "realistic." On the contrary, it's a prime expression of the human tendency to live in and through illusion. This might explain why, even as I laugh scornfully at those ads' images of men's and women's faces lighting up in romantic hope, I can feel a little catch in my throat. It is at these moments, after all, that we're most liable to confuse reality with our daydreams. For a fortnight, or a night, or an hour, we recklessly sweep aside all doubt and revel in the feeling that now, with this person, we have everything we've ever yearned for. There is nothing realistic about that.

And we have a whole armoury of methods for fending off our doubts about this feeling. With little conscious awareness of what we're doing, we turn the person before us into the very embodiment of our deepest needs and wishes. In turn, we present ourselves as *their* imagined ideal, assuring them we're exactly who they've been looking for. We withhold inconvenient truths and throw out embellishments and distortions that may come back to haunt us somewhere down the line, when we're made to weather storms of hurt reproach: "When we first met, you said you *loved* free jazz!" "Yeah, and *you* said you'd always *dreamed* of going on a yoga retreat!"

Perhaps, watching those ads, my eyes grow misty at the thought of that moment when our illusion seems infinitely more real than any so-called "reality," when we enjoy the delirious sensation of merging with this new acquaintance we seem to have known for ever. All our hopes, desires, anxieties and vulnerabilities become theirs, and a row or disappointment seems virtually inconceivable.

This tendency to filter potential partners through the lenses of our own needs and wishes is a primary expression of who we are. As we've already seen, illusions are woven into our sense of reality from the beginning of life. As small children, we hold fiercely to a conviction in the physical, intellectual and moral perfection of our parents, and show an impressive capacity to deny even the most glaring evidence to the contrary, as though anything would be easier to bear than the knowledge that they were ordinary human beings.

And don't we repeat this childish tendency in reverse the moment we become parents? When we speak of falling in love with our newborn babies, our words are more exact than we know. Because our parents and babies are initially objects of our blind love, we are liable to confuse who they are with who we wish they were.

Time tends to modify these illusions. As the years go by, the new baby who seemed to be the incarnation of love, beauty and serenity will reveal himself to his parents as spoiled, sullen and sarcastic, while the parents who seemed so wise and kind at first will eventually appear uptight, out of touch and embarrassing.

It's inevitable that marriage comes to be caught in this same tension between idealism and disillusion. We place all our hopes in a new partner, and then find ourselves—sometimes very quickly, sometimes much more gradually—disappointed by the reality.

This liability to disappointed ideals, as we've seen, is one of life's great hazards. The ambitions of Julien, Gatsby and Esther unravelled in that widening gap between the imagined future and the tawdry reality that they saw their lives becoming.

So how is a marriage to avoid lurching from the wild hope of those first heady days to disappointment when the daily reality fails to live up to it? The gap that inevitably opens between the glorious promised future and the eventual reality can corrode and eventually kill a marriage.

But strangely, that same gap can also enrich a marriage. The reality of daily living with someone eats away at our illusions about them; or at least, that's the cynical way of putting it. Another way is to say that as we get to know them more deeply, a person becomes more human and more complex to us. This might make us love them a lot more or hate them a lot more; often it does both.

Many years ago, walking along the banks of the Thames or the Seine, you stared into the face of the person you'd met just a few weeks earlier and felt the electric charge of new love. Fast-forward many years later, when you're exhausted parents to fractious children, eardrums pierced by plaintive wailing and gleeful yelling, beset by credit card bills, boiler repairs and work emails. An enduring love may be a matter of looking at the all-too-real face before you, washed out and fed up, and recognising it as the same one.

i "Awful nearness": Dorothea Brooke

DB, twenty, was reluctant from outset to conduct this assessment, wondering politely but firmly if it hadn't been the initiative of her "well-meaning but misguided" uncle. Pushed back indignantly at what she saw as attempt to "pathologise" her marriage to a much older clergyman, insisting (as though assessor had implied otherwise) that her husband was "noble," "brilliant," "far above me in ideals and achievements," protesting no one had any right to impugn him or his motives. Fought back tears as she said this, a losing battle as she became increasingly distressed, especially as she related some ongoing family dispute involving husband and his young cousin. Assessor found this story hard to follow. Danger of moderate to severe depression? Offer of antidepressant medication rather haughtily rebuffed.

According to Freud, the greatest and rarest achievement of the mind is to channel its erotic energy, or libido, into creative or intellectual projects. It's hard not to think of this process, which he called "sublimation," when we first meet the idealistic Dorothea Brooke, heroine of *Middlemarch* (1871).

Orphaned and raised by her genial but distracted uncle, Dorothea craves an object on whom she can bestow her love and altruistic zeal. She finds it in Reverend Casaubon—or rather, she imagines she does. To her proudly conventional and pragmatic sister, Celia, who never cares to see more than the bald facts, Casaubon is ageing, charmless and bald. But filtering his face through the lens of her own fantasies, Dorothea sees nobility, even greatness.

Reading Casaubon's proposal letter to Dorothea, it's hard to fathom how it could stir such a passionate response in a young woman of twenty:

> I have discerned in you, an elevation of thought and a capability of devotedness, which I had hitherto not conceived to be compatible either with the bloom of early youth or with those graces of sex that may be said at once to win and to confer distinction when combined, as they notably are in you, with the mental qualities above indicated.

It's a stroke of quiet comic genius, this rendition of an uptight clergyman's love-talk. But Eliot is also subtle enough to hint at what might appeal to Dorothea in the

note: perhaps she is relieved not to read the vapid nonsense churned out by chinless young gentlemen to make
delicate young ladies swoon—so relieved, she overlooks
the letter's absurd pomposity.

And so Dorothea has her own peculiar version of a
whirlwind courtship, hurtling into marriage at breakneck
speed, rendered insensible to her suitor's shortcomings
not by the usual blind spots of lust or greed but by a sense
of superiority to any such base motives.

Married offstage, she disappears from the novel for the
next hundred pages, turning up again as a honeymooner
in Rome. That term, though, while strictly correct, is
grossly misleading, for no bride could be further away
from the state of giddy lightness we normally associate
with a honeymoon.

In her elevated vision of her wifely role, Dorothea
had cast herself as the dedicated assistant to Casaubon
in his epic scholarly project, *Key to All Mythologies*. But
wandering Rome's temples of art or stranded alone in
their apartment, it dawns on her that all her hopes of
educating herself and serving the great cause of human
knowledge have been deluded. Casaubon doesn't want
her assistance, not least because he fears she'll discover
his lifelong project is an incoherent mess.

The narrator's commentary on Dorothea's predicament is both caustic and compassionate. It's not, she
points out, that Casaubon has suddenly revealed some
hidden malignancy since Dorothea so willingly declared
her devotion to him and his cause. She cannot complain

he's not the man she married, because he's nothing if not that—not a whit less humourless, self-involved or emotionally dead.

No, the problem with marriage, says the narrator, is that it means getting to *know* the person you marry. Dorothea and Casaubon marry after a handful of chaste conversations spaced over "a few imaginative weeks." Here, a brief courtship isn't so much a way of getting to know your prospective spouse as of spinning all kinds of stories around them, mostly of the wishful kind.

If from one angle Casaubon is the exact same man she married, from another he's entirely different: previously a creature of her imagination, he is now a fact of her experience. The narrator states that in marriage, "we begin by knowing little and believing much, and we sometimes end by inverting the quantities."

Perhaps this is a difficult point to appreciate in the worldly atmosphere of our time, when so many couples don't so much take a leap of faith into marriage as shuffle into it by default, often following years of sharing child-rearing duties and bathrooms. In the modern West, it seems much less common to commit to marriage "knowing little" of one another.

But this is to reduce Eliot's insight. A brief and chaste courtship may be an obvious way to marry someone without really knowing them, but it's hardly the only one. Two people can rub along together for years, becoming familiar with one another's culinary, musical and sexual tastes, all the while knowing little and believing much.

In the absence of anything to really disturb their idea of who the other is, the relationship can sustain itself for months and even years in a state of contentedly thin mutual knowledge.

But as the events of life inevitably befall each partner—bereavements, illnesses, successes, failures and bursts of illicit desire, along with all the imperceptible external and internal changes wrought in us by daily ageing—those quantities of belief and knowing are slowly but surely inverted. This is the point at which marriage becomes, as that grim phrase has it, "hard work."

Dorothea and Casaubon vividly remind us that every marriage must undergo this discomfiting transition into believing less and knowing more about one another, and there is no guarantee it will survive the experience. This is of course true of all long-term couples, married or not. But there is nothing like the public avowal of commitment to another, and the tight emotional, legal and financial bonds it creates, for instilling the sense of another person as an integral part of our inner landscape. The moment a couple pronounce their wedding vows is the moment they consent to believe less and know more about one another.

That close to half of marriages end in divorce reminds us that the effect of this leap is unpredictable at best. Towards the end of *Middlemarch*, Eliot gives us another candid take on the strange experience of marital intimacy, this time through the mouth of Dorothea. When she pays a visit to Rosamond Lydgate, the doctor's wife and would-be adulterer, she offers a rather shocking bit of counsel: "Marriage is so unlike everything else," she tells her. "There is something even awful in the nearness it brings."

There's an interesting ambiguity to what Dorothea says here. Its obvious meaning is that there's something claustrophobic, restricting and exhausting about being in such intense proximity to someone else. To know someone this well deprives us of the comfort of our illusions about them. But the equally powerful and more subtle sense of her words is that marriage brings us too awfully close to ourselves.

This intensifying knowledge of another person, and of ourselves in turn, can both enrich and diminish a marriage, sometimes at the same time. To experience at close hand the events of someone else's life is to discover not only more about who they are but more about ourselves. And these simultaneous discoveries may be life-affirming or horrifying, may fill us with disgust and shame or love and admiration.

We get a sense of this dual awfulness during that disastrous Roman honeymoon, as Dorothea confronts her husband about his *Mythologies* project. When will he start sifting and organising the "rows of volumes" of his notes, instead of simply adding to them? Having lived with the project a few weeks after admiring it from a distance, Dorothea now perceives its chronic interminability and is stricken by distress. Her complaint, writes the narrator, "in a most unaccountable, darkly feminine manner, ended with a slight sob and eyes full of tears."

In the hands of a lesser writer, Casaubon's response would merely affirm his vanity and self-importance. Eliot instead pulls the rug from under our complacent contempt for him, letting us into his painful vulnerability and confusion. It isn't simply that Casaubon doesn't know what to say or do in the face of her distress; it's that her words reveal her to be, as the narrator puts it, "as blind to his inward troubles as he to hers."

In directly alluding to the hopelessness of his great enterprise, Dorothea unknowingly strikes through to his worst fears about himself and his project, forcing him to see the very thing he's shut his eyes and plugged his ears to as tightly as possible: that he may have wasted his life. In another great moment of insight, the narrator comments on his wounded sensitivity:

> We are angered even by the full acceptance of our humiliating confessions—how much more by the hearing in hard distinct syllables from the lips of a near observer, those confused murmurs which we try to call morbid, and strive against as if they were the oncoming of numbness!

It is hard enough, in other words, to be confronted with the bad stuff we already know about ourselves. But to hear the things we try *not* to know about ourselves—and from the very person in whom we've placed our love and trust—is infinitely more terrible.

This is the true weight of Dorothea's later observation of "something even awful in the nearness" that marriage brings. Being so close to someone else will almost inevitably mean being too close to ourselves. Without meaning to, Dorothea holds up a grossly magnified mirror to Casaubon's soul, forcing him to see at close hand the scale of his self-delusion.

We've been aware all along that Casaubon is deaf and blind to the nuances and complexities of his young wife's character. What we now see, rather more unexpectedly, is that she is equally oblivious to "those hidden conflicts in her husband which claim our pity."

It isn't just the difference in age or their naive expectations of one another that doom this marriage. What seals their shared misery is that their illusions about one another are too flimsy to survive their dawning perceptions of who the other really is. Casaubon imagines he is taking a bride "with the uncritical awe of an elegant-minded canary bird"; Dorothea, for her part, pledges to marry not so much a man as a grand projection. "All Dorothea's passion," writes the narrator at the point she accepts Casaubon's proposal, "was transfused through a mind struggling towards an ideal life."

Casaubon, expecting nothing but adoring affirmation, is devastatingly unprepared for Dorothea's stinging reproaches; while Dorothea, having invested heart and soul in a spiritual ideal rather than a man, cannot cope when her husband turns out to be all too human.

Psychoanalysis suggests illusion and fantasy to be a

characteristic of all relationships. As he was developing his psychotherapeutic technique, Freud noticed that the ways his patients related to him—wishing to please him, for example, or being contemptuously dismissive of him—repeated the patterns of much older relationships. Quite unconsciously, they would remake Freud in the image of the formative figures of their early lives, so that he would draw onto himself the feelings of love, hate, anxiety and longing they once directed against parents, siblings and others.

This tendency, which he called transference, is by no means confined to the consulting room, although the consulting room is an arena in which it can be played out and examined. In fact, every new relationship is also an old one, consisting, as Freud has it, of "new editions of old traits." Transference is a fact of life for everyone.

Surprisingly for a book so rich in detail, *Middlemarch* tells us almost nothing about the parents Dorothea and her sister lost when they were "about twelve years old." The sisters remember their mother through her jewellery rather than her words or touch, while their father is conspicuous only by their silence about him.

With such a threadbare memory of her lost parents, Dorothea is primed for a peculiarly vague and airy transference. Her passion is channelled "through a mind struggling towards an ideal life." It's as though her erotic life has been formed not by her relationships to once-live adults she can remember longingly, but by their absence.

She is desperate for intimacy but doesn't really know what it feels like.

It's striking that someone so intensely alive should seem so unaware of herself as an adult, sexual woman. Losing her parents early and raised by a distracted bachelor, as a child she enjoyed little of the sensual comfort and pleasure of being held and caressed. Perhaps that is how, as a young woman, she can be so excited at the prospect of marriage to someone so palpably asexual; it is as though she were pledging herself to an abstract spiritual entity, the supposed embodiment of "an ideal life." She is bitterly disappointed to discover Casaubon is an actual person. Things can only go downhill at that point.

The love Dorothea and Casaubon think they feel for each other is a creation of their own unconscious needs and vulnerabilities. Under such conditions, hope and reality become enemies rather than allies; the gap between them can only be a source of anger and dismay.

In an ordinarily loving marriage, with its fair share of frustration, resentment and rage, there is an intricate interplay between illusion and reality, to the point that they become hard to distinguish. A fantasy we carry within us of our partner as a figure of beauty, courage and brilliance can coexist with a clear-eyed perception of their beer gut, chronic need to please and embarrassingly large gaps in basic general knowledge.

A marriage—like any significant relationship—runs

aground when these facets of the couple's mutual perception become disconnected from one another. I am struck by how consistently so many patients' discontent in a relationship seems to register itself in complaints about some aspect of their partner's physical person: she's getting fat, he snores like a pig, her laugh is fake, he never stops farting.

It's as though the "awful nearness" of marriage has disenchanted their partner, stripped away all the illusions and reduced them to a bare sum of ugly physical facts. At this point of crisis, it's as though each can only see the other from a purely external perspective. This is what we might call intimacy gone bad. To love another person's face is to see it clearly both objectively and subjectively. See it without objectivity and some day you'll notice with dismay that it doesn't quite match up to your private vision. See it without subjectivity and it will become an indifferent arrangement of features, no different from anyone else's.

Dorothea eventually finds happiness in marriage with the young, fiery and handsome Will Ladislaw, Casaubon's outcast cousin. Her second marriage brings out two obvious points of contrast with her first: first, she marries him having been exposed to the most troubled and concealed dimensions of his character and personal history; second, she lets herself feel with him the sexual passion she had disowned in marrying Casaubon. This time round, her love may be able to survive knowing more and believing less—not a bad definition of intimacy—about both her husband and herself.

ii "Perfectly free": Isabel Archer

Difficult in first instance to determine what has induced husband of IA, twenty-three, to direct her to this assessment, though subject herself was insistent that decision to attend was "entirely my own." Possessed of great wit and insight, but for most of assessment very withheld in response to questions about own history and especially marriage. While not more explicitly forthcoming, began to weep towards end of session, insisting all the while she hadn't "the faintest idea what's the matter with me." Distress seemed to be triggered by discussion of husband's "perfect judgement in matters of taste." Gathered herself and left assessment abruptly, having declined both medication and talking therapy, forcing smile and saying she was "perfectly all right." Social services? Some concerns here about emotional abuse.

Yes, the plot of Henry James's *The Portrait of a Lady* (1881) is strikingly similar to that of *Middlemarch*, published just a decade earlier. Given that James was an avowed admirer of Eliot and has his heroine read her very early on in the novel, the resemblance is unlikely to be coincidental. Both protagonists make disastrous marriages in a spirit of idealism and misguided defiance, and both end up paying dearly.

But James is far too ambitious and bold a novelist to want simply to rework someone else's story. The skeletal narrative is placed in the service of a very different and much darker novel.

One major difference between Dorothea and Isabel is that the former enters marriage actively embracing a subordinate position in the hierarchy of husband and wife. Isabel, on the other hand, imagines that marrying a man as noble in spirit as Gilbert Osmond will free her to be who she is—in contrast to Lord Warburton and Caspar Goodwood, both of whom represent for her a future of conformity and constriction.

"Freedom in marriage"—isn't this a straightforward contradiction in terms? Doesn't marriage imply an agreement to curtail certain personal freedoms—of movement, of sexual desire, of domestic habit? Why would anyone get married to protect their freedom? The question is especially pertinent for women, for whom marriage has historically always meant a contraction of any freedom and independence they may have previously enjoyed, as it still does in many parts of the world today.

Then again, in most societies, remaining single has rarely been a liberating alternative. In both *Middlemarch* and *The Portrait of a Lady*, the Victorian spinster or "old maid" appears as a pitiful figure, a fixture of the family home consigned to a lifelong childhood of dependence and deference to her parents and married siblings.

Of course, a lot has changed since then, and most single women are no longer subject to such suffocating restrictions on their financial, social and sexual independence. But the meaning of freedom for women remains fraught and contradictory, as experience in the consulting room constantly reminds me.

For the first two years of her therapy, Laura, a woman in her mid-thirties, spent much of her time on the couch turning over the same ambivalence about her partner, Colin. She described the sonic torture of his fingernails rhythmically scraping the hair on his stomach as he stared gormlessly at the TV. She lamented the hole-ridden, oversized sportswear he insisted on changing into as soon as he got home, his constant moaning about how tired he was, his lack of imagination in initiating sex and then in the act itself. "He says he wants to marry me," she would tell me indignantly, "but how can I possibly say yes to someone so lacking in passion, so completely undynamic?"

But no sooner had she resolved to end it than she would tearfully berate herself for her harshness. She had no idea why she was so mean about him, he was so sweet with his goofy smile, always doing little thoughtful things to make her happy, and she needed to get over the idea that being tender was the same as being boring in bed . . . Really, what kind of monster was she, talking so casually about dumping the nicest man in the world?

In any given session, she might pinball several times between hypercriticism and sentimentality. Her frenetic movement between hate and love served the purpose of keeping her indefinitely suspended between yes and no. What possible benefit could there be to this indecision? The answer, I think, was that it helped keep alive her dream of the ideal man—unmatched in looks, intelligence and talent.

Laura's fantasy expressed both an inflated sense of herself, as though no one less than perfect could possibly be worthy of her, and an underlying feeling of chronic inadequacy, as though the flawed reality of her actual man merely showed up her own failings. She was stuck between the rock of deserving so much better and the hard place of not deserving him at all. This was undoubtedly an awful place to be—but, as I pointed out to her, it kept her options open. It meant she could be in a relationship while remaining emotionally outside it.

Why not leave him, then, and have all the fish in the sea to choose from? This was an enticing prospect for as long as she stayed with Colin; from that distance, it signified lightness, fun and excitement. But she was clear-eyed enough to know that once her imagined single status became reality, she'd be immediately oppressed by the anxiety of being left alone and unloved. The prospect of "tiring myself out meeting the usual parade of bores, fools and liars" on the internet was depressing.

But perhaps she could try out someone else. A guy in the office was constantly flirting with her, she told me, had even made a clumsy, drunken pass at an after-work drinks thing recently. "So?" I said. She paused. "Well," she sighed. "He's a bit of a dick, really."

Did Laura want the freedom that comes of a clear-sighted decision, or the freedom that comes of remaining uncommitted? This is the conundrum James explores in *Portrait*. For Isabel Archer, freedom is an ideal to be cherished, but this ideal is always compromised by the fact of living in the real world.

Isabel turns down two ardent lovers, each with his own problems and limitations, for an ideal man who turns out to be a bit of a dick, really.

Isabel wants to believe this choice is fully consistent with her zealous protection of her personal freedom. When first we meet her, she feels less that she has no desire to marry than that she has no need to. The difference is crucial. If she wants to marry, she should feel free to do so; but needing to marry, whether for status, security or companionship, is a fatal compromise of her freedom: "she held that a woman ought to be able to live to herself."

Notice that little detail of James's famously fastidious diction, so foreign to our twenty-first-century ear—"*to* herself" rather than the much more familiar "by herself." Where the latter suggests lonely isolation, the former hints at following one's own intuitions and desires. Isabel is determined never to bend herself to a life that doesn't feel like her own. It is the precise difference between not wanting to marry and not needing to.

In fact, says the narrator, even deeper than her wish to live to herself lies the belief "that if a certain light should dawn she could give herself completely." To say yes, in other words, she would really need to feel she couldn't say no.

We can see the contours here of two very different and in many ways conflicting senses of what it means to be free. The freedom associated with personal independence implies the capacity to make intelligent choices consistent with our own interests. But "giving oneself completely" in the name of love is not the act of a robust mind.

Paradoxically, real freedom in love involves a kind of compulsion, a feeling we can do nothing else but surrender to it. In falling in love, we find ourselves suddenly untethered from the tiresome obligation to be sensible and balanced in our feelings and behaviour. Do we not frequently look back on the heady early days of love affairs and think, "I never felt so free"?

There is, in other words, the freedom to choose and the freedom of surrender, and it's very difficult to have one without renouncing the other.

When Isabel finally does consent to marry, she believes she's made a choice faithful to both her independence of mind and her feelings. She evidently loves Osmond, but this is no delirium. In her mind, her choice is an expression of clear-eyed discernment. When her cousin Ralph attacks her fiancé as a "sterile dilettante," she counters that "he has the kindest, gentlest, highest spirit." In other words, she isn't some love-struck young girl; she's chosen Osmond with the utmost degree of thoughtfulness.

Too late, Ralph realises that in denigrating Osmond,

he's only entrenched Isabel's determination to marry him. It isn't that love has blinded her to reason. On the contrary, Ralph observes, she's all too reasonable; the logical consistency of her defence of Osmond is hard to fault. She hasn't so much fallen madly in love as formulated a very sound argument for loving someone. We hear this thought through Ralph:

> She was wrong, but she believed: she was deluded, but she was dismally consistent. It was wonderfully characteristic of her that, having invented a fine theory about Gilbert Osmond, she loved him not for what he really possessed, but for his very poverties dressed out as honours.

In this regard, Isabel is a lot like Dorothea: both women base their decisions on elegant, idealistic distortions of reality. But in Dorothea, this looks like an error of reason by a wilful, unworldly young girl. Ralph's belated insight is that Isabel's error is not one of reason but of intuition. She is so busy spinning elaborate theories about Osmond, she fails to see him at all.

Isabel takes the fact that Osmond has "no property, no title, no honours, no houses, nor lands, nor position, nor reputation, nor brilliant belongings" as proof of the perfect disinterestedness of his love and the integrity of his character. She doesn't let it occur to her that his having so little might induce toxic envy and venality, or at least give him a glaringly obvious reason to marry a young heiress.

Isabel's mistake in accepting Osmond helps shed light on her earlier refusals of Lord Warburton and Caspar Goodwood. Perhaps Isabel's high valuation of thinking over instinct serves her best with Warburton. The grand, politically progressive Warburton offers her an undoubtedly agreeable life—a doting husband, membership of the nobility and dazzling wealth.

But for Isabel, this would be an unacceptably frivolous motive for surrendering her freedom. To marry Warburton would be to place a velvet rope round her life, protecting her from all the world's risks and possibilities. "It's getting—getting—getting a great deal," she tries falteringly to explain to the hopelessly enamoured nobleman. "But it's giving up other chances."

By "other chances" she emphatically doesn't mean other men, she adds, but simply "the usual chances and dangers" of an ordinary life. Isabel is telling Warburton she has neither good enough reason nor strong enough feeling to marry him. Her independence of mind preserves her from convincing herself to marry him for the shabby motive of living, as he puts it, "in a comfortable sort of way."

As we've seen, the same independence fails to preserve her from Osmond, who offers not the material comfort which, as a newly minted heiress, she already possesses, but (supposedly) beauty and nobility of mind. She marries him, as Ralph notes, on the back of a bad theory about him.

What about Goodwood, the young, square-jawed

American industrialist who follows her tirelessly around Europe, doggedly but hopelessly pressing his case? On the face of it, she refuses him for the same reason she does Warburton: that marrying him would compromise her liberty. Popping up everywhere, he makes her feel as though she's under his constant watch. It doesn't help that he responds by claiming, "It's to make you independent that I want to marry you."

Spoken by a powerful man to a woman, the self-contradictory phrase "make you independent" is bound to sound absurd, if not downright creepy, to today's readers. In his resolute refusal to get the message that, no, she doesn't want to marry him, Goodwood could come across as arrogant and overbearing.

But James won't let us dismiss him as a mere nuisance. Isabel, he hints, is running away not only from his threat to her liberty, but from the intensity of her feelings for him. When he tracks her down to a London hotel, she parries his every verbal thrust until she finally succeeds in getting rid of him.

But instead of breathing a sigh of relief after his leaving, Isabel "by an irresistible impulse, dropped on her knees before her bed . . . She was not praying; she was trembling—trembling all over." This moment of erotic dispossession anticipates the end of the novel, when Goodwood follows her once more to Gardencourt and implores her to leave Osmond to be with him. Even as she continues to resist him, Isabel is overcome by his kiss:

This was the hot wind of the desert, at the approach of which the others dropped dead, like mere sweet airs of the garden. It wrapped her about; it lifted her off her feet, while the very taste of it, as of something potent, acrid and strange, forced open her set teeth.

James's evocation of female rapture intimates the difference between Goodwood and the other suitors. Goodwood's embarrassing lack of style and refinement conceals a potent, almost violent erotism. He is the very opposite of her "sterile dilettante" husband.

Perhaps this explains why Isabel, denying us a happy ending, runs away from him and back to her gilded prison in Rome. The marital prison, as she tells her friend Harriet, is the consequence of a disastrous mistake, but a mistake for which she can and must take responsibility: "I married him before all the world; I was perfectly free."

You cannot be "perfectly free," at least not in the sense Isabel's talking about, with someone who lifts you off your feet. This is the crux of the clash between those two different kinds of freedom. When we speak of love making us slaves and fools, we imply that sexual desire is the enemy of freely exercised reason. Isabel will not be tyrannised by her feelings; she prefers to be the prisoner of her own free choices. She knows the sensible freedom of self-possession, but not the ecstatic freedom of dispossession.

This gives us a clue as to why she chooses a man for his imagined aesthetic and intellectual superiority, rather than one who appeals to her sexually. Given that we tend to think of sexual desire as a poor basis for marriage, we might see this as very sensible. But sexual desire has one crucial advantage over a judgement of character: it makes people do all sorts of stupid things, but it is always honest. That may be Isabel's reason for escaping; the last thing she wants is to be in the grip of feelings she can't deny.

Psychoanalysis tells us that human sexuality is dangerous and unruly, and that our minds, wary of being tyrannised by it, try to distance themselves from its intense physical and emotional effects. But both Dorothea and Isabel remind us that if we try to be too reasonable about sex, we end up doing the most unreasonable things.

Dorothea imagines she's marrying a man of great spiritual grandeur. Isabel imagines she's marrying a man of unique moral and aesthetic fineness. Both believe their marriages will be a means to true self-realisation; in this they turn out to be catastrophically wrong. Casaubon is intimidated and distressed by Dorothea's aspirations to intellectual development. Osmond, more shockingly, hates Isabel for the simple fact of being herself. He resents her evident unwillingness to align her opinions and feelings seamlessly with his: "He said to her one day that she had too many ideas and she must get rid of them."

If a sterile dilettante like Osmond has any sexuality at all, it's a cold and calculating one, a perverse glee in the control and manipulation of another. Isabel spends much of the novel fleeing from the fierce desert wind of

Goodwood's desire, not realising that there's as much danger in being led by "fine theories" as by lust.

We must find ways to reconcile two very different senses of being free. There is the freedom of reason, which helps us think and judge clearly, and there is the freedom of madness, which helps us throw off the burden of rules and be guided by impulse. Most people agree that long-term relationships can't survive without the first freedom; this is what allows for understanding and compromise, for making our own claims while listening to those of others.

But Isabel's story offers a clue as to what can happen when reason operates to the exclusion of madness, when love is all fine theories and no desert wind. The madness of love is often dismissed as the temporary aberration of a relationship's beginning, dissolving as familiarity and routine set in. But if a couple can't maintain contact with that first madness or, as in the cases of both Isabel and Dorothea, they never really experienced it in the first place, their life together is liable sooner or later to feel more like a dry contractual arrangement, friendly at best, than a lifelong love.

iii "A dark, almost evil thing": Will Brangwen

WB, twenty-two, seemed gravely troubled. Difficult to comprehend, often speaking in anguished gestures and facial expressions rather than words. Alluded at one point to "falling into the void," reference here unclear.

Went on to speak of wife, alternately criticising and praising her before breaking down in tears, lamenting own transformation into "helpless infant." After calming down, suggested sanity was being preserved only by interest in church architecture and wooden handicraft. Follow-up required urgently, with view to offer a course of personal as well as marital therapy.

It turns out that the pursuit of intimacy and freedom, experiences we associate with happiness and fulfilment, can easily leave us unhappy and unfulfilled. Real intimacy, Dorothea learns, is nothing like her fantasy of spiritual and intellectual companionship, but an "awful," claustrophobic proximity. Freedom is Isabel's most cherished possession until it leads her into her own personal hell.

A craving for intimacy afflicts us from the minute we enter the world. Ejected from the womb, we seek the same enveloping protection in tight proximity to our mother's skin. But as we grow older, we are pulled between a desire to escape the constrictions of this closeness and a desire to recreate it. Most of us become familiar at some point with the predicament that results: the absence of intimacy induces feelings of emptiness and depletion while a surfeit of intimacy can make us feel suffocated.

Few writers have explored this paradox of intimacy more fully or boldly than D. H. Lawrence. In his fiction, essays and poetry, Lawrence developed a kind of metaphysics of love and sex, at the heart of which is the idea that intimate love begets a sense not of reassuring familiarity but of radical and disturbing strangeness.

Like many keen readers, I first read Lawrence in late adolescence. The appeal is obvious: no one captures more forcefully the turbulent landscape of the emotions as we experience them at that time of life. And yet I now realise that I was far too young for Lawrence at that age. He unsettled me so much, I could respond to him only with defensive flippancy. Every casual touch, every word, every glance between a man and a woman (and between men, and between women, and between adults and children, and between humans and animals) seemed so heavily freighted with signs and wonders. Did bones really have to melt, hearts and guts to tear every time a boy kissed a girl, or even looked at one? C'mon, Dave, lighten up—sometimes a snog is just a snog! Recalling running commentary like this at least reassures me I wasn't nearly as precocious as I sometimes remember myself being.

It turns out that it takes some experience of intimate life to understand what Lawrence is talking about. Loving someone over the long term—most obviously a lover, but equally a child or a friend—cultivates a region of subterranean contact between the individuals involved that they might be only fitfully aware of.

So much discussion about relationships these days seems to be based around observations of the overfamiliarity they breed: the same jokes, the same stories, the same arguments, the same excuses, the same gross habits. And then, after a glass of wine or two, the same old body, the same moves in bed, the same lack of imagination. No doubt there is some truth to this story, or it wouldn't be told so often by so many.

But isn't there also something defensive about it? Perhaps we're closer to Lawrence's intuitions about relationships than is comfortable for us to acknowledge. Might we not prefer to laugh at the predictability of the person we love because the alternative would be to touch on the very different and frightening reality of our intimacy?

Lawrence's point is that as our knowledge of a lover deepens, so does their essential mystery: "he knew she was his woman," he writes of Tom Brangwen and his wife, Lydia, in *The Rainbow* (1915), "he knew her essence, that it was his to possess. And he seemed to live thus in contact with her, in contact with the unknown, the unaccountable and incalculable."

"The unknown, the unaccountable and incalculable" may be much more important elements of a lasting relationship than we realise. But what exactly does this mean for the everyday conduct of a marriage?

The marriage of Will Brangwen to Anna Lensky, seesawing giddily between pleasure and pain, love and hate, cannot be called happy in any straightforward sense. But it is infinitely richer and more nourishing than the emotional and sexual void of Dorothea's marriage to Casaubon, or the cruelty and manipulation of Isabel's to

Osmond. And this difference is surely made above all by the way their marriage shelters within it a place for the unknown and unknowable.

You may be surprised to see Lawrence, who infuses love with so much anguish and pain, identified as the writer who brings us closest to what a good marriage might mean. Does it follow that marriage and suffering are inseparable? And if so, why should we not conclude—as many people have—that it's not worth the effort?

Among the affinities between psychoanalysis and the novel is their refusal of easy answers to the difficulties of life. Both remind us that the first step in learning how to live is the recognition that there is no circumventing the confusion and pain that come with being alive. This is in large part because they both understand the human being as divided, pulled between irreconcilable impulses and desires—security and adventure, dependence and independence, solitude and sociality.

These internal divisions, while being central to what it means to be human, prevent us from ever achieving an unbroken state of happiness. Because we must make choices, we must also endure losses. As parents, for example, we can feel both deep joy in our children while yearning for the freedom and independence we enjoyed before they arrived.

Perhaps this is what Tolstoy meant when he said, "Happiness is an allegory, unhappiness a story." I've always preferred this unsourced quote to its more celebrated cousin, the first sentence of *Anna Karenina*: "Happy families are all alike; every unhappy family is unhappy in its own way."

What does the first Tolstoy quote mean? An allegory is a tale whose purpose is to impart some universal lesson, unfolding in a timeless region peopled by Everymen rather than real human beings. An allegory exists in a world free of ambiguities; therefore, if happiness is an allegory, it means that a truly happy person can exist only in a flattened, one-dimensional world.

For better or worse, we are condemned to live in three dimensions—in a world of stories rather than allegories. Stories, Tolstoy is suggesting, are the realm of individual men and women in a complex reality. In stories, happiness and unhappiness exist not in binary opposition but as inextricable threads in the same fabric.

But does this mean that we are all unhappy? If "unhappy" is solely a synonym for sad or miserable, then hopefully not. But if we think of unhappiness more as "non-happiness," then it becomes the state in which we are pulled between different feelings—not just sadness, but also joy, anxiety and excitement. Perhaps this is closer to the state in which we're not conscious of any defined feeling but "just are."

And this could be what Freud was getting at in 1895, some years before anyone had heard of psychoanalysis (or Freud), when he said his aim in therapy was "transforming your hysterical misery into common unhappiness." Many people coming across this statement are rather horrified, seeing it as confirmation of both the negativity of the psychoanalytic outlook and the ineffectiveness of its method. After all, is "common unhappiness" really the best we can hope for?

As I read it, common unhappiness here doesn't simply mean being slightly less miserable; it is closer to that ongoing state of "nothing in particular" we need if we want to be available to the full range of feeling, positive and negative. This emotional variety makes for a richer life than a bland state of permanent happiness. And as an aim, it's a good deal more realistic.

If an ideal marriage is one in which each partner is perpetually bathed by the other in unconditional love, positivity and support, well, good luck with that. To me, it sounds suspiciously like a mirror image of the hellish claustrophobia we find in the marriages of Dorothea and Isabel. We may see more loving smiles than hateful grimaces, but there is the same atmosphere of emotional restriction, to which is added a sense of subtly coercive expectation. What could be lonelier than giving or receiving a loving smile when what you're really feeling is sad or angry?

This pressure to be happy, or rather to be seen to be happy, reflects a binary understanding of happiness and unhappiness as strict opposites. It's a view aggressively pushed by our consumer culture, which is forever projecting beautiful bodies, bathrooms and beaches, exuding a happiness from which all the stains of anxiety, ugliness, pain or age have been expunged.

Tolstoy reminds us that the relation of happiness to

unhappiness is more accurately and more humanely conceived as one of two parts of a single reality. Do we really want our deepest relationships to be lived in the emotional equivalent of perpetual sunshine? It seems both truer and more life-enhancing to experience the variety of the seasons.

I remember, around the age of ten, being invited to a school friend's house for Sunday lunch with his family. Not long before we sat down to eat, he whispered, as he rolled the dice onto the Monopoly board, that his parents were getting divorced. He probably felt the low-level soundtrack of slamming doors and muffled obscenities needed explanation.

Now, staring stiffly into a mound of potato salad, the silence cut only by the clink of glasses and cutlery, all I could think about was how desperately I wanted to get out of there. The lowest point came when my friend's mother, usually so warm and lively, asked me in a low monotone how I was finding school. As I started to stammer an answer, she abruptly stood up and walked out of the room, her eyes to the floor. I stopped talking. No one else said a word. I couldn't bear to look at my friend or anyone else.

For all my inability to understand the knotted history and dynamics concentrated in it, that scene left a painfully vivid impression of marital breakdown that stays with me to this day. I felt the force with which rage could numb tongues and block hearts, drain people of words and thoughts. Sitting there helplessly, I picked up some sense of the parents' emotional paralysis, of how resentment and recrimination had become their invisible straitjackets. Without being able to name it as such, I had a glimpse of the unconscious forces that shaped the life of relationships. This is the wordless territory of Lawrence, where feelings reach a pitch and depth of intensity that outstrip our powers of communication.

In its portrait of three generations of the Brangwen family, *The Rainbow* reduces domestic detail to a minimum. We don't hear much about each couple's outward-facing lives as workers or members of a community, or of the everyday labour of parenting. Lawrence's perspective on married life is not social, or even psychological in the sense that he says little about what his characters are consciously thinking. Instead he narrates as though from the inside their unconscious lives, revealing the impulses and desires and longings that are secret even to themselves.

The sixth chapter of *The Rainbow*, "Anna Victrix," takes us from the first days of Will and Anna Brangwen's marriage through to the birth of their second child. The passage of time is kept deliberately vague, as though married life operated on a kind of other-worldly calendar cut off from the time of the external world. Living in intense proximity to his inner self, Will experiences the world beyond his wife and home as the incidental trappings of a "fabricated world, that he did not believe in."

It's not that Will is lacking an external life; he works as a lace designer and spends much of his time restoring the local church. But these activities are significant for him and for Lawrence only for what they reveal about the deepest strata of his psychic life. Even vignettes of the couple's petty quarrels feed into this portrait of their interior lives as individuals and as a couple.

The chapter begins with the idyllic honeymoon period, those first heady days after the wedding in which the couple withdraw from the world into their marital bed. These pages are an intensely moving evocation of the power of erotic love to lay waste to everything but itself. The honeymooners are sole survivors of an apocalypse, "and being alone in the world, they were a law unto themselves, they could enjoy and squander and waste like conscienceless gods."

But each in turn becomes agitated by an awareness of a world outside the cottage. Will feels growing shame at the rapid dissolution of established routine: "One ought to get up in the morning and wash oneself and be a decent social being." These protestations turn out to be useless in resisting the siren call of the marital bed and the perfectly sealed intimacy of the couple. But just as he's surrendering giddily to the dissolution of his established life, his new wife gets up and dressed, leaps enthusiastically into "a real outburst of house-work" and decides to give a tea party.

Faced with this eruption of domestic zeal, Will feels

suddenly superfluous and unwanted. The exchange that follows will no doubt ring bells for cohabiting readers:

> "Shake the rug then, if you must hang round," she said.
>
> And fretting with resentment, he went to shake the rug. She was blithely unconscious of him. He came back, hanging near to her.
>
> "Can't you do anything?" she said, as if to a child, impatiently. "Can't you do your wood-work?"
>
> "Where shall I do it?" he asked, harsh with pain.
>
> "Anywhere."
>
> How furious that made him.
>
> "Or go for a walk," she continued. "Go down to the Marsh. Don't hang about as if you were only half there."

What could be more ordinary, banal even? Versions of this row are repeated in households everywhere, all the time: woman gets busy, man stands about uselessly, woman becomes irritable, man retreats into a bubble of self-pity and hurt pride. If you're in a long-term partnership and don't recognise some version of this dispute, your relationship is either a shining example of domestic cooperation or a ticking time bomb.

But the ordinariness of the scene is made extraordinary by Lawrence rewriting it as a skirmish in an ongoing war of unconscious forces. Beneath the familiar surface of marital bickering is a violent revolt against the pressures of intimacy. As soon as Anna tries to recover a self and a life separate from her husband, his presence, so enticing just a few days earlier, drives her to an irritation "beyond bearing," which she unleashes in blind fury. Will reacts with a rage of his own, "black and electric":

> There followed two black and ghastly days, when she was set in anguish against him, and he felt as if he were in a black, violent underworld, and his wrists quivered murderously. And she resisted him. He seemed a dark, almost evil thing, pursuing her, hanging on to her, burdening her. She would give anything to have him removed.
>
> "You need some work to do," she said. "You ought to be at work. Can't you *do* something?"

Reading this overwrought passage, it's easy to see why some readers bristle at Lawrence. Why can't he be more of a realist, in both the literary and the everyday sense? Why this wild disproportion between the external content of the row and the couple's internal experience of it? Surely this creates a skewed and exaggerated picture of the everyday texture of married life?

But there's another way of looking at it, which is that Lawrence's apparent exaggerations give us a picture of married life that is all too accurate. By taking the perspective of subjective immersion in the quarrel rather than distanced observation of it, he gives shape and tone to inner states we have difficulty understanding and putting into words—those most profoundly private and vulnerable experiences of oneself that come of being in an intimate relationship.

These are just the routine conflagrations that are part of marriage. But we do ourselves and our marriages no favours by laughing them off and reducing them to sitcom fodder. If we read Lawrence openly rather than defensively, it's hard not to see that he's on to something here. At one level of consciousness, Anna knows that Will's getting in the way is nothing more than a petty annoyance; at another, it is a torment that makes her want to annihilate his very presence in the world.

We can dismiss Lawrence's characters as drama queens, or we can recognise ourselves in their dangerous, wordless extremities of feeling. Marriage is the willing entrance of two people into locked-in proximity. It places us in open-ended close range of another's needs, desires and anxieties, all of which arouse and amplify needs, desires and anxieties of our own. Thought about this way, why *wouldn't* it provoke feelings of desperation, horror, isolation and murderous rage?

It's not about the feet getting in the way of the Hoover. It's more that when those feet are in the way, the resulting twinge of irritation touches the edge of something much bigger and more frightening: all my external and internal space is shared with this person. Everything that happens to them happens to me. I cannot make an important decision without factoring them in. Everywhere I turn, they're there. It's not just the hallway carpet; they are *always in the way*.

And just to complicate things further, if the apparent meaning of this complaint is "I don't need this person, why can't they just get out of the way?," its deeper meaning, as Will especially makes clear, is more often "Why must I need this person? Why do they intrude on me and invade my space and disturb my peace by meaning so much to me?"

Lawrence had an enduring if ambivalent fascination with psychoanalysis, writing about it extensively. He is certainly very close to the spirit of psychoanalysis in showing us that a marriage's best chance of thriving is when it confronts and works through these fears and longings. Will and Anna come to understand that their horror of one another is inseparable from the intensity of their desire for one another; that to love the other is also to be dangerously vulnerable to them.

Lawrence relates the couple's difficult path to this insight with disarming simplicity. Anna loves him more as she learns to stand aside from his black fits, to "ignore him, successfully leave him in his world, whilst she remained in her own." Will, in turn, "had a black struggle with himself, to come back to her. For at last he learned that he would be in hell until he came back to her."

This returns us to the paradox of intimacy we noticed earlier: in deepening our closeness to another, we not only make them more familiar to us, but also come to sense their strangeness and irreducible difference from us. Anna learns gradually to respect this difference and to take her distance accordingly. Faced with the darkness in him that has frightened and enraged her for so long, she comes to ignore him, to allow each of them to occupy separate worlds.

This ignoring is a curiously and counter-intuitively intimate gesture. It can come only from knowing someone to their core, which turns out also to mean knowing what we *cannot* know about them, and what we must leave them to. This creates the space for Will to discover in his own time and space how much he needs and loves his wife. "Then," writes Lawrence, "he was grateful to her love, humble."

And this brings us to perhaps the most surprising aspect of Lawrence's idea of marriage, namely that it's curiously optimistic. This isn't the optimism that sees marriage as making life easier—more companionable, secure and protected—but a darker, more risky optimism. It encourages us to see marriage as a journey, through the experience of another, into ourselves, into the outer edges of our emotional lives. A journey of this kind is always perilous, exposing us to internal and external forces that may be hard to bear. But face the peril head-on, Lawrence hints, and there is a different, deeper kind of security to be won. This is the intimacy that not only revels in close contact, but equally respects the need for separateness and distance.

It's intriguing to note that of the three characters discussed in this chapter, Will gives the least thought and deliberation to the decision to marry. For Dorothea and Isabel, marriage turns out to be the bitter fruit of a lot of serious thinking. Dorothea enters marriage under the illusion that it will provide her with the loving intimacy she craves, only to find herself shuttered in claustrophobic servitude. Isabel believes that marriage will be the ultimate fulfilment of her freedom, only to find it puts an end to it.

Will, in contrast, marries a young woman his age because he falls in love with her. It's not that he is any better prepared than Dorothea or Isabel for all the surprises marriage will spring—after all, who could be? But, unlike the two women, he doesn't impose on his marriage the expectation that it will fulfil some grand and illusory ideal.

Dorothea and Isabel are too hamstrung by their idealism to meet the harsh realities of marriage. Unhampered by such grand ideals, armed only with his passion and his vulnerability, Will can make himself available to all the varieties of abject suffering and matchless joy marriage can bring. He may not always be happy in marriage but, unlike his female counterparts, he is always fully alive in it. And perhaps that's enough, for him, for Anna, and for us.

7

Adulthood Part 3: Middle Age

July 2018, evening. The white glare has relented a little over the last hour, but the air feels as close as it has all day. I'm walking home from work, flapping my shirt front as barely coherent phrases—"climate change," "apocalypse," "two degrees"—bounce off the walls of my mind.

My watch says it's past eight, later than usual. I need to rush to relieve the babysitter; the kids should be in bed, the house quiet. That'll be nice, I sigh to myself, anticipating the warmed sardines on toast I'll enjoy in blissful solitude.

Turning the corner into my street, I glance down the hill, registering the two hazy figures fifty yards ahead of me only when they stop to face each other. My instant response is to pick up the pace, as I lean into the faint breeze wafting over my face. My eyes lock on to the glorious evening sky as my ears are hit by the rhythmic squelching of lips and urgently heavy breathing.

The pair of figures are a couple—late teens, early twenties, who knows? As I get older, the subtle variegations of youth are dissolving into an undifferentiated blur. In a single surreptitious glance, I take in a fog of pink cotton and black polyester mesh, sculpted pectorals and pierced belly button. And then, before I know it, my legs and eyes and breath have slowed to a crawl, my quick peek has become an involuntary gape as the girl throws her head back deliriously and I see that, yes, his hand really is burrowed right under her tiny skirt.

Get a grip, I tell myself or perhaps them, once again speeding ahead, feeling the burn in my cheeks, nothing to see here! I'm just approaching the front gate when I hear a young male voice at my back: "S'up, Grandad, did you fancy a go?"

I turn on my heel, the comeback miraculously elegant and fully formed: "That won't be necessary, but thank you for saving me the drive to an Essex car park at four in the morning to peer into the fogged back windows of an old Astra. Who'd have thought the day would come when I could see a live sex show in broad daylight, and all just a few feet from my bedroom window!" With a triumphal wave, I pivot back and stroll the path to my front door.

Well, that at least is what I imagined having said a couple of minutes later, as I irritably shook the fish out of its tin and into the pan, trying hard to erase the memory of my actual comeback, more on the lines of a subaqueous gargle, followed by, "Yeah, well, maybe you've heard of this thing called *indoors*? You know, with, like, *walls* and *doors*!" They had both laughed loudly. At rather than with me, I think it's safe to say.

In my agitation, I wolfed down the sardines without tasting them, then slumped against the back of my chair, feeling their poorly digested mass under my ribs, as I stared blankly at the kitchen tiles.

In fact, all my physical and emotional soreness was now concentrated around my middle. The year had begun with minor surgery and now I was waiting for a date to remove a troublesome gall bladder that had caused me months of unpredictable pain. That neither procedure was medically serious somehow amplified the sense of slow but inexorable decline. These were signs that the body's systems were becoming sluggish and unreliable.

As I recall that feeling now, the first words of a novel come to mind: "Running out of gas." Part of the interior monologue of Harry "Rabbit" Angstrom as he watches the traffic from his Toyota showroom, they open John Updike's *Rabbit Is Rich*. The words capture the gathering anxiety that the machines—the bodies, the minds, the social structures—we've relied on to carry us through life are running down. Running out of gas: the distilled lament of almost anyone in middle age.

It's what I inferred in my young antagonist's "S'up, Grandad?," and then in the echo of my kitchen, sitting in a pool of my own exhaustion and self-pity. Here was my own mordant comedy of lust, envy and offended potency, a bit as though I'd accidentally stumbled into a low-grade Updike novel.

I recalled a recent Monday morning session with Gareth during which he spoke about the weekend he'd just spent away with his wife in an old country house hotel in the Scottish Highlands.

"After dinner, Polly turned to me on the sofa and whispered, 'That woman, by the door frame!' I turned and looked at Polly a bit quizzically, so she glanced across at the woman in question and said, with a mischievous glint in her eye, 'I may have to go and give her a slap, the way she's eyeing you up. Brazen slut.' I should have been flattered, not by the woman, but by Polly noticing me as someone who might be desired by another woman. Instead, I turned round and said, 'You are joking, aren't you? She's what, forty-five!' The thing is, Polly is forty-four. As I don't need to tell you, *I* am forty-six."

"Only somewhere in your mind, you're not."

"Ha, that's what she said. 'Oh yes, of course,' she said. 'What would an old bag of forty-five be doing making eyes at a boy of twenty-two?' Her whisper was no longer really a whisper by that point. I felt the eyes of the rest of the room on us."

After a silence, he went on: "I thought once we went back to the room it would have been forgotten, that she might even see the funny side. But her anger turned into this distant sadness. I suppose she had heard me imply that I'd prefer a younger woman, that she was no longer desirable to me. Which is not true, but also not what this was really about. I mean, it's about me, not her."

He took a deep breath. "It's like . . . like I occupy parallel realities. In one, which I suppose we could call life in general, I inhabit the body and mind of a man in his forties: greying, slightly paunchy, well established in a solid and unglamorous career. I see him in the bathroom mirror each morning and have this moment of disappointed surprise before adjusting to a kind of easy equanimity. I'm not, hmm, Justin Bieber or whoever young girls or young boys lust over these days. I can live with that.

"And then there's the other reality . . . where I'm still that twenty-two-year-old, yes. Where I strut onto the tube, see an attractive woman in her twenties and can't understand why she looks straight past me. Where a signal of interest from a woman my age induces confusion, if not mild outrage."

Gareth sighed. "It's not about the younger or older woman, not really. It's about some place in me that categorically denies the last twenty years have passed. An entirely private reality inhabited by me alone. Or at least by a bit of me."

Slumped in my kitchen chair, I could hear, or rather feel, the resonance of Gareth's words. Facing myself in the mirror each morning, I'm not especially fazed by the grey hairs or loose flesh, the lines or any other markers of age. It's only when I see myself in the mirror of someone else, say an ostentatiously carnal young man, that I'm shocked and a little offended to discover I'm no longer in the bloom of youth. As Gareth says, something in me simply doesn't know, or want to know, that I've got older.

We are in the region of one of Freud's greatest insights about the unconscious mind. The unconscious, he said, is "timeless": that is, literally lacking in any sense of time and its consequences.

To be in time is necessarily to suffer losses—long-term, cumulative losses like our youth, vigour and looks, as well as the loss of loved and important figures in our lives. But loss is also the very texture of our moment-to-moment reality—the hour we just wasted (or fully used) is one we'll never get back. To all of which the unconscious says, well, bollocks.

The unconscious enjoys what Freud calls "exemption from mutual contradiction," or, put more simply, it lets you have the very cake you just ate. It thinks in wishes rather than realistic perceptions, and so laughs off the merest hint of limits on its own gratification. In the unconscious you can enjoy the authority and respect of fifty years and the youth of twenty-five. You can gain everything while losing nothing. This, of course, is the message of the anti-ageing industry, whose peculiar genius has been to weaponise the unconscious, to assure us that we can be fifty and still be twenty-five.

In our unconscious, we are happily oblivious of what age is doing to us, of the slow accretion and depletion of our powers and energies as we approach, reach and then pass our youthful prime. Like some positive-thinking guru, the unconscious never accepts there could be anything to lose or to lack.

In that moment after dinner, Gareth was the dupe of his unconscious, wondering why a middle-aged woman would be looking at a young man like himself. He wasn't helped by the position that he, like all of us, occupies inside his body—able to see others in full, but only the edges of himself. He could perceive the age of the woman opposite while in a protected bubble of his own permanent youth.

In the previous chapter, we witnessed the promises and fantasies that propelled Dorothea, Isabel and Will into marriage run up against the difficult reality of shared daily life. Death ended the first marriage; the other two were left at the cusp of decades in which to live out this reality. It is during these decades, after the great uncertainties of young adulthood (who will I be? what will I do? who will share my life?) have been settled, that we find the protagonists of this chapter.

It is easy to get lost in the illusion of endless youth, to forget that we're in an ageing mind and body. Until something or someone comes along to pierce it, placing us before an unforgiving mirror on our own mortality. At the gate of my house that evening, I saw myself reflected in that horny boy's eye as grey, uptight and resentful at someone else possessing the lust and vigour that was once mine.

In his writings on the life cycle, Erik Erikson sees us pulled at each stage of life by two fundamental and competing impulses. What he calls "middle adulthood," spanning roughly between the ages of forty and sixty-five, involves mediating between the tendencies to "generativity" on the one hand and "stagnation" on the other.

These alternative destinies imply different responses to the dawning fact of mortality. Even if we're fit and healthy and optimistic enough to feel that old age and death are a long way off, the undeniable physical and mental facts of ageing will force a shift from the abstract knowledge that we're all going to die to the personal knowledge that I myself am going to die. As the exchange outside my house made clear, when the younger generation laughs at their elders, the implied punchline is always, "Ha! It's all behind you, and all in front of me . . ."

As Erikson hints, there are two poles of response to this realisation. At one extreme lies despair, first at the past as a catalogue of wrong turns and missed opportunities, then at the future as an unbroken prospect of decline and continued disappointment: it's all gone and there's nothing left to do but wait it out to the bitter end, getting worse all the while.

At the other extreme is hope, the feeling that we have established a solid place in the world on which we can build and eventually leave a significant mark. As we go through the decades of middle age, don't we experience both these opposed states of mind, as well as many shades between?

Confronting our mortality can be an occasion for self-pity: Erikson's "stagnation"; and for renewed curiosity and determination: "generativity." It can leave us feeling that there's nothing to live for, or everything: that life is an extended cosmic joke, or a remarkable adventure.

Erikson can give the impression that these attitudes are opposed to one another, which they certainly can be; but I suspect that few of us pass the age of forty-five without moving unpredictably through one and then the other of these states, sometimes within the same day, if not the same hour.

Popular perceptions or clichés of middle age, though, tend heavily towards the pole of stagnation. The phrase connotes tired habits and attitudes, a resignation to the life we have rather than the one we want, alongside weary acceptance of the world as it is rather than as we'd like it to be.

The real dangers of such stagnation are being shown to us today by the youth-led movement for climate justice. My generation's casual habits as consumers and apathy as citizens are being brutally exposed for their complicity with planetary destruction. Retreating to the comforts of a centrally heated house with a nice car on the drive has lost any veneer of harmlessness it might once have had. The young climate strikers are shaming us out of complacency.

There is of course nothing new in this confrontation between generations. Each era brings a different iteration of the same scenario, whereby the middle-aged take over the reins of worldly power and are accused by the youth of using it to protect rather than question and alter the existing arrangements.

The middle-aged are mocked and disdained for their abandonment of spontaneity and idealism, for their blind maintenance of the status quo and for holding back justice and progress.

How might literature help us think about and even experience middle age differently? Part of the problem is that we've allowed a surfeit of jokes and greetings cards, where our energy levels drop as suddenly and unforgivingly as our stomach muscles, to create a perception of middle age as a kind of inner death.

i "A thing there was that mattered": Clarissa Dalloway

CD, fifty-two, reported mild to moderate depression following a recent period of serious illness from which she appears to have recovered. Protested at various points that she didn't really know why she was here, that she was "quite well" and that all this seemed a "fuss about nothing." Further questioning, however, revealed significant concerns. Despite busy life dedicated to support of MP husband, appears emotionally isolated. Flinched when asked about her sexual life, "scarcely see how this is relevant," before acknowledging she sleeps alone. Towards end of assessment, revealed frequent thoughts of death, insisting though that these were "perfectly natural" and "nothing to worry about." Seemed relieved to receive prescription for antidepressant medication and leave.

The first of our books under discussion, while fully alive to the compromises and disappointments of middle age, refuses to equate midlife with imaginative and emotional atrophy. From the outside, the eponymous protagonist of *Mrs. Dalloway* would seem to be the very embodiment of middle-age cliché: the wife of a Tory MP, her life is stultifyingly conventional; she is weighed down by disappointment and regret, brooding incessantly on the lost loves of her youth. And yet our time inside Clarissa Dalloway's mind is an experience of remarkable emotional intensity and sensory vividness.

Virginia Woolf published *Mrs. Dalloway* in 1925, at the age of forty-two—ten years younger than her protagonist. During the previous six years, she had published a series of celebrated essays on the nature of modern fiction, mounting a concerted attack on what we would call "realism" (and which she calls "materialism") in literature and art.

There is an obvious link to be made between this critique of realism and Woolf's preoccupation at the time with middle age. After all, isn't one of the great truisms of middle age that it's the period during which we become more "realistic"—as expressed, for example, in the old aphorism that anyone who isn't a socialist before twenty-five lacks a heart and anyone who remains one after forty-five lacks a head?*

---

* Often ascribed to Churchill but of uncertain provenance, having appeared in many iterations in both French and English since the late nineteenth century.

To be more realistic in this sense means to accept the world as it is and stop hankering after the world as you'd like it to be. It means recognising grown-up truths: that self-interest is a stronger and more reliable motive for human beings than altruism or compassion, for example, or that values and principles are all very well but you have to make a living. It means, in short, seeing things straight, in the harsh light of day.

Woolf's essays are a kind of sustained riposte to this lazy common sense, by way of an elegant skewering of the leading fiction writers of the generation that preceded her—Arnold Bennett, H. G. Wells and John Galsworthy. Woolf is using an argument about the future of literature to ask a more fundamental question: what is it to be a human being? How should we conceive of a person's character?

The Edwardian novelists, she says in her 1919 essay "Modern Fiction," reduce character to a series of superficial outward or "materialistic" indicators—physical features, gestures, phrases, dress—of a person's true being. The problem with trying to capture a person in external signs of this kind is that "life escapes": a diverting story is told at the expense of "life or spirit, truth or reality." Instead of conveying the elusive wanderings of the soul, the Edwardian novelist gives us a formula providing the reassuring pleasures of "a plot . . . comedy, tragedy, love interest," along with an eye for external detail ensuring "that if all his figures were to come to life they would find themselves dressed down to the last button of their coats in the fashion of the hour." This is a human world made up exclusively of solids, from which all liquid and gaseous elements have been banished.

I can't help noticing how much Woolf's version of the Edwardian novel sounds like the worst caricature of a middle-aged man: set in its ways, blindly committed to routine, devoted to appearances, narrow in its ideas and imaginative scope, reductive in its view of both the soul and the world. Novels of this kind have a perfectly honed set of tools to describe what the world looks like, only "these tools are death," for they tell us nothing about what the world *feels* like.

These Edwardian novels have a certain ambition. They ask big social questions, make grand statements about inequality, class and injustice; but this means their characters' lives, and especially their inner lives, are annexed to something outside of them. They aren't so much works of art, she suggests, as ciphers for a campaigning message: "In order to complete them, it seems necessary to do something—to join a society, or, more desperately, write a cheque." Most of us are familiar with the present-day equivalent: watch a documentary about, say, the proliferation of food banks, get upset, sign an online petition and forget about it.

The Edwardian character has been reduced to a crudely painted marionette having its strings pulled by an author lacking the imaginative force to bring them to life. No wonder a new generation of novelists couldn't wait to leave this clapped-out, tired novelistic house.

Some, Woolf observes, were so exasperated they felt only full-blown demolition could remedy the problem: "the strong are led to destroy the very foundations and rules of literary society."

But Woolf doesn't see herself as a breaker of windows. She prefers a radical refurbishment of the interior. This is achieved by a kind of receptive attention to the texture of everyday inner experience, as she suggests in one of the most famous passages in (and about) modern literature:

> Examine for a moment an ordinary mind on an ordinary day. The mind receives a myriad impressions—trivial, fantastic evanescent, or engraved with the sharpness of steel. From all sides they come, an incessant shower of innumerable atoms . . . Life is not a series of gig-lamps symmetrically arranged; life is a luminous halo, a semi-transparent envelope surrounding us from the beginning of consciousness to the end. Is it not the task of the novelist to convey this varying, this unknown and uncircumscribed spirit, whatever aberration or complexity it may display, with as little mixture of the alien and external as possible?

What will immediately strike anyone who's been on either side of the therapeutic couch is how much this famed description of a mind quietly at work resembles the experience of a psychoanalytic session. This isn't altogether surprising—Woolf's brother Adrian Stephen was a key figure in the early British psychoanalytic movement, and the Hogarth Press, which she founded with her husband, Leonard, became the first British publisher of Freud and other psychoanalytic writers. Like Woolf's novelist, in any given session a psychoanalyst is trying to follow the associative, non-sequential, shapeless movement of an ordinary, wandering mind.

But what does any of this have to do with middle age? Well, it's not coincidental that so many of Woolf's novels, but *Mrs. Dalloway* above all, explore the psychic lives of middle-aged characters. The aspect of middle age that is so often decried or mocked—its settled, uneventful, rule-bound tendencies—is exactly where Woolf finds bottomless imaginative richness. In young adulthood, we tend to be constantly busy, internally and externally. Our character and identity are still in formation; we are devilled by our desires, driven by our ambitions, forging careers, lifelong loves and friendships and families. None of this gives us much time to sit still and pay close attention to the internal or external world, to take in its colours and sounds, to be receptive to its sensory and emotional ebbs and flows.

Let's recall that Erikson's point about middle age is that to be settled—in character, in place, in habits, in work, in interests, in loves and hates—can beget generativity just as much as stagnation. It can be the platform for a renewed attentiveness to people and things, a kind of imaginative rebirth.

*

Key elements of Woolf's own life resurface in her protagonist's. Like her creator, Clarissa is upper class, vivacious, birdlike, and frail in the aftermath of a debilitating illness. But these social and physical resemblances are not the only autobiographical echoes in *Mrs. Dalloway*. As Woolf had during her previous bouts of psychosis, Clarissa's spiritual counterpart in the novel, the traumatised First World War veteran Septimus Smith, hears the sparrows in Regent's Park "sing freshly and piercingly in Greek words."

By scattering different elements of her story among her characters, Woolf makes startling connections between people and states of mind that appear to be oceans apart; the stodgy conservatism of Clarissa meets the outcast madness of Septimus. By placing Septimus's story alongside Clarissa's, Woolf reveals a secret solidarity between these two supposedly diametrically opposed minds, one trapped inside the narrow tramlines of caution and compliance, the other wandering its wildest edges. Although Clarissa and Septimus never meet, their pairing invites us to recognise the strangeness lurking unseen in even the most apparently conventional life.

Clarissa and the various men who orbit around her— Peter Walsh, who loved and lost her long ago; Richard, her well-meaning, emotionally constipated husband; the sycophantic Hugh Whitbread—are each exemplars of middle-aged disappointment, of a shrinking of the scope of emotional and imaginative life.

Long past the age of marriage and childbearing, celibate and cloistered in a single bedroom, Clarissa experiences "the oddest sense of being herself invisible; unseen; unknown." She is fearfully attuned to "the dwindling of life," a reference not only to the daily contracting lifespan, but to the draining away of its sensory vividness. She feels increasingly incapable "of stretching, of absorbing, as in the youthful years, the colours, salts, tones of existence." "The whole world," Woolf writes, "seems to be saying 'that is all' more and more ponderously."

Peter Walsh reflects peevishly to himself on Clarissa's "coldness," "a sort of timidity, which in middle age becomes conventionality." Middle age, Peter implies, embraces convention as a kind of refuge against the fear and risk of being authentically oneself. This sense of middle age as mediocrity, compromise and disappointment insists throughout the book.

But the paradox of *Mrs. Dalloway* is that it is in precisely this rather unpromising inner landscape that we can find remarkable experiential riches—if only we dare discover them. The desperate, inchoate "unhappiness" Clarissa feels is simply the warp to the weft of the overwhelming "love of life" that can just as easily overwhelm her. Even her loss of youthful energy and hope becomes an eerie kind of joy, as in this beautiful passage close to the end of the novel:

> Odd, incredible; she had never been so happy. Nothing could be slow enough; nothing last too long. No

pleasure could equal, she thought, straightening the chairs, pushing in one book on the shelf, this having done with the triumphs of youth, lost herself in the process of living, to find it, with a shock of delight, as the sun rose, as the day sank.

There is something almost unbearably moving to me about this image of Clarissa pottering aimlessly, suddenly possessed by an unaccountable, senseless happiness. Perhaps its intense effect on me, as though I were merging into Clarissa's beatific mood rather than just reading about it, has something to do with my approaching her age; I don't recall it registering much when I first read the book as an undergraduate.

Reading it now, I feel as though I've been building decades' worth of insider knowledge of this moment. A smear of burnt orange in the cold early-morning sky as I'm walking to my practice; the cardamom waft of milky chai during my afternoon break; the deep yellow of the tiles I'm staring into as I brood, abruptly dissolving my despondency in sunshine. What Clarissa means by the joy of "having done with the triumphs of youth" is a sense of happiness no longer being projected into an endlessly deferred, elusive future; suddenly, fleetingly but unmistakably, it's right here, just waiting for us silently in the faces of the people and things around us.

Perhaps the strangest thing of all is that the ultimate source of this overwhelming happiness lies in the deepening awareness of our mortality. We all know we're going to die; our casual conversation is peppered with references to life being too short, to only living once. But it isn't until we enter middle age, when our bodies begin to betray us and the generation that preceded us starts to die off, that mortality becomes palpable in the air we breathe.

Across that single June day, death insistently pierces the peaceful, contented surface of Clarissa's consciousness. At one point she contemplates the eerie, unremarked wonder of the days passing in the same sequence, the miraculous background hum of time going by. That she can rise from bed, take a walk, meet Hugh Whitbread in the park, receive a visit from Peter in the morning, a bunch of roses from her husband in the afternoon: "it was enough. After that, how unbelievable death was!—that it must end; and no one in the whole world would know how she had loved it all; how, every instant . . ."

Clarissa, or Woolf, just trails off here, as though the world in its fullness has taken us into a region beyond the reach of words. That death should steal in to bring it all to an irrevocable end is "unbelievable"; and yet death is also the strange gift that, in depriving us of the world, makes us feel how much we love it. Nothing makes us love a thing or a person so much as the prospect of losing them.

Which means that while *Mrs. Dalloway* is infused with the presence of death, it isn't a morbid novel. It shouldn't induce a fear of death but, on the contrary, attune us to the inextricable presence of death in life. At the moment her party is in full swing, Clarissa picks up the laughter of Sir Harry Ainsty, "which, as she heard it across the room, seemed to reassure her on a point which sometimes bothered her if she woke early in the morning and did not like to call her maid for a cup of tea; how it is certain we must die."

There are moments, Woolf intimates, when the sudden awareness of death's certainty bothers us. But, in the middle of the party, seeing "old Mrs. Hilbery stretching her hands to the blaze of his laughter," this troublesome knowledge is felt as oddly reassuring. Why? Perhaps because it seals the value of life, reminds us forcefully that it needs to be lived and loved, not passed through like an infinitesimal and meaningless interval between one silence and another.

But how do we square this with the parallel ending of the book, the suicide of Septimus Smith? Certainly there's no easy comfort to be gleaned from it, especially knowing that sixteen years later Woolf herself would take her own life during a bout of similar madness. Septimus's terrible verdict on the world as a cesspit of cynicism and cruelty, embodied in the menacing self-certainty of the psychiatrist (modelled on Woolf's own) Sir William Bradshaw, isn't to be dismissed as a tragic symptom of Septimus's delusional state.

In fact, it's through Sir William, who attends her party soon after Septimus's suicide, that Clarissa and Septimus, who never set eyes on each other, come into a kind of posthumous spiritual contact. Hearing the Bradshaws casually discussing how the young soldier had "thrown himself from a window," landing on the "rusty spikes," she feels a visceral disgust—not for the gruesome nature of his death, but for the way in which she and the people around her have failed to see what his suicide now makes her see: that to live life indifferently or casually is an offence against the universe:

> A thing there was that mattered; a thing, wreathed about with chatter, defaced, obscured in her own life, let drop every day in corruption, lies, chatter. This he had preserved. Death was defiance. Death was an attempt to communicate, people feeling the impossibility of reaching the centre which, mystically, evaded them; closeness drew apart; rapture faded; one was alone. There was an embrace in death.

Septimus's violent death has conveyed in a flash the urgent preciousness of her own life, the "thing . . . that mattered," that is so easily lost in cynicism and self-satisfaction. The "embrace in death" Clarissa remarks on is surely an embrace by Septimus of her, a reaching across from the dead to the living to remind them not to let life drain away slowly in corruption, lies and chatter.

Stagnation and generativity: middle age can be the stage at which we let life be taken over by unthinking complacency and it can be the point at which we refuse it, when the dawning truth of our limited time on earth alerts us to life as a thing that matters.

*

One of the great paradoxes of psychoanalytic work, at once baffling and entirely human, is that people enter it seeking change and then use it to demonstrate to themselves and their therapist that change is impossible. The force for potential renewal thus morphs into grim entrenchment in the unhappiness that brought them to me.

This is when the work is hardest and most dispiriting, as though its secret and sinister purpose were to infect me with the very misery I'm trying to alleviate. Often enough, I hope to help a patient see that life is worth living, only to find myself half-persuaded that it isn't. This is the feeling of powerlessness in the face of another's determined effort to seal themselves in their own unhappiness.

This dynamic, I've found, is more liable to set in with patients in middle age. Disappointment with the state of their life, measured against the high hopes they once had for it, leads to a knowing cynicism towards the very idea of hope or change. More than once, I'm told early on in a treatment that if I were honest, I'd concede that their life is an irredeemable failure and give up on them.

This was certainly Emmy's line of attack through the course of six years' work together, when things began falteringly to shift. Twice weekly she would arrive at the end of the day and bemoan her sorry fate. When I first met her, she was approaching her forty-seventh birthday and working as a successful government lawyer. She had just come out of a relationship, which had broken down in large part, she said, "on account of my dithering over having a child or not."

Her partner was eight years younger and eager to be a mother, but Emmy had stalled from one year to the next, always pleading some new and impassable obstacle—a new job, a dying parent, stretched finances. "I was deaf and blind enough to think I was getting away with it. Then I came home from work one evening and there she was, zipping up a suitcase, with that look on her face." By this point in her story, Emmy was battling bitter tears. "And then last month I found out she was pregnant."

The psychoanalyst Christopher Bollas makes a helpful distinction between fate and destiny as ways of telling our own story. When we narrate life as fateful, we imply that we're in the grip of alien forces over which we have no control, that we have no say over how the course of our life unfolds. This experience of reality will inevitably inhibit our capacity "to work, find pleasure, or form intimate relationships." Psychoanalysis, for Bollas, is tasked with moving the patient from this fatalism to what he calls an experience of one's own destiny—that unconscious "sense of direction" in us which tells us who we are and what we want.

Sessions with Emmy soon settled into the groove of self-confirming, fatalistic misery in which she always seemed to find herself stuck. Every development in her life was absorbed into the same fateful narrative. If she began seeing someone, their interest would soon fall off: "She only calls me when she's bored or horny, there's no future there." Of course, Emmy showed no more eagerness herself. "What would be the point? It's obvious she's not interested."

It was as though surprise had been systematically excluded from Emmy's horizon of possibilities. It often seemed that our work was simply being sucked into the same black hole of fate as everything else in her life. When I pointed out that she seemed to be willing me to become another item on her long list of disappointments, she snorted and said, "Feel free to go ahead and prove me wrong."

Ostensibly her career told a more gratifying story, but this too was mired in a gnawing sense of under-achievement and lack of recognition. She remarked that her colleagues found her "unclubbable," competent and reliable but no fun. This, she felt sure, was why her career progress had been so lacklustre in spite of the regard in which she was held.

Thus Emmy whiled away many sessions trashing the record of her own life, a litany of bad luck and stupid choices, but above all her own inadequacy to the task of living. "What do I have to look forward to now," she would ask rhetorically, "beyond a decade or two of more plodding mediocrity and slow decline? Sometimes I wonder why I carry on. But you needn't worry. Topping yourself takes courage I don't have."

She would sometimes follow these bursts of emotional nihilism with an apology: "It must be grim to listen to the same stuck record." "Well," I once replied, "I only hear it a couple of times a week. You have to listen to it all the time."

Her unrelenting excoriation of herself and her life placed her in the position of her mother, who had bathed her daughter's entire youth in an ether of constant, unfavourable comparison. There seemed to be no friend of Emmy's who didn't apply herself more dedicatedly to her studies, no cousin who didn't have nicer table manners. " 'I never see that next-door girl without a smile, not like you, always so sour-faced,' she'd tell me. And through it all you could guarantee my dad would hover silently in the background, occasionally flashing me the odd nervous smile, otherwise reliably slipping out as soon as my mother started: 'Just nipping to the study!' I suppose the focus on me gave him a bit of a break, poor bastard. He'd get it once I went to bed—'If you made more effort we might have some friends,' 'If you had a bit of oomph you'd have been promoted and we wouldn't be living in this shabby excuse for a house,' and on and on."

Emmy's ambivalence about having a child could be traced directly to these experiences. "I suppose there was always the anxiety that I'd become that kind of mother."

"But haven't you anyway?" I said. "The child you now berate as a source of permanent disappointment is yourself. And I expect you've been waiting for me to do the same."

"Well, yeah. I imagine I must be disappointing to you. You must have thought you could help me, and I'm always letting you know that you can't . . ."

"A bit like your father—a nice, well-meaning bloke hovering behind you, listening to your mother blasting away at you, powerless to step in and do something."

She laughed as tears now flowed liberally down her temples. "I so wanted him to step in, it's true. I suppose I want you to do something, but I'm not ready to let you. I'm not ready to stop being angry, because without my anger I haven't a clue who I'd be or what I'd do."

She was right. She needed to hold on to her anger as long as she needed, to work it through in her own time. Her mother had steamrollered her anger, her father evaded it; she needed someone who could bear it alongside her, leave her feeling it had finally been heard and received. When she did reach this point, after more than six years of therapy, she was left with the more sober reality of her sadness—she wouldn't have a child, nor would the world be dazzled by her brilliance.

But she had friends and curiosity and pleasures and desires, and some gratitude for all these things, which meant she had some inkling of what Bollas calls a destiny, a "sense of direction" and an openness to something new and unexpected. Her mortality could stop being the unfunny joke that underlined the essential futility of her life and become the reminder that it needed living.

ii "*I am alive!*": George

G, fifty-eight, declined to provide a surname. Responded to the assessor scornfully, complaining of "fatuous" and "ludicrous" questions, especially in regard to recent loss of his long-term partner. Expressed many contentious and provocative opinions on various topics while evading discussion about his own emotional state. When asked if he was having difficulty coming to terms with getting older, responded (presumably sarcastically) that he "loved" seeing his flesh sag and his face look tired. In response to assessor's remark that he seemed angry and unhappy, G became visibly agitated, directing a stream of insults at him before abruptly getting up and leaving. For referral to social services.

Up to this point, I've not been unduly troubled by the problem of so-called spoilers. Few of the books I've discussed turn on a shock twist; and given that my focus is on characters rather than plots, I've been able in some cases to say very little or nothing about how a novel ends. But it isn't possible to discuss Christopher Isherwood's *A Single Man* (1964) without giving away its unexpected and rather devastating last page. Like *Mrs. Dalloway*, it describes a single day in the life of its middle-aged protagonist and ends in a death. But in this case, the death is the protagonist's own.

Why give away this narrative secret? Surely there's plenty to say about George, the British professor of English literature now living in LA, and his experience of ageing, without revealing his sudden death in the closing paragraphs? And if his death is so important, why doesn't the book belong in the next chapter, on old age and dying?

But at fifty-eight, George is not old; nor, as far as he knows, is he dying. In one of the novel's crueller ironies, he visits Doris, a terminally ill friend (or rather enemy— the woman with whom George's late partner, Jim, had an affair) in hospital during her final hours. *"I shall follow you soon,"* George thinks to himself as he holds her hand, with no inkling of quite how literally true this will turn out to be. Every last word of the novel acquires its full meaning only in the light of its ending.

"I am alive . . . I am alive!" George says to himself triumphally as he goes from the dying Doris to the gym, affirming "the body that has outlived Jim and is going to outlive Doris." Contemplating his fellow "age-mates" in the locker room, he notes his relative youth and vigour:

> What's wrong with them is their fatalistic acceptance
> of middle age, their ignoble resignation to grandfa-
> therhood, impending retirement and golf. George is
> different from them because . . . *he hasn't given up.*

This is not, in other words, a novel about being old or contemplating an impending death; it invites us instead to imagine our life as though it could end tonight, in our sleep, without us at any point knowing a thing about it. Death strikes George randomly and meaninglessly, the culmination of a roughening of the major branches of his coronary artery that had, entirely unbeknown to him, begun years ago.

A Single Man is very much a book about midlife in more than one sense. It reminds us that as long as we're alive, we're in the middle of life, that we can never attain some privileged vantage point outside it that would reveal to us what it all means. Only death completes life and gives it a final shape, which we never get to see—we don't get to hear our own eulogy or read our own obituary.

This may be a commonplace enough observation, but sudden death gives it reality and urgency. Anyone who has reached middle age is likely to have experience of at least one shocking and unforeseeable death of someone they knew. In recent years I've known a father in his sixties to keel over at his son's wedding party, a young mother struck by a fatal aneurysm while walking to her child's kindergarten, a man swept to his death in full view of his family by the waves on a Moroccan beach.

The horror I've felt in the involuntary visualising of each of these scenes has to do with the brutal incursion of death into a space of pleasure, joy or celebration, or just ordinary living, its annihilation, at a single stroke, of human hopes and desires. A person immersed in their own life is banished from it instantly and without warning. The effect of this is a violent severance of life from death. There is no period of slow decline, no space in which to contemplate the meaning of one's time on earth and its impending end. The person who just a few seconds ago was right in the centre of life is now permanently banished beyond its borders.

George is hardly unaware of the vicissitudes of the ageing process; he ruminates constantly on his ebbing vitality and physical decline, his vulnerability to exhaustion and his grief for those he has lost. "The harassed look is that of a desperately tired swimmer or runner," he notes at the beginning of the novel, contemplating his waking self in the mirror.

And age brings emotional as well as physical fragility—he is "humiliated and sick to his stomach" recalling himself chasing and roaring at the misbehaving little boy from the neighbouring house, unable to recognise the irritable, cantankerous old git he's unaccountably turned into.

During that opening moment in the bathroom mirror, George discerns the past faces that haunt the face before him:

> the face of the child, the boy, the young man, the not-so-young man—all present still, preserved like fossils on superimposed layers, and, like fossils, dead. Their message to this live dying creature is: Look at us—we have died—what is there to be afraid of?

The point here, though, is that George can commune with the "dead" child, boy and younger men lurking inside the contours of his face; talking and listening to these younger selves is his way of working through their loss. The death ahead of him is different: "But that happened so gradually, so easily," he answers his younger versions. *"I'm afraid of being rushed."*

Yet another cruel irony: at the break of day, George finds himself in touch with the terrible fear that will be realised at the end of it. The tragedy awaiting him is that he *is* indeed going to be "rushed," ushered hastily out of life before he has a chance to say goodbye to it.

What should we take from this? Perhaps a profoundly atheistic vision of life; a "single man" not just in the marital but in the existential sense, abandoned to himself in a lonely, random and absurd universe. Experience, he tells the young student Kenny, whose seduction will turn out to be the final act of George's life, fails to make us wiser. We accumulate it, and "it can be kind of marvellous," but "you can't *use* it." What he means, I think, is that we are too much inside our experiences to be able to get the kind of distance on them that would allow us to understand them and so ensure they feed change and growth. Far from getting wiser, says George, "I, personally, have gotten steadily sillier and sillier and sillier."

We are all, literally, midlife, whatever age we happen to have reached: that is, we are all too much in the muddle of life to obtain the clarity that would give us the assurance that now, finally, we get it, now we know what we're doing. This is our predicament, but also our gift.

George's nocturnal death doesn't make a mockery of all the emotional investments he's made during the preceding day in loving, hating, learning, friendship and bodily pleasure; on the contrary, it affirms them. It reminds us to enjoy life and to involve ourselves in it as fully and deeply as we can. Life is worth loving precisely because it is so small and insignificant. As another much older and even more controversial book has it, in more than one place: "Let us eat and drink, for tomorrow we die."

iii "Running out of gas": Harry "Rabbit" Angstrom

A difficult assessment. HA, forty-six, seemed unable to keep his attention focused on the matters at hand, veering off at various tangents at any opportunity. Some concerns about the current domestic set-up, especially since son has returned home, having dropped out of college against HA's pointed and strenuous objections. Mention of son triggered long, somewhat rambling monologue, berating the young man for his incompetence and bad attitude. Long and involved incident related, difficult to follow, about son's purchase of number of vintage cars at expense of family business. Clearly a combustible situation. Risk assessment? Marriage seems to have stabilised after much turbulence, and is doing quite well professionally. But referral for family therapy seems to be in order.

But even biblical wisdom isn't without its complications. Eat? Having learned the hard way a few too many times that my digestive system is no longer up to the challenge, I've foresworn the red meat and hard cheeses I once consumed in stupid quantities with impunity and glee. Drink? I wouldn't pretend to have been a heavyweight even in the bloom of youth, but these days I'm barely halfway into a second beer before my head and gut are sending me coordinated pleas to stop. I'm finding that in middle age there are few more effective reminders that tomorrow we die than the pleasures of eating and drinking.

In middle age, it seems, we become acutely aware of pleasure as a problem. In youth, we are much more likely to be governed by what Freud called the "pleasure principle." The desire for pleasure induces tension, which is relieved only when we get what we want—when hunger is satiated by a good meal, for example, or sexual arousal by an orgasm. But this alternating rhythm of excitement and gratification can be hard to sustain after a while. It is the rhythm of youth—of late nights and later mornings, of drink and drugs and strange beds.

This explains why, as we get older, most of us warm increasingly to the benefits of delaying gratification—or what Freud calls the "reality principle." The toll extracted by these swings between heightened tension and exhaustion becomes too much for our nervous system to bear. We don't renounce pleasure, but we prefer to receive it in low and even doses, a state closer to quiet contentment than ferocious excitement.

In the course of his first thirty-six years, Harry "Rabbit" Angstrom, protagonist of our next novel, has experienced life at its wildest extremities—high school sports stardom, the accidental death of a child, his own and his wife's marital infidelities, and a near-hallucinatory, drug-fuelled experiment in improvised group living that ends in a house fire and a tragic death. These turbulent journeys through pleasure and pain unfold in *Rabbit, Run* (1960) and *Rabbit Redux* (1971).

Rabbit Is Rich (1981) is the third of the tetralogy that would end in 1990 with *Rabbit at Rest* (conceivably the most egregious instance of title as spoiler in literary history). It sees our protagonist restored to the very suburban contentment from which he's spent most of his adult life trying to escape. He has returned to his wife Janice and is, as the title tells us, rich, "even if" (as Updike comments in a later afterword to the tetralogy) "only by the standards of his modest working-class background," managing his late father-in-law's Toyota franchise. They are living with his mother-in-law, their idyll of complacent ease disturbed only by the arrival on the doorstep of his angry, brittle son, Nelson, and Melanie, a female companion who may or may not be Nelson's girlfriend, and whose place will soon be taken by Pru, his fiancée.

When I first read the Rabbit tetralogy in chronological order about twelve years ago, I remember being struck by *Rabbit Is Rich*'s distinct shift of tone. The Rabbit of the previous two novels was cocksure, reckless and often cruel, compulsively tearing up his own life, enslaved to his erotic and escapist impulses, heedless of the havoc he wreaked in the lives of those around him.

After all that, the overweight, quietly prosperous, friendly car salesman of *Rabbit Is Rich* took me by surprise. He remained a man of healthy appetites and dubious attitudes, but the voracious indulgences in illicit sex and other dangers had given way to the easy comforts of the family home, the marital bed and the country club, where he golfs and drinks and sits poolside with other couples, ogling his friend's much younger, bikini-clad wife. Who'd have thought it? Rabbit had become, of all things, harmless.

Perhaps it was his thorough domestication that led me, when I reread the book this year, to remember the Rabbit of this instalment as creaky with the ravages of age. I recalled the overhanging belly, the crankiness, the unmistakable weariness, the *running out of gas*. And I read on, laughing smugly to myself that it wasn't all *that* many years before that'd be me—ha!—when the inner chuckle abruptly gave way to a double take.

I'd read this book before, so I knew that the Rabbit of this book was much older than me. But here he was said to be forty-six, which was demonstrably absurd, because that would make him three years younger than me. C'mon! I implored no one in particular. Look at this guy! He is clearly older than me! He becomes a *grandfather*, for goodness' sake, which I most certainly am not, whatever that dumb kid might have called me.

In returning to Rabbit, I'd fallen prey to the same involuntary error as my patient Gareth: seeing my own ageing self in the mirror of someone else, I took temporary, panicked refuge in the grandiose illusion that time had passed for everyone but me. If Rabbit was the same age as when I'd first read it, surely I was too!

This isn't the way I normally respond to a book I'm rereading after a long interval; in fact, mostly it's just the opposite. To read *Alice* now, having first met Alice at ten, is to be made wistfully aware of the chasm of time between our first and most recent encounters, the loss of the child's eye which bonded me to her in recognition and understanding. In the same way, I can feel the comically vast distance between my late-adolescent self, staring earnestly into the mirror of young Werther's breathless erotic rapture, and the wry cynic I feel myself to be reading the same book now.

Perhaps this was also a strategy for dealing with the increasingly audible whispers circulating in the cultural ether against Updike as yesterday's man, one of the Great Male Narcissists, in David Foster Wallace's memorable phrase, of American letters. An indisputably brilliant wordsmith, yes, but, his critics have long been saying, his writing is too saturated by racism and misogyny, and by what Wallace called a "radical self-absorption . . . in both themselves and their characters," a function of their patrician sense of entitlement and unconcern for the world beyond themselves.

"Just a penis with a thesaurus" ran the famous summary dismissal of one of Wallace's disdainful female friends. More recently, the Canadian writer Patricia Lockwood penned a merciless evisceration of Updike in the *London Review of Books*, laying out the various ways his linguistic virtuosity served as cover for his uncritical ventriloquising of successive smug misogynists with a striking resemblance to their creator.

It needled me, almost as if I were the secret target of her playful scorn. How's that for "radical self-absorption"? Updike, Lockwood observed, seems to sow confusion among his detractors and defenders alike. In a line that immediately achieved viral status, she wrote:

> No one can seem to agree on his surviving merits. He wrote like an angel, the consensus goes, except when he was writing like a malfunctioning sex robot attempting to administer cunnilingus to his typewriter.

That week, I complained to a male writer friend about that line, in what I can best describe as a defensive high-pitched whine. "It's symptomatic that a line like that would get ten million shares or likes or whatever, that the guy gets skewered for bad writing by a line that *pretty much exemplifies bad writing*," I said, my (one pint of) beer-fuelled shrillness rising as I lamented *the sheer bloody incoherence* of the simile. "Wow," my friend said, "you seem really upset by this."

Which took the wind out of my sails and set me thinking. It occurred to me in the sober light of day, as I turned over the pages of *Rabbit Is Rich*, that Lockwood is thirty-seven, that Wallace was thirty-five when he wrote his Great Male Narcissist article and that I'd first read the Rabbit books at thirty-six. I wanted to be on the side of the younger readers, coolly disparaging these white male giants of literary self-satisfaction; but reading this piece only brought home that I was on the side of the old, malfunctioning sex robots. I had indeed aged since I'd first read *Rabbit Is Rich*, was older than the sad old grandad who evidently really did "want a go" with a woman young enough to be his daughter. Lockwood was the one out in front, driving the electric car of literature's future; I was puttering behind, sitting in the back of an old banger that was running out of gas, listening to Rabbit bitching from the driver's seat. It was all so unfair.

And yet I take some comfort from the fact that most of Updike's detractors are too attentive and curious as readers not to notice the many glories of his prose. It can't be denied that the Rabbit of *Rabbit Is Rich* sees women through the same shamelessly unreconstructed, toxic sexual political filter he always has. But the novel also reveals Updike—or Rabbit, or both—as a kind of laureate of middle age, of the strange transcendent grace of the graceless, recalcitrantly ageing body. No one captures more lovingly the terrors and banalities and defiance of midlife, the way it brings on a belated and therefore melancholy joy in the world around us.

Mortality stalks Rabbit's consciousness at every moment in this novel, even as he seems to be reflecting on nothing more than Toyotas, golf swings, the price of precious metals, the grating entitlement of his petulant, resentful son. As in *A Single Man*, we are just three pages in before the protagonist is contemplating his ageing head in the bathroom: "In the shaving mirror a chaos of wattles and slack cords blooms beneath his chin in a way that doesn't bear study. Still, life is sweet."

I love the way Rabbit so often follows up an intuition of a primordial void so terrible it "doesn't bear study" with a saccharine platitude, as though having stared his own death in the face he's earned the right to trivialise it. "Life is sweet" is "what old people used to say, and when he was young he used to wonder how they could mean it." But now he knows; for Rabbit as for Clarissa, far from spoiling life, the intimation of his mortality is what makes it sweet.

As Rabbit has grown older, the animal lust and rage that animated his youth appears now not in reckless action but in stray traces of thought—mental driftwood. Driving home, he is tailgated by "some pushy road-hog" who turns out to be "a young blonde with a tipped-up tiny profile . . . a little girl at the wheel." He sees no sense in reacting to the provocations of these "kids in a hell of a hurry, pushing. Let 'em by, is his motto." Then, right after this little sigh of Zen equanimity and tolerance: "Maybe they'll kill themselves on a telephone pole in the next mile. He hopes so." A little casual misogyny, a touch of cheery psychopathy; this is the ugly truth of the middle-age stream of consciousness.

But it doesn't mean very much in real-world terms. All this chauvinism and murderousness has been relegated to the dustbin of Rabbit's unspoken thoughts, inaudible

to anyone else, barely noticed by himself. Running out
of gas means renouncing the drive to force yourself on
the world, to shape it in your own image. And Rabbit is
curiously happy to make this renunciation. Responding
to the young Melanie's sadness at President Carter's pro-
nouncement that "things are going to get worse instead
of better," Rabbit's friend and colleague Charlie (who
also happens to be Janice's former lover) replies mordantly that "for old crocks like us, things are going to
get worse in any case."

Rabbit is "genuinely surprised" at Charlie's equation
of ageing with things getting worse. For Rabbit, the loss
of youth's possibilities, far from presaging the end of his
life, enables it to begin in earnest: "the stifled terror that
always made him restless has dulled down. He wants less.
Freedom, that he always thought was outward motion,
turns out to be this inner dwindling." The young, with
the world at their feet and all the resources and energy
to realise their ambitions and desires, end up enslaved by
them; true freedom comes only with "this inner dwindling," when you're liberated from the compulsion to do
anything very significant or strenuous.

"Middle age is a wonderful country," Rabbit reflects
later on. At fifteen, he thinks to himself, "forty-six would
have seemed like the end of the rainbow, he'd never get
there, if a meaning of life was to show up you'd think it
would have by now." The hard-won wisdom Rabbit has
uncovered with age is that it's at the end of the rainbow,
where we can take measure of the shrunken dimensions

of the life we've actually led rather than the life we've fantasised about, that we can truly begin to live. Life can begin when we give up on the burdensome hope of revealing its real meaning.

"Yet at moments," Rabbit continues, "it seems it has"—that is, the meaning of life seems momentarily illuminated—only "there are just no words for it, it is not something you dig for but sits on the top of the table like an unopened dewy beer can."

Perhaps there are just no words to convey the feeling of gratitude I have for this beer can made of words, for Rabbit and for Updike, notwithstanding everything that can be said against them. It's true enough that Updike's characters can induce anger, disgust even; but it would be a great shame for his indulgence of middle-aged male narcissism to obscure the quiet beauty of that can.

Like the chairs Clarissa straightens distractedly, Updike's beer can tells us that life's fulfilment won't be found at the elusive end of a rainbow; it is right in front of us, here and now, if only we care to look.

What Clarissa's, George's and Rabbit's experiences teach us is that to be properly open to this revelation, we must pass through the disappointment of our youthful fantasies of greatness and fame, which, as Rabbit observes, will have brought us only restless anxiety. Perhaps it's at the point we "settle," that we take the peculiarly radical step of surrendering to the life we have in all its unexceptional ordinariness, that we can feel free to do and be whatever we want. Perhaps to be truly generative, we need to take the risk of stagnation. Only once we stop chasing after the next, elusive goal can we listen to ourselves for long enough to hear what we want now. It may just be that we already have it.

8

Old Age and Dying

One consequence of my parents' divorce was that I would spend large chunks of my adolescent summers with my father in Jerusalem. My days there, as languid and aimless as summers at home, usually began with a late-morning visit to my grandparents' apartment in the centre of town, a functional, simply furnished rectangle and a sanctum of shaded cool in the punishing midsummer heat. A push on its heavy front door blew a brief, bracing gust of wind in our faces, carrying notes of cardamom and sage from the tiny kitchen, from which my grandmother would emerge spreading her arms and her indiscriminate effusions of love and culinary promise in English-dusted Arabic.

My grandfather, a decade older, and frailer than she, was seated at the round table to the right, looking up from his newspaper with a gentle smile. During the war, following a wave of murderous rioting against Baghdad's Jews, Grandpa had risked his life and lost his property getting his family out of Iraq. When I was a small child, he struck me as endowed with an impossibly worldly seriousness, his enigma polished by square-shouldered suits and frequent trips to Geneva.

I had to remind myself that this mellow old man had once been that quietly imposing younger man. "Did you see?" he would ask, pointing to the headline before slowly and deliberately reading it aloud, his finger alighting on each syllable: "Hun—dreds—Killed—in—Jap—an—ese—Air—Crash," say, or "Gun—man—Kills—14—in—Shoot—ing—Ram—page."

And then, to my unfailing amazement, he would let the paper fall to the table and laugh—or rather, emit the strangest approximation of a laugh: "*Hyuh . . . Hyuh . . . Hyuuuuuh . . .*" It was hard to discern in this outburst any trace of spontaneity or happiness or bitterness or sarcasm or triumph or hilarity or any other of the feelings we generally associate with laughter. Each of his guffaws and the intervals between them seemed to drag out interminably, as though he were being played in slow motion, leaving the hearer with the sound but not the sense of laughter.

My father, trying to suppress his own smile, would ask him what was so funny about this awful piece of news. My grandfather would look up at him, the puzzlement and mild rebuke in his sweet, reedy voice out of sync with the persistence of his smile: "Funny? . . . It isn't funny! It's terrible!"

I wonder why this scene should come to me as I begin this final chapter on, well, our final chapter. In some ways it's obvious: the laugh was an intimation of decline, of what the English euphemise, as though marking the comic potential in the creeping disintegration of our mental and emotional faculties, as "going a bit funny."

To spend time with a very old person can sometimes feel like bearing witness to a series of frustrating (and unbearably sad) disconnections between an intended act and its fulfilment. Various necessary things—glasses, appointment times, names—elude perception and memory. Thoughts and feelings rush to the surface only to be deprived of the words to express them.

Middle age will already have given us some intimation of this fate, in all those casual betrayals of our body and memory. That crunching soccer tackle, which you would barely have registered not long ago, now electrifies your entire skeleton with unimagined pain. That conversation with the person who talked to you so familiarly at last night's party as you maintained an unconvincing smile and silently begged the gods to reveal their name or at least how on earth you knew them. Eventually it's going to be like this all the time, only with a gentle walk taking the place of the soccer tackle, the forgotten names of family and lifelong friends added to those of acquaintances.

In Clarissa, George and Rabbit, we discovered different ways of managing life once the terms on which we live it have settled, along with our own place in the world. Clarissa's concealed loneliness, George's crankiness and Rabbit's wry resignation to his declining vigour and potency showed us the different ways our selfhood can shape itself, once most of the big decisions have been made and the world is no longer ours to conquer. They paved the way for our final question: what makes life worth living even as we sense the approach of the end and the dwindling supply of remaining days?

In our youth-centric culture, this has all become fodder for amusement as well as horror. We are persecuted by an ideal of the seamless integration of mind and body—the effortless coordination of the body's parts, the mind's different faculties. We admire the dancer, the athlete and the raconteur their capacity for perfect absorption into their activity, to the point we can no longer, as Yeats put it, know the dancer from the dance.

In old age, however, dancer and dance become increasingly easy to tell apart; whatever the aged dancer is doing as they misstep and hesitate, it doesn't look like any dance we recognise. What is being eroded is the sense of internal flow, of one step in a sequence of movements rolling imperceptibly into the next. For decades of youthful and adult life, most of us take for granted our capacities to walk or speak. One foot or one word simply goes in front of the other. Old age returns us to that earliest stage of life when none of this was obvious or simple, when it required the greatest effort of deliberation and concentration.

When my grandfather, then in his mid-eighties, was asked why he was laughing at such terrible news, he was confused. He wasn't aware that he'd laughed, and certainly wasn't aware of finding anything to laugh at in air disasters or mass shootings. It was as though the sequences of information and response had been scrambled, as though the internal cue cards directing us to be sad or happy or angry or frightened had become unreadable.

For my father and me, for almost anyone who doesn't have to see the exposed, creaking joints of their own mental activity, this non sequitur was funny, as violations of the laws of logic and propriety tend to be. Inappropriate laughter, as many of us discover on solemn occasions, makes us laugh despite ourselves.

But this leaves untouched the question of what, if not the tidings of horror themselves, might have made my grandfather laugh. And given I'll never know now, all I can do is speculate. What if this habitual laughter at these eruptions of human suffering were less a failure of his conscious mind than a small gift from his *un*conscious mind?

In a short and strangely moving paper on "Humour," written in 1927, when he was seventy, Freud offers some hints as to the nature of this kind of laughter. His argument rests on a distinction between "joking" and "humour." Jokes are the products of the id; they express our concealed sexual and aggressive impulses. Humour, on the other hand, is an expression of the superego.

We normally think of the superego as an inner parent reproving us for being naughty, lazy or immoral. But in humour, the superego can instead induce a healthy laughter at ourselves—more specifically, at our narcissism. The superego reminds the ego of the essential insignificance of what it desires; in the wider scheme of things, it says, what we want doesn't matter much.

This can often be a cruel message, especially at good moments in our lives. If we ace exams or get a promotion, the internal voice telling us we don't deserve it can have a malignant effect on our sense of self-worth. This is why we so often think of the superego as the villain of psychic life: it turns feeling good into an occasion to feel bad.

But humour has the opposite effect, Freud argues, salving life's wounds and humiliations. Humour is how the superego wards off our suffering by reminding us that, in the wider scheme of things, nothing is that big a deal. "Look!" Freud has the superego say to the ego. "Here is the world, which seems so dangerous! It is nothing but a game for children—just worth making a jest about!"

From this perspective, it isn't the suffering of the victims that sparked my grandfather's laughter. This, after all, was the one thing he was clear about, insisting when asked that he saw nothing funny in these traumatic news items. He may not have known why he was laughing, or even *that* he was laughing, but he knew very well why he wasn't.

So perhaps it wasn't anything or anyone but himself that drew his laughter. Our ego places us at the centre of the world. In humour, the superego reminds us that we're not masters of this world; as Freud repeatedly reminded us, we're not even masters in our own house. As a response to human pain and injustice, humour in this sense is neither callous nor belittling; it is a way of coming to terms with the limits of our own power. In the face of those positive-thinking gurus who insist "You can do anything!," the superego insists that you can't.

This is a counsel less of despair than of humility. The fact that our powers to change and improve the world around us are limited makes our efforts to do so more rather than less meaningful.

And in old age, when we may in any case be feeling powerless, displaced from the centre of life, watching ineffectually from the sidelines, perhaps unable to see or hear much of what's going on, this may be an especially important consolation. I imagine that my grandfather, confronted with these dispatches of the world's daily cruelty and rage, and the impotence of his own despair, found a kind of internal refuge in laughter.

Old age, as long as we can get there, has a lot to teach us, if only for its moment-to-moment reminders of our essential fragility, of the limits on our time on earth and on what we can do with it. For most of our lives, "life is short" is just a bumper-sticker platitude; in old age, it becomes the deepest and most intimate truth of daily existence.

In common with childhood, the image of old age in our culture is Janus-faced. One face shows idealised wisdom, serenity and kindness, the other abject folly, haplessness and ill temper. Different commentators on old age place the emphasis on one or other of these faces.

For Ralph Waldo Emerson, writing in 1862 as he was approaching sixty, the last phase of life sets the stage to live as we've always aspired to live. The aged person "has weathered the perilous capes and shoals whereon we sail," and in so doing has removed the "chief evil of life," namely fear. The dread of death and the disordering ravages of the "sexual instinct" wear away, making space for "grander motives."

Emerson relates a meeting with the sixty-three-year-old Wordsworth. The poet tells him of his friends' concern for a recent fall in which he'd lost a tooth: "He had replied, that he was glad that it had not happened forty years before." Getting older means the chance to be liberated from vanity, driving ambition, the desire for riches and status, and so many other anxieties that pinch and constrain the full expression of our personality. Throwing off the tyranny of appearances and expectations, old age gives us the best chance of becoming who we are.

Just over a century later, in 1970, at the age of sixty-two, the philosopher Simone de Beauvoir presented a very different picture in *Old Age*, a broad historical and sociological study of the treatment of the elderly in the modern world. The twin blows of biology and society, she argued, banished the elderly to a place of isolation and marginality. A culture premised on youth, dynamism and productivity can only meet the slowness and frailty of the aged with contempt, while physical and mental deterioration deprive them of any sense of existential continuity. "When memory decays," wrote de Beauvoir, the entire storehouse of life experience and knowledge "sinks and vanishes in a mocking darkness; life unravels stitch by stitch like a fragile piece of knitting, leaving nothing but meaningless strands in the old person's hands."

In the ways it's perceived from outside as much as experienced from within, old age is split between these two visions: on the one hand, a place of authority, and liberation from the anxieties and desires of our youthful selves; on the other, of mockery, contempt and subjection to the vagaries of physical and mental deterioration.

Erik Erikson's psychoanalytic account of this stage of the life cycle, developed in his old age in collaboration with his wife, Joan, points us towards a reconciliation of these perspectives. Like each of his previous stages, old age is pulled between two opposed possibilities, in this case integrity and despair.

Integrity as Erikson defines it is "acceptance of one's own and only life cycle," and of the primary relationships, chosen or not, made during its course. It implies an affirmation of these formative figures, most obviously our parents, for who they are, "free of the wish that they should have been different."

The inability to affirm the life and parents we have rather than those we would have preferred—what we commonly call regret—is the basis of despair. It manifests as rage at the shortness of life and its failure to afford us more chances to get it right. It is inevitably bound up with the deterioration of the body's organs and muscular-skeletal system, alongside the "mocking darkness" that comes with the unravelling of our mental powers.

It's likely that here, as in all life stages, most of us will move between these attitudes rather than settle exclusively in either one of them. But what ensures, and what prevents, our internal compass orienting us more towards the horizon of integrity than of despair? This might require us to imagine ourselves at the end of our lives, asking ourselves another question: have we lived a life that's been truly our own?

And this is the question troubling Lady Slane, protagonist of Vita Sackville-West's *All Passion Spent* (1931).

i "A little holiday": Lady Deborah Slane

It is unclear to us why DS, eighty-eight, was referred for assessment. Referral was made at instigation of one of her six children, who cited recent widowhood and very advanced age. Daughter concerned also referred to mother's recent "questionable judgements," such as decision to take new quarters on her own rather than reside with any of her children, and "eccentric" resolutions re distribution of personal fortune. Questioned as to her emotional state, DS acknowledged her grief but was notably lucid and robust in her reasoning when asked about new residence. Cognitive testing left the assessors in no doubt as to soundness of mind. When asked about her daughter's anxiety, responded with what seemed to be distinct measure of irony, "Carrie is always very concerned for my welfare." Given that DS has live-in help and a small network of friends around her, we can identify no significant safeguarding issues here and feel confident in confirming soundness of mind. No action required at present.

There's a nice irony to Sackville-West having written *All Passion Spent* at the age of thirty-nine, when her own passions were so far from spent. At the time of the novel's publication, she was involved in a ménage à trois with the journalist Evelyn Irons and Irons's lover Olive Rinder.

Sackville-West's open marriage to the diplomat Harold Nicolson embodied the spirit of experiment that fuelled the erotic and creative life of the Bloomsbury Group. In addition to numerous short-lived affairs with women and men, Sackville-West had had significant relationships with the married writer and socialite Violet Trefusis and, most famously, with Virginia Woolf. These complicated sexual entanglements hummed in the background of a remarkably prolific career as novelist, memoirist and gardener (her garden at Sissinghurst in

Kent remains one of the most stunning achievements in modern horticultural design).

The turbulent course of Sackville-West's personal life couldn't be more different from Lady Slane's. We meet the latter at the age of eighty-eight, recently widowed, and soon learn that she has been a model of propriety and self-sacrifice, married for nearly seven decades to a former viceroy of India and prime minister, and mother to six children. And yet it's hard to miss the obvious, if superficial, affinities between Sackville-West and her protagonist: both are aristocrats, both diplomat's wives.

The differences, however, are more glaring still. The diplomatic career of Sackville-West's husband never approached the giddy heights of Lord Slane's. And as we've seen, Sackville-West herself could hardly have resembled less the selfless and reserved Lady Slane. Except that the Lady Slane we meet isn't the domestic goddess of her previous seven decades, but an aged widow; and it is just now, at the tail end of her life, that she begins to resemble her real-life creator in perhaps the most fundamental way: she resolves to do as she likes.

All Passions Spent, in other words, can be read from an autobiographical perspective as an ingeniously oblique self-justification, in which a similarly well-born and privileged woman who's lived her entire life in the compliant vein Sackville-West always rejected belatedly resolves to live in the defiant spirit Sackville-West embodied. One

can be a great matriarch and professional wife of a political grandee, the novel hints, only at the expense of a life
of one's own.

After the death of their father, the Slane children,
themselves in their sixties, are seen and heard in hypo-
critical and self-serving disputations over who is going to
look after their supposedly infirm, hopelessly unworldly
mother. These discussions end when Lady Slane announces to her incredulous children that she won't be
living with any of them, but in a house of her choosing
in Hampstead.

While assuring her superciliously that she is of course
her own mistress, her eldest son, Herbert, asks her to
consider how her choice to live alone rather than with
one of her "devoted children" might look "in the eyes
of the world." "I have considered the eyes of the world
for so long," replies his mother, "that I think it is time
I had a little holiday from them. If one is not to please
oneself in old age, when is one to please oneself? There
is so little time left!"

This new and final phase of life will exclude visits
from all grandchildren and great-grandchildren, whose
noisy chatter can't be permitted to intrude upon the contemplative repose of the "completely self-indulgent" old
age Lady Slane has set her heart on.

Of course, Sackville-West is writing Lady Slane into
life when she herself is roughly the age of one of her
grandchildren. Mired in the agitation of her own life, she
imagines a state in which all such agitation has dissipated,

a life in which she might be, as Lady Slane puts it, "content merely to *be*." "Repose," her new landlord and friend, Mr. Bucktrout, remarks, "is one of the most important things in life, yet how few people achieve it?"

Sackville-West's agitation and Lady Slane's repose may be opposite states, but they have in common a radical willingness to ignore "the eyes of the world." At eighty-eight, the character is finally living the ethos of her author—pleasing herself, living her life as though it belonged to her alone. For Sackville-West, emotional authenticity was expressed in passionate entanglements, whereas Lady Slane finds her true voice by ruthlessly cancelling the demands and intrusions of others.

This may sound like a state of physical and emotional coldness, but reclaiming the space that has always been filled by the needs of others allows for a new and heightened awareness of the minutiae of her own everyday life: the ring of the back-door bell, the arrival of book parcels, the question as to whether to serve muffins or crumpets to her tiny circle of elderly friends. Running alongside these apparently trivial events and concerns are her bodily aches and pains,

> for which she was beginning to feel quite an affection . . .
> all the small squalors of the body, known only to oneself, insignificant in youth, easily dismissed, in old age became dominant and entered into fulfilment of the tyranny they had always threatened. Yet it was, rather than otherwise, an agreeable and interesting tyranny.

What makes the twinges of her lower back and teeth and finger and toe so interesting and even agreeable is that they return her to herself after decades of absence: "all these parts of the body became intensely personal: my back, my tooth, my finger, my toe." And beyond this reclamation of her selfhood, these "contemptibly tiny things" are "ennobled . . . by their vast background, the background of Death."

The imminence of death confers a peculiar sublimity on the vagaries of daily routine and the irritations of being inside a body, engendering a limitless curiosity and love for the simple fact of being. The contracting scope of Lady Slane's life, its very lack of any strong sources of perturbation or excitement, lends a new intensity and beauty to its every moment. This is a key aspect of what Joan Erikson calls the "integrity" of old age: "It stretches our being," she writes, "into contact with the real, surrounding world: with light, smell, and in touch with all animate beings. Everybody, everything matters intensely, more than ever before."

But how could the loss of bodily strength and robustness be an occasion for anything but sadness and despair? A short detour into another famous life may help us here.

The great American poet Walt Whitman, having achieved fame for his thrillingly propulsive verse, was paralysed at the age of fifty-three by a stroke. The bard of the body, who had wandered with such fluidity through the physical and emotional lives of men and women, young and old, rich and poor, through the endless variety of racial and sexual identities, was now unable to move.

Much of his late poetry reads like the work of a man stuck, in more than one sense. The lines that had wandered off the page now truncate; the poems that seemed less to come to an end than to stop in the middle, as though assuring us of their limitlessness, shrink to a few lines. In many poems, the tone of giddy intoxication gives way to one of cranky weariness.

In one five-line poem, Whitman imagines himself as a "Dismantled Ship," "old, dismasted, gray and batter'd . . . disabled, done . . . rusting, mouldering." He is even more mercilessly self-deprecating in one of his late prefaces to *Leaves of Grass:**

> here I am these current years 1890 and '91, (each successive fortnight getting stiffer and stuck deeper) much like some hard-cased dilapidated grim and ancient shell-fish or time-bang'd conch (no legs utterly non-locomotive) cast up high and dry on the shore-sands, helpless to move anywhere—nothing left but behave myself quiet, and while away the days yet assign'd . . .

---

* *Leaves of Grass* was the title Whitman gave to the continually updated work in progress that was as much his life as his work. The qualities of *Leaves of Grass*, he wrote in an 1871 note, are not those of a work of art, but of a "living and full-blooded man . . . You do not read it, it is someone that you see in action . . ."

The hard-boiled humour does little to mitigate the tone of bitterness and loss emanating from these pages. Whitman is recording the slow dying of his imaginative as well as physical mobility. He wrote in the preface to the last edition of *Leaves of Grass* that his "paralytic seizure" of 1873 induced a "physical debility and inertia (laggardness, torpor, indifference, perhaps laziness)" that has "remain'd ever since."

There are poems of gratitude from this period that make efforts to convey his frailty as a joyful blessing. If they fail to convince, it's because they are little more than wistful glances back at the heights of his past. But in the very last poem of *Leaves of Grass*, Whitman plays poignantly on the paradox of old age as both loss and gain.

In "Good-bye My Fancy!" he bids farewell to his own imagination as he contemplates his impending demise. But in the course of the poem he reconsiders—perhaps he's been hasty in his goodbye, for if he and his imagination have been inseparable in life, why shouldn't they be inseparable in death? Why shouldn't they meet whatever lies beyond together, even "learn something"?

No sooner has he told his fancy "Good-bye" than he wonders if he's been "too hasty," for if the two of them have lived inseparably, they will surely die just as inseparably and "remain one." "May-be," Whitman ventures, "it is yourself now really ushering me to the true songs."

What looks like me saying goodbye to my fancy, Whitman is saying, may in fact be a little trick that my fancy is playing on me. The trick is to lull the poet into thinking it's "me" that's written the poem, whereas in fact it's "my Fancy." And if that's the case, then his farewell to the imagination is really evidence that his imagination is still alive.

This is just another way of saying that the imagination lives beyond the individual. There is nothing supernatural about such a view; if this weren't the case, we would have no literature, or other art, or any civilisation at all. But it points to why I've interrupted our discussion of Lady Slane to talk about the old age of a poet so different in biography and spirit. It's because they both tell a story about the legacy of the imagination, the ways it allows us to live beyond the span of our biological life.

Whitman envisions his existential goodbye as an imaginative hello, confident in the knowledge that his poems will outlive him, that his imagination, just as the poem prophesies, will continue to speak for him, to lead him into all the posthumous adventures that come with an illustrious literary reputation. Few poets, after all, can boast such a rich and varied afterlife—since his death, an astonishing array of composers, photographers and filmmakers as well as other poets have fed off the abundance of *Leaves of Grass* in numerous settings, adaptations and riffs. Immortalised in photographs of his long-bearded, untamed face atop his sturdy frame, he is as great and recognisable an American icon as Abraham Lincoln or Marilyn Monroe.

And what about Lady Slane? She too turns her dying into an occasion for an imaginative renewal that will allow her to live beyond her death, albeit in a manner very different from Whitman. FitzGeorge, an eccentric and plain-speaking old art collector, visits her at home and reminds her of the impassioned gaze they had cast at one another more than fifty years previously during a visit to Fatihpur Sikhri.

The surfacing of this memory of unrequited passion disturbs Lady Slane's "old-age peacefulness," the more so when FitzGeorge links it to her renunciation of the artistic ambition she'd nurtured before being railroaded into marrying Henry Slane. "Face it, Lady Slane," he tells her. "Your children, your husband, your splendour, were nothing but obstacles that kept you from yourself. They were what you chose to substitute for your real vocation."

FitzGeorge confronts the woman he loved so long ago with the brutal truth that her life, though outwardly rich and eventful, was lived at the expense of her self. Marriage and motherhood in Lady Slane's era and milieu couldn't accommodate meaningful ambition or creativity. Now, having refused visits from grandchildren and great-grandchildren, she follows their social and professional progress through the society columns, noting with quiet dismay the engagement of her great-granddaughter and namesake Deborah, as pretty and accomplished as she had been, and as likely to renounce her own ambitions.

Shortly after FitzGeorge's death, Lady Slane receives a surprise visit from Deborah. Rather than send her away, she makes a spontaneous exception to the ban on visits from the young. Deborah reveals she's broken off her engagement to a man she didn't love in order to pursue a career as a musician. For Lady Slane, this is a chance to break the cycle of history and a reclamation across generations of suppressed female creativity, the promise of a kind of posthumous realisation of her own creative life. She has even unwittingly facilitated this outcome by giving away her fortune and eroding Deborah's status in the marital marketplace.

Seeing that Lady Slane has fallen asleep, Deborah slips out, aware as she does so of the "enveloping music" swelling in her mind's ear. This will turn out to be the old lady's final sleep, to which she can now submit without resistance, knowing that the life she herself was kept from will be continued—and perhaps fulfilled—beyond her death.

Lady Slane brings home to us the possibilities contained in old age, both for coming to terms with the life we have had and for claiming that life as inalienably ours. To leave the legacy of a life lived as one's own: this, it turns out, may be the true meaning of living beyond death.

It probably isn't much of a surprise that only a very small proportion of the people I've seen in psychotherapy could be described as elderly. One of these was a man of eighty, with thick, silver hair and a bearing and expression so grave I can honestly say I never once saw him smile. Wearing an immaculate suit, he sat opposite me for a few weekly sessions, each time turning over the same single story, gleaning the same conclusions and casting the same ruthless judgement on himself.

It took place on a train one night two years previously, when his wife suddenly complained of pains in her chest. Though she had no history of heart trouble, her pallor and perspiration alarmed him. "What if it's your heart?!" he implored her. "No," she assured him, "it's just a nasty bout of indigestion, that's all." She didn't want him wandering carriages looking for doctors, making a fuss, and for what? She was going to look pretty silly causing such a commotion for a tummy ache.

"What I can't forgive myself for," he told me in our first and in every subsequent session, "is that I knew not to trust what she was saying. I knew my own instinct was right, that she was in danger, that she needed urgent medical attention, hospital no doubt. But I let her persuade me. I could see she was frightened and that was why she wanted me with her." He looked down, suddenly unable to meet my gaze. "So I told myself I was putting her first, that I should listen to her wishes rather than my own. But the truth is, I was too gutless to face what was happening until it was too late. By the time I finally called for help, she had no chance. She was dying before my eyes, and I just watched it happen."

My twelve or so sessions with Adam were a kind of murky cubist collage, presenting the same scene from different, superimposed angles. In one, he recalled the fatefully missed signals of heart trouble from across her last decade, missed because of his habitual distraction by some work project or other. In another, he ruminated on his hidden unconscious motives for failing her that night. "What if," he wondered, his eyes once again boring into the floor, "I . . . secretly wanted her gone?" "But does that ring true to you?" I asked him. He paused. "Well, no, but what do I know about my unconscious mind? There is that idea in psychoanalysis, isn't there, that we harbour all these secret, terrible feelings." I told him I thought he was trying to recruit psychoanalysis, and me, as allies in his ongoing war against himself.

Each session played out a catalogue of successive retellings and speculations and forensic self-examinations, bound together by the single motif of his crushing, irredeemable guilt.

During our first meeting, Adam had been unwilling to say much about his history. His wife's last night had taken up all available space in his head, rendering everything else irrelevant. In our penultimate meeting, though, his usual round of self-excoriation over his negligence and stupidity led him to an important association: "I abandoned her just as I had my father."

I asked him what he was referring to and he shook his head wearily. "Well, I told you my mother died when I was nineteen. Cancer. I was about to take up my place at college. I was the only child, so Dad was suddenly left alone in the house. The day after the funeral we were in the parlour, as my mother called it. He was sitting on the sofa, staring into thin air. I remember thinking he was barely there. It was quite unbearable. I asked him if he wanted me to stay at home a while and he just sat there in silence for what seemed like an age. Finally he said, 'No, son, no. No, you go and . . .' I don't think he even finished the sentence. A year later he had a heart attack and died. You see, had I only listened to my first instinct, I'd have stayed on at home a while. I didn't have to leave. I could have gone the following year, or the one after that. But I wanted to get out of there and . . ." He paused for a painfully long moment. ". . . have a good time."

I was only recently qualified when Adam came to me. It may have been that no one could have helped him, but I certainly doubted I could. I didn't know what would be useful to say, only what wouldn't be—that it wasn't his fault, that he shouldn't blame himself. Friends, of course, had been telling him this since the day Rita had died: "They could have no idea, poor things, how much worse they made me feel. I barely speak to anyone any more for fear that they'll give me the same bloody platitudes." He paused, looking at me meaningfully, and said, "I'm thankful to you for not feeding me that absurd . . . pap."

But this left me none the wiser as to what he did want from me, other than to listen to his pain. In what turned out to be his final session, I pointed out that with each session, he seemed to be trying harder to persuade us both that his wife's death left him beyond understanding or forgiveness—the more so given what had happened to his father.

"Yes, you're right about that," he said, leaning forward and looking me hard in the eye. "I thought I'd forgiven myself for him, but after Rita died, the guilt over her somehow revived all the guilt over him. You should know you're not the first therapist I've seen. It always seems to go the same way. I think I have this secret hope each time I start to tell the story that some detail will miraculously emerge, something about the events themselves or my own feelings, that will finally exonerate me from guilt and allow me to live the rest of my life in peace. But no sooner do I start than I push as hard as I can in the opposite direction, daring you or the other therapists to argue with me. And at least you didn't do that, which is why I've stayed with you longer than any of the others. And the thing about my father . . . I've never talked about it, not even to Rita really."

"Stayed longer?" I said. "You sound like you're talking about this in the past tense."

Adam said nothing for a while, then: "I think for this to be really worthwhile, one should want to feel better about oneself, and I'm not sure I do."

I replied that this was indeed the big question, and now that he'd put his finger on it, our work could properly begin. He raised his eyes to the ceiling and in a tone of firm resolve said, "I will ponder that. Thank you."

But the following week, Adam didn't return. At the time his session was due to start, an email arrived, thanking me for my kindness over the last weeks. He felt he had gone as far as he could. He was talking about his therapy, and perhaps too about his life.

I had no option but to respect Adam's choice. But I've wondered ever since whether he wanted me to feel some small sense of his terrible regret; just as he'd failed to save his wife and his father, I'd now failed to save him. Perhaps punishing himself, denying himself even a second of the "good time" for which, in his mind, he'd abandoned his father, was his way of managing the burden of his sadness. Perhaps it was easier to see the losses he'd been afflicted with as punishment for his criminal neglect than to bear their sheer arbitrary cruelty. It gave at least a semblance of meaning to what had happened. Without it there was only a void.

Still, I do wish he'd come back. I would have liked the chance to try to forge a different, less punishing meaning to his loss, to find a way for him to make peace with his regrets after so many years of enmity with them.

ii "Hankering for oblivion": Don Fabrizio Corbera

FC, a retired gentleman in his early seventies, was referred to us for suspected depression, following concerns flagged by close associates, both friends and family. Terse and somewhat disdainful in first instance, became more animated and somewhat rageful in response to questions regarding life circumstances. Particularly bitter at developments in extended family over last two decades, lamenting declining fortunes, deterioration in both status and value of land assets. Spoke of "arrivistes" stealing everything, should be monitored for any increase in paranoid symptoms. Tone became more contemplative when asked about personal interests, spoke of upstairs observatory and astronomy. While this provides him with regular, high-level cognitive activity, we are concerned this may be too rarefied and solitary a pastime for a man of FC's years, and would recommend referral to over-seventies community centre drop-in. Note, however, that FC's response to this proposal was unenthusiastic.

Walt Whitman and Lady Slane showed us that death can open a space for renewal. They were able to imagine themselves living beyond their own allotted span through their creative work or the generations that succeeded them.

Adam lived a much more negative relationship to his own death: overwhelmed by guilt and self-disgust, he gave off the sense of wanting to erase every last trace of himself from the world. He'd met Rita when they were in their early forties and her two children were already in their late teens. She had no wish for more, which had been fine with him. He was, eventually, a game enough step-grandfather to her grandchildren, but since she'd gone, neither he nor her children had made much effort to keep in contact. Without siblings, maintaining relationships only with a few friends and ex-colleagues, Adam was, as he put it, "the end of the line, thankfully."

This is something he had in common with the protagonist of our next novel, Don Fabrizio Corbera, Prince of Salina. The biographical source of *The Leopard* (1958) is clear: its author, Giuseppe Tomasi di Lampedusa, was himself a minor Sicilian prince, the last of the house of Lampedusa. The novel was based on the life of his great-grandfather.

If *All Passion Spent* is a novel about wresting a future from the dead weight of the past, *The Leopard* is about how the past can suffocate the future. For this reason, it makes sense to approach the novel backwards, beginning with the Prince's death. Given that this is announced in the novel's table of contents, it is hardly a spoiler. But death is everywhere from the very opening of the book; no sooner do we enter the Villa Salina than we're breathing the air of decay.

Unlike the other two characters under discussion in this chapter, for most of the novel Don Fabrizio is neither aged nor near death. He is in his late forties when we meet him, "very large and very strong," a model of vital force. Don Fabrizio seems to gather in himself the full range of powers and qualities, both animal and human. He has the physique and height of an ox, the wiliness of a politician, the presence and confidence of a great actor, the sublime intellect of a scientist.

But the paradox of this man so full of life is that he's in such intimate proximity to death. The old world around him, of which he is an integral part, is dying, and he's fighting a losing battle to preserve it. When the novel leaps forward twenty-one years to the "Death of a Prince," it doesn't feel unexpected; on the contrary, this is the event we've been anticipating all through the novel. The chapter begins:

> For a dozen years or so, he had been feeling as if the vital fluid, the faculty of existing, life itself in fact and perhaps even the will to go on living, were ebbing out of him slowly but steadily, as grains of sand cluster and then line up one by one, unhurried, unceasing, before the narrow neck of an hour-glass.

Lampedusa might be giving a poetic rendition here of a key and controversial psychoanalytic idea: the death drive. This was a notion Freud introduced in his extraordinary essay *Beyond the Pleasure Principle*, written against the dark background of traumatic personal and historical experiences. Freud had borne witness from a distance to the mass destruction of the First World War and up close to the death in 1920 of his beloved daughter Sophie at the age of twenty-seven, a casualty of the Spanish flu pandemic sweeping Europe. He published the essay later that year.

The premise of *Beyond the Pleasure Principle* is that there's a secret tendency in us to return to the inanimate condition of matter before life began. This is a secret even to ourselves; over millions of years of biological evolution, the drive to return to a nothingness has hidden behind a much more visible drive to life—those familiar impulses to grow, develop and expand into the world around us.

For a dozen years, the Prince's slow, seeping death has disguised itself as a will to live. The ebbing of vital energy, Lampedusa suggests, doesn't manifest in pain or even discomfort: "on the contrary this imperceptible loss of vitality was itself the proof, the condition so to say, of a sense of living." Life has become almost indistinguishable from its opposite. Lampedusa's rendition of the Prince's death leaves us feeling almost as though Don Fabrizio were born to die.

The story of *The Leopard* is really the story of Don Fabrizio's attempts to preserve his aristocratic status and privilege in the face of the radical changes sweeping the land, most notably the unification of Italy (the Risorgimento) and the coming of republican democracy. He is guided in this task by the youthful wisdom of his beloved nephew Tancredi, who has fought alongside Garibaldi's Redshirts: "Unless we ourselves take a hand now," warns Tancredi, "they'll foist a republic on us. If we want things to stay as they are, things will have to change."

Don Fabrizio chooses to open himself and his estates to the forces of progress. Having ingratiated himself with the newly united kingdom of Italy, the Prince is rewarded with a visit from Cavaliere Chevalley di Monterzuolo, a government representative, who invites him to join the new Senate of the Kingdom.

The Prince declines the invitation with a startling speech about Sicily and the Sicilians. He tells Chevalley that, having been colonised by successive invading forces for 2,500 years, "We're worn out and exhausted." For the people of Sicily, doing things well or badly isn't the issue: "the sin which we Sicilians never forgive is simply that of 'doing' at all." The essence of the Sicilian character, he goes on, is total inactivity:

> Sleep, my dear Chevalley, sleep, that is what Sicilians want, and they will always hate anyone who tries to wake them, even in order to bring them the most wonderful of gifts . . . All Sicilian self-expression, even the most violent, is really wish-fulfilment; our sensuality is a hankering for oblivion, our shooting and knifing a hankering for death; our languor, our exotic ices, a hankering for voluptuous immobility, that is for death again; our meditative air is that of a void wanting to scrutinise the enigmas of Nirvana.

Everything the Sicilians do, the Prince rather outrageously suggests, is a concealed expression of the wish for oblivion, silence and death. Their history of repeated invasion and conquest has made them peculiarly intimate with some death-driven tendency in the human psyche.

The Prince seems for much of the novel to be an exception among Sicilians in this regard. He is single-mindedly dedicated to plotting and strategising, seeking the right moves and alliances to preserve his family's pre-eminence in the face of the new levelling forces at work in the land.

But all this connivance flies in the face of reality: there can be no reconciliation between the feudal culture his family once presided over and the emerging bourgeois democracy. The aristocracy are dying, the middle class are ascendant. Needing to believe he's in control of his family's fate, he doesn't see that every compromise and adaptation he makes is another death blow to the traditions of the house of Salina. He deludes himself that he's on the side of life and the future, unaware that he's working in the service of decay and decline.

During a hunting expedition, the Prince confides to his friend Don Ciccio Tumeo, the parish organist, that he has approved marriage between his nephew and Angelica, daughter of aspirational new money. Don Ciccio sees this for the catastrophe it is, at least for the Prince and his family's interests: it is, he declares bluntly, "unconditional surrender" and it presages the end of the Salina family line. The Prince's reaction is oddly contradictory. He at once accedes to the truth of what Don Ciccio says and stubbornly repudiates it: "Tumeo was right; in him spoke clear tradition. But the man was a fool: this marriage was not the end of everything, it was the beginning of everything."

Despite his defensive stance, the Prince knows better. In the deepest cells of his being, he knows that he and his family are in the final stages of their own endgame. This is the truth he comes to own fully as an old man on his deathbed, as he contemplates his family's ebbing significance.

"For the significance of a noble family," he thinks to himself, "lies entirely in its traditions, that is in its vital memories, and he was the last to have any unusual memories, anything different from those of other families." In the new culture of liberal, democratic progress, everything will be levelled out, flattened and generalised—even memory and inner life; one family's photos and stories look much like another's. The singular man in the mould of Don Fabrizio will be superfluous, irrelevant, deprived of a legacy to bequeath the future. His reflections on the decline of tradition are so devastating because they are also unflinching observations of his waning powers and impending death.

The crowning irony of the novel comes in the final chapter, which jumps forward a further twenty-seven years to the Villa Salina, now inhabited by the three elderly, quarrelsome spinster daughters of the Prince. The one concrete bequest of the Prince to the future was his beloved Great Dane, Bendicò, stuffed and mounted and left mouldering for decades in a wooden case.

Concetta, the Prince's eldest daughter, orders the disposal of Bendicò, who has "really become too moth-eaten and dusty." The decomposing body is thrown from the window into the yard for collection by the dustman:

During the flight down . . . its form recomposed itself for an instant; in the air there seemed to be dancing a quadruped with long whiskers, its right foreleg raised in imprecation. Then all found peace in a little heap of livid dust.

The painful beauty of this passage surely has something to do with Lampedusa's own intimacy with feelings of abject superfluity. It was out of his experience as the last of a minor royal line of Sicily that he wrote the novel. Like the Sicilians of whom the Prince speaks, Lampedusa was apparently unconcerned to "do" very much up to this point. He was a man of exceptional cultivation, a gentleman scholar of French literature, on which he wrote various papers and books, including a study of Stendhal, as well as odd short stories. None of these were published in his lifetime.

Lampedusa began work on *The Leopard* in 1954 and completed it in 1956. It was rejected by the two publishers to whom he'd submitted it. More painfully still, he was diagnosed with lung cancer in 1957, from which he would die a few months later. It is hard not to see in the disposal of Bendicò a bitterly self-deprecating image of the fate of his own novel, unwanted and unloved.

And yet here, from the midst of that "little heap of livid dust," comes a final twist of hope. Lampedusa's friend Elena Croce sent the book to the renowned writer Giorgio Bassani, who immediately recognised its greatness and ensured its publication. *The Leopard* received the Strega Prize, a prestigious literary award, in 1959.

The novel was saved from that heap of dust and, unlike poor Bendicò's recomposed form, was returned to the long life it continues to enjoy. It turns out that Lampedusa's final gesture was, like Whitman's, a way of wresting life from death. Perhaps he was anticipated in this by his own great creation, Don Fabrizio, who witnesses his coming death with such defiant courage and imagination. Throughout his life he's been shadowed by death, but in dying he comes strangely and beautifully alive.

Lady Slane, Whitman, Don Fabrizio, Lampedusa, even Bendicò: each of these figures gives us a glimpse of how we might survive our own death—through the memories, the works and the succeeding generations that allow us to live beyond ourselves.

Perhaps this is the moment to return once more to the poem by Wallace Stevens, reproduced in full here, that gives this book its title.

> Last evening the moon rose above this rock
> Impure upon a world unpurged.
> The man and his companion stopped
> To rest before the heroic height.
>
> Coldly the wind fell upon them
> In many majesties of sound:
> They that had left the flame-freaked sun
> To seek a sun of fuller fire.
>
> Instead there was this tufted rock
> Massively rising high and bare

Beyond all trees, the ridges thrown
Like giant arms among the clouds.

There was neither voice nor crested image,
No chorister, nor priest. There was
Only the great height of the rock
And the two of them standing still to rest.

There was the cold wind and the sound
It made, away from the muck of the land
That they had left, heroic sound
Joyous and jubilant and sure.

"How to Live. What to Do," as I suggested in the Intro-
duction, offers an oblique lesson in ways to see the world.
The man and his companion (is this a friend? a lover? a
child? a dog? It strikes me as rather wonderful that we
don't get to know) have left one "flame-freaked sun" to
seek another, "a sun of fuller fire."

They have been searching, in other words, for nature's
fireworks, for some extravagant display of godly power
and majesty. But what stops them in their tracks isn't
an other-worldly spectacle, but a simple, imposing rock
dimly illuminated by the moon. And this encounter has
a transformative effect, for the two onlookers seem to
realise that this vista, bare and rugged as it is, is what
they've been searching for all along.

This isn't a drama of sound and fury, but of the world
stripped to its essential elements. Instead of "a sun of
fuller fire," they have a "tufted rock / Massively rising

high and bare / Beyond all trees." This sight is stripped of all adornment beyond the rock and its two resting onlookers. It is unaccompanied by celestial choirs, or by anything other than the cold wind: "heroic sound / Joyous and jubilant and sure."

On an epic spiritual mission to find "more," the man and his companion have stumbled across the truth and beauty of less.

Poetry is, as Stevens saw it, a way of penetrating to things as they really are. The poem is encouraging us to pay attention to things without the overlays of previous experiences or cultural associations, to behold them in their absolute singularity, their difference from any other thing.

To enter this purified space is to leave behind the mental noise and confusion—the "muck," as the poem has it, of the land we inhabit most of the time. To be alive to the world in front of us in this way is to tune in to the elemental music of the world, even if it's "just" the sound of the "cold wind." When we can hear it for what it is, this sound is more beautiful, more "joyous and jubilant and sure," than any choir.

iii "A little willingness to see": John Ames

JA, seventy-six, a local pastor, referred by doctor following recent diagnosis of angina pectoris. Reported low, though likely realistic expectations with regard to remaining span of life. Nonetheless, no sign of depression. On contrary, evidently very much at peace with prospect of end of life. However, suffering insomnia and anxiety for those he's leaving behind. Concerns include insufficient financial provision, possible presence of troubled young man next door in life of young son (and wife?) following his death. To be monitored by social services.

The central questions of old age are starting to sound suspiciously like the central questions of life: what kind of mark do we wish to make on the world? How and for what would we like to be remembered? How have we mattered to the people around and beyond us?

These are also the questions raised insistently by the last character to be discussed in this chapter and this book: Reverend John Ames of Marilynne Robinson's 2004 novel, *Gilead*. It seems remarkable to me that I'm conferring the privilege of the last word on the elderly minister of a small Congregationalist church in a small Iowan town in 1956.

But then Robinson's novel *is* remarkable, imagining a figure from the margins of history, geography and religion and endowing him with a voice and vision and character at once so singularly his own and so universally human. And given that the novel consists of his own last words, it makes sense that they should guide us towards a kind of conclusion.

Gilead might help us understand why Stevens's poem is called "How to Live. What to Do": that is, it might help us make the connection between the kind of attention the poem commends and its title's confident announcement of an agenda for practical life.

There is *only* "the great height of the rock," the poem tells us; but this "only" doesn't mean that something is lacking. In fact, we can best get the measure of this "only" by cross-referencing to a passage in *Gilead*, in which Ames writes of a certain way of using the word "just," as in "the sun just *shone*," "the tree just *glistened*," "the girl just *laughed*." We use the word in these instances, says Ames, "to call attention to a thing existing in excess of itself, so to speak, a sort of purity or lavishness." Learning how to live, Stevens's poem and Robinson's novel both suggest, is a matter of making ourselves receptive to this "purity or lavishness."

Gilead takes the form of a letter, written to a single addressee, the young son born to Reverend Ames in his dotage. Ames has angina pectoris, a condition which casts a shadow of precariousness over his remaining life; at any moment, his heart might fail, meaning he doesn't know when his letter might be permanently interrupted.

More positively, it also ensures that his letter is an open form, available to whatever comes into his mind, including the events unfolding around him as he writes. So while the letter is something of a last word, and begins by announcing itself as such ("I told you last night that I might be gone sometime, and you said, Where, and I said, To be with the Good Lord"), it's an ambiguous last word, a farewell that is continually intruded upon by new developments in the world around him. Even as he's approaching death, Ames is plunged again and again right back into life.

"I do regret that I have almost nothing to leave you and your mother," Ames writes early on in his letter. He is referring to a material legacy, but this statement is contradicted by the very pages we're reading. What Ames is writing is the richest of legacies: an expanding, deepening set of meditations on how to live.

And the writing itself becomes a journey for Ames. Towards the end of the novel, he resolves to "put an end to all of this writing" (meaning we can't infer from the novel's last words—"I'll pray and then I'll sleep"— that Ames has breathed his last). He continues: "The expectation of death I began with reads like a kind of youthfulness, it seems to me now."

What does he mean? In what sense was his expectation of death "youthful"? Perhaps Ames is talking about the exaggerated certainty that comes with being young. He had started the letter from the conviction that his time on earth was over, only to be surprised by new effusions of life, including the very act of writing and thinking about it. His persistent openness of mind and heart ensures that what begins as a meditation on his life and its wisdom gradually becomes a story of the living present.

But these philosophical and narrative elements aren't in conflict. On the contrary, the story that starts to insinuate itself into Ames's mind and letter only complicates and enriches the more meditative passages. It concerns the return home of his namesake and godson, John Ames (or Jack) Boughton, son of Presbyterian preacher Reverend Boughton, Ames's boyhood friend and neighbour.

Jack Boughton is the tearaway child and destructive adolescent who has come home, following a long absence, a bitter, broken man. Intensely wary of Jack at first, Ames finds compassion and understanding slowly brewing in him. Jack's troubled story becomes the thread Ames weaves into his reflections on envy, suffering and forgiveness.

Ames tells us at the outset that he's "lived seventy-six years, seventy-four of them here in Gilead, Iowa, excepting study at the college and at seminary." Notwithstanding this apparently restricted life, lived in the confines of church doctrine and duty, Ames reveals to us an emotional life of great range and depth. His devout belief in an afterlife doesn't prompt him to dismiss this world as a fleeting vanity, but to love it more deeply and more desperately. "I want your dear perishable self to live long," he tells his son, "and to love this poor perishable world, which I somehow cannot imagine not missing bitterly."

This love will abide, Ames imagines, even in the "incorruptible" state of heavenly life:

> I can't believe that, when we have all been changed and put on incorruptibility, we will forget our fantastic condition of mortality and impermanence, the great

bright dream of procreating and perishing that meant the whole world to us.

He is saying, I think, that being a worldly human with a fleshly body is merely different from, rather than inferior to, being an incorruptible spirit. The "rainbow colors" visible in "the shimmer on a child's hair, in the sunlight," and "in the dew, sometimes . . . the petals of flowers . . . a child's skin"; "the singularity . . . courage and loneliness" of any human face—these are some of the ordinary, and so typically unnoticed, ways in which the "mortal loveliness" of this life finds expression. As in Stevens's poem, Ames is inviting us to find occasion for joy, jubilation and surety in the sights and sounds of the commonplace world. Both are telling us that learning how to live begins with paying close and loving attention to what is in front of us.

But maybe Robinson's novel wants to take us a step further, for while Stevens extols the sublimity of the ordinary non-human world in the form of the rock, his only hint of the beauty to be found in and between human beings is the shared journey of "the man and his companion."

In *Gilead*, it is human existence that induces the greatest awe and reverence. Towards the end of the novel, Ames recalls the morning he first set his eyes on Lila, his much younger wife, who had first come to the church as a homeless wanderer. That morning, he tells his son, and the journey towards their marriage that followed, "enlarged my understanding of hope, just to know that such a transformation can occur. And it has greatly sweetened my imagination of death, odd as that may sound."

Perhaps, beyond any supernatural or religious inferences, the sudden, transformative force of human love can sweeten the prospect of death simply because it leaves an immeasurable legacy. With his long farewell, Ames ensures that his wife and child will both continue to feel the depth of his love beyond his death.

"Wherever you turn your eyes," writes Ames as the book comes to a close, "the world can shine like transfiguration. You don't have to bring a thing to it except a little willingness to see." This little willingness to see is the core of Ames's bequest to his son, and Robinson's to us. Knowing how to live and what to do begins by relinquishing the impulse to believe that what we most want lies in some elusive "sun of fuller fire" far away, as opposed to the one that rises for everyone, every morning.

Recently, an elderly man working with me asked an intriguing question: why, at the very moments that he is most at peace, has he been struck by the urge to spoil it all? Sitting quietly on a park bench with his wife, his thoughts would turn abruptly to a good-looking woman in his office; absorbed in a novel or poem, he would suddenly recall some tedious errand or work task. "Why," he asked plaintively, "would I want to go from a state of contentment to a state of agitation?"

The question strikes me as an apt one to end a chapter on old age and a book on the span of life. My patient is

hardly alone in this tendency to disturb his own contentment. This is a habit and an itch and a yearning wired
into the human condition. Perpetually seeking that "sun
of fuller fire," we pass over the rock before our eyes,
tune out the wind in our ears. We have a mysteriously
abundant willingness to pursue what we don't have, but
not that "little willingness to see" what is already there.

One of the ways psychoanalysis has helped me, and
hopefully some of the people I've worked with, is in
directing my attention and curiosity towards that which
is already there, towards what we see and hear all the time
and so fail to see or hear at all. In retrospect, it strikes
me that I went into analysis in large part because this
was such a struggle for me. Always wondering if I was
missing something, if there was a better place or way of
life somewhere other than where I was, I couldn't allow
myself to inhabit fully the life I already had. The books
and ideas and experiences I've explored in these pages
have all, in some way or other, helped me to do this.

The basic task of psychoanalysis, to listen to the
unconscious, can be understood in many different
ways—discovering the concealed meanings of our
nightly dreams or daily words and actions, or the sexual
and aggressive motives, undetected even by ourselves,
that direct our behaviour towards others.

But more basically still, listening to the unconscious
means we take it as a given that every human being, to
invoke Whitman's famous words, "contains multitudes,"
that each of us is an inexhaustible mystery to ourselves

and everyone else. This is surely also the great life lesson of literature. It shows us how to live not by instruction but by the example of the generous, expansive curiosity it extends to people and things alike.

If we can live in this spirit of curiosity, we don't need to be told "what to do"; we can discover it, each in our own way, for ourselves.

Acknowledgements

This book was the brainchild of Andrew Goodfellow at Ebury, to whom I'm deeply grateful for entrusting me with such a wonderful idea, and for overseeing its realisation so thoughtfully. My thanks too to Clare Bullock for bringing to every chapter, page and line of this book the kind of granular attention and insight every writer hopes for from an editor, as well as boundless enthusiasm for novels and ideas. I feel frankly spoiled to have worked with two such responsive and dedicated editors. And in Lesley Levene, I've once again had the benefit of a uniquely sharp-eyed copy editor and her seamless command of English usage.

I also feel very fortunate to have in Zoe Ross such a tirelessly supportive and proactive agent, who is so well versed in my writing and interests; it was through her the idea for this book first reached me.

In writing this book, I've had the benefit of numerous rich conversations around life and literature with friends who spend too much time reading and writing. Lara Feigel and Margie Orford read various drafts and provided an embarrassment of invaluable feedback and suggestions. Karen Whitely, Angie Simon and Beth

341

Guilding all read chapters and responded with characteristic generosity and intelligence.

I couldn't have written this book without my family; not only because they supported and tolerated the time it took away from them, but because they have taught me more about life and relationships than any education or training. Ethan, Reuben and Ira are each in their own way the most stimulating imaginable interlocutors on politics, philosophy, music, football, food, superhero franchises, string theory (nope, me neither) and everything else. Whatever I can claim to know about how to live and what to do I owe mostly to Abigail Schama, my constant companion through the mad adventure of grown-up life. This book is dedicated to her.

Notes

Chapter 1 Childhood Part 1: Play

9 "Let's pretend": Lewis Carroll, *Alice's Adventures in Wonderland and Through the Looking-Glass*, ed. Peter Hunt (Oxford University Press, 2009), p. 126

11 "It's the stupidest": ibid., p. 68

11 "Things flow about so": ibid., p. 179

13 do what she would: ibid., p. 137

13 as if deliberately: Franz Kafka, *The Castle*, trans. Willa and Edwin Muir (Minerva, 1992), p. 17

15 there was nothing to be done: Carroll, *Alice's Adventures*, p. 137

15 suddenly came to a stop: Kafka, *The Castle*, p. 17

17 "when *I* use a word": Carroll, *Alice's Adventures*, p. 190

31 If his mother was not there: William Maxwell, *They Came Like Swallows* (Vintage, 2001), pp. 11–12

32 If his mother were not there to protect: ibid., pp. 8–9

33 His mother was not satisfied: ibid., p. 13

35 "My village": ibid., p. 104

36 hovering on the edge: ibid., p. 103

36 Robert sighed: ibid., p. 104

38 In the long run: ibid., p. 147

38 They rented a farmhouse: ibid., pp. 172–3

44 When he was nearly thirteen: Harper Lee, *To Kill a Mockingbird* (Vintage, 2004), p. 3

45 "until you climb into his skin": ibid., p. 31

45 about six and a half feet tall: ibid., p. 13

47 In Maycomb, if one went: ibid., p. 162

48 "I could never ask you": ibid., p. 82

48 "Simply because we were licked": ibid.

49 "folks can say Dolphus Raymond's": ibid., p. 219

Chapter 2 Childhood Part 2: Schooling

56 a great favourite with him: Charlotte Brontë, *Jane Eyre: An Autobiography* (Pan, 1967), p. 254

56 miserable cruelty: ibid., p. 53

56 Ere I had finished this reply: ibid.

57 "spiritual edification": ibid., p. 80

58 "to mortify in these girls": ibid., p. 82

58 "not a member of the true flock": ibid., p. 84

58 "to gain some real affection from you": ibid., p. 87

59 "Hush, Jane!": ibid.

59 "when I should be listening": ibid., p. 74

60 I tired of the routine: ibid., p. 103

61 "you were no beauty": ibid., p. 110

70 loves not realities: Ralph Waldo Emerson, *Essays and Lectures* (Library of America, 1983), p. 261

73 "Will I wake him up?": Roddy Doyle, *Paddy Clarke Ha Ha Ha* (Vintage, 1994), pp. 50–51

74 I didn't understand: ibid., p. 27
75 When the brothers: ibid., p. 133
76 "Look at that": ibid., pp. 168–9
76 It was a new feeling: ibid., p. 169
77 "the minute you get home": ibid.
77 "I'm not going to show": ibid.
77 "Paddy Clarke—": ibid., p. 223
78 the man of the house now: ibid.
85 authorized curriculum: Muriel Spark, *The Prime of Miss Jean Brodie* (Penguin, 2000), p. 5
85 no thoughts of anyone's personalities: ibid., p. 75
87 "He must have committed": ibid., p. 17
87 Sandy looked back: ibid., p. 30
88 It occurred to Sandy: ibid., p. 31
89 "We'd look like one big": ibid., p. 102
90 "*was* rather naughty": ibid., p. 122
90 unified compliance: ibid., p. 123

Chapter 3 Adolescence Part 1: Rebellion

104 every look, every movement: Elizabeth Bowen, *The Death of the Heart* (Vintage, 1998), p. 60
104 In her home life: ibid.
109 "You and I know each other": ibid., p. 219
109 "How can I keep on feeling": ibid., p. 220
110 "You could always have struggled": ibid., p. 225
111 Inwardly innocent people: ibid., p. 112

118 "You're a very bright boy": James Baldwin, *Go Tell It on the Mountain* (Penguin, 2001), p. 22

118 was his identity: ibid., p. 23

118 His father's arm: ibid.

119 hardhearted, stiff-necked: ibid., p. 131

120 a sickness in his bowels: ibid., p. 224

120 "The Lord done raised you up": ibid., p. 212

120 who blocked the way: ibid., p. 256

129 "Your lives are set out for you": Kazuo Ishiguro, *Never Let Me Go* (Faber, 2005), p. 80

130 we were all pretty relieved: ibid., p. 81

130 people out there: ibid., p. 82

131 the way they gestured to each other: ibid., p. 119

132 special guardians: ibid., p. 242

132 the actual model: ibid., p. 138

Chapter 4 *Adolescence Part 2: First Love*

143 We need books . . . that affect us: Franz Kafka, letter to Oskar Pollak (January 1904), *Letters to Friends, Family and Editors* (Schocken Books, 1977), p. 16

147 because his own desire or needs: Johann Wolfgang von Goethe, *The Sorrows of Young Werther*, trans. Michael Hulse (Penguin, 1989), p. 55

147 that jot of rational sense: ibid., p. 64

147 To lift the curtain: ibid., p. 113

149 His tranquil manner: ibid., p. 57

154 dark-haired, greying: Ivan Turgenev, *First Love* in *First*

Love and Other Stories, trans. Richard Freeborn (Oxford University Press, 2008), p. 145

154 expectant and shy: ibid., p. 146

155 The unexpectedly rapid fulfilment: ibid., p. 149

156 "In your eyes": ibid., p. 182

157 "It's him! It's him at last!": ibid., p. 190

158 I harboured no bad feelings: ibid., p. 196

165 me: I can't believe you're breaking up: Sally Rooney, *Conversations with Friends* (Faber, 2017), p. 89

166 already preparing compliments: ibid., p. 3

167 to arrange my face in a way: ibid., p. 6

167 felt a sting of self-consciousness: ibid., p. 29

168 emotionally cold: ibid., p. 83

169 I love my fellow human beings: ibid., p. 294

Chapter 5 Adulthood Part 1: Ambition

177 slight young man: Stendhal, *The Red and the Black*, trans. and ed. Roger Gard (Penguin, 2002), p. 25

177 he would have died: ibid., p. 28

178 would it one day be his?: ibid., p. 72

178 an obscure and penniless lieutenant: ibid., p. 32

178 "it is necessary to be a priest": ibid.

178 "a sombre flame in the depths": ibid., p. 54

180 timid, rancorous, unfriendly: Stendhal, *The Life of Henry Brulard*, trans. John Sturrock (New York Review Books, 1995), p. 102

180 he didn't love me as an individual: ibid., p. 78

180 I loathed my father: ibid., p. 33

182 derived from the joy: Stendhal, *The Red and the Black*, p. 101

182 take pity on a family: ibid., p. 338

183 A clear spring sent to quench: ibid.

183 the most brilliant young woman: ibid., p. 349

194 so close that he could hardly fail: F. Scott Fitzgerald, *The Great Gatsby* (Penguin, 2008), p. 194

194 was already behind him: ibid.

194 orgastic future: ibid.

194 stretch out our arms further: ibid., p. 195

197 cruel body: ibid., p. 8

197 "careless people": ibid., p. 62

198 more real to him now: ibid., p. 185

198 a ragged old copy of a book: ibid., p. 186

198 "Jimmy was bound to get ahead": ibid., p. 187

199 shiftless and unsuccessful: ibid., p. 105

199 constant, turbulent riot: ibid., p. 106

199 represented all the beauty: ibid., p. 107

199 quick and extravagantly ambitious: ibid.

199 gleaming like silver: ibid., p. 160

199 "Her voice is full of money": ibid., p. 128

202 the summer they electrocuted: Sylvia Plath, *The Bell Jar* (Faber, 2012), p. 1

205 I noticed, in the routine way: ibid., p. 16

206 I was supposed to be having: ibid., p. 2

206 steering New York: ibid.

207 "I don't really know": ibid., p. 30

207 plan after plan started: ibid., p. 118

207 an Olympic lady crew champion: ibid., p. 73

Chapter 6 Adulthood Part 2: Marriage

217 I have discerned in you: George Eliot, *Middlemarch* (Penguin, 1985), p. 67

219 a few imaginative weeks: ibid., p. 227

219 we begin by knowing little: ibid.

221 "Marriage is so unlike": ibid., p. 855

221 rows of volumes: ibid., p. 232

221 in a most unaccountable: ibid.

222 as blind to his inward troubles: ibid.

222 We are angered even: ibid.

223 those hidden conflicts in her husband: ibid.

223 with the uncritical awe: ibid.

223 All Dorothea's passion: ibid., p. 51

224 about twelve years old: ibid., p. 30

231 she held that a woman: Henry James, *The Portrait of a Lady* (Penguin, 1986), p. 106

231 that if a certain light should dawn: ibid., p. 107

232 "sterile dilettante": ibid., p. 396

233 She was wrong, but: ibid., p. 398

233 no property, no title: ibid.

234 "It's getting—getting—getting": ibid., p. 186

234 "the usual chances and dangers": ibid.

234 "in a comfortable sort of way": ibid.

235 "It's to make you independent": ibid., p. 214

235 by an irresistible impulse: ibid., p. 216

235 This was the hot wind: ibid., p. 634

236 "I married him before all the world": ibid., p. 536

237 He said to her one day: ibid., p. 477

241 he knew she was his woman: D. H. Lawrence, *The Rainbow* (Penguin, 1986), p. 96

242 Happy families are all alike: Leo Tolstoy, *Anna Karenina*, trans. Richard Pevear and Larissa Volokhonsky (Penguin, 2012), p. 1

246 fabricated world: Lawrence, *The Rainbow*, p. 235

247 and being alone in the world: ibid., p. 191

247 One ought to get up: ibid., p. 189

247 a real outburst of house-work: ibid., p. 191

248 "Shake the rug then": ibid., p. 192

249 There followed two black and ghastly days: ibid.

251 ignore him, successfully: ibid., p. 252

252 Then he was grateful to her love: ibid.

Chapter 7 Adulthood Part 3: Middle Age

256 Running out of gas: John Updike, *Rabbit Is Rich* (Penguin, 2006), p. 1

265 life escapes: Virginia Woolf, "Modern Fiction," *Selected Essays*, ed. David Bradshaw (Oxford University Press, 2008), p. 8

265 a plot . . . comedy, tragedy, love interest: ibid.

265 that if all his figures were to come to life: ibid., pp. 8–9

266 these tools are death: Woolf, "Character in Fiction," *Selected Essays*, p. 48

266 In order to complete them: ibid., p. 44

267 the strong are led to destroy: ibid., p. 51

267 Examine for a moment: Woolf, "Modern Fiction," *Selected Essays*, p. 9

269 sing freshly and piercingly: Virginia Woolf, *Mrs. Dalloway* (Oxford University Press, 2000), p. 31

270 the oddest sense of being herself: ibid., p. 9

270 the dwindling of life: ibid., p. 38

270 The whole world seems to be saying: ibid., p. 51

270 Odd, incredible: ibid., p. 243

272 it was enough: ibid., p. 160

273 which, as she heard it: ibid., p. 230

273 old Mrs. Hilbery: ibid.

273 thrown himself from a window: ibid., p. 241

274 A thing there was that mattered: ibid.

281 *I shall follow you soon*: Christopher Isherwood, *A Single Man* (Vintage, 2010), p. 77

281 *I am alive . . . I am alive!*: ibid., p. 82

281 What's wrong with them is: ibid., p. 83

283 The harassed look: ibid., p. 2

283 humiliated and sick to his stomach: ibid., p. 11

283 the face of the child, the boy: ibid., p. 2

283 But that happened so gradually: ibid.

284 it can be kind of marvellous: ibid., p. 130

284 I, personally, have gotten steadily sillier: ibid.

287 even if only by the standards: Updike, "Afterword," *Rabbit Is Rich*, p. 433

290 No one can seem to agree: Patricia Lockwood, "Malfunctioning Sex Robot," *London Review of Books*, Vol. 41, No. 19, 10 October 2019

292 In the shaving mirror a chaos: Updike, *Rabbit Is Rich*, p. 4

292 some pushy road-hog: ibid., p. 29

293 "for old crocks like us": ibid., p. 85

293 the stifled terror that always made him restless: ibid., p. 86

293 Middle age is a wonderful country: ibid., p. 208

294 Yet at moments: ibid.

Chapter 8 Old Age and Dying

308 "I have considered the eyes": Vita Sackville-West, *All Passion Spent* (Virago, 1983), p. 67

308 completely self-indulgent: ibid., p. 67

309 content merely to *be*: ibid., p. 134

309 "Repose is one of the most important": ibid., p. 98

309 for which she was beginning to feel: ibid., p. 194

310 all these parts of the body: ibid., p. 195

311 old, dismasted, gray and batter'd: Walt Whitman, "The Dismantled Ship," *Leaves of Grass*, ed. Sculley Bradley and Harold W. Blodgett (W. W. Norton, 1973), p. 534

311 here I am these current years: Whitman, "Preface Note to 2d Annex," "Good-bye My Fancy!," *Leaves of Grass*, p. 537

312 paralytic seizure: Whitman, "Prefatory Letter to the Reader, Leaves of Grass 1889," *Leaves of Grass*, p. 560

312 May-be it is yourself: Whitman, "Good-bye My Fancy!,"
Leaves of Grass, p. 558

314 "Face it, Lady Slane": Sackville-West, *All Passion Spent*,
p. 220

315 enveloping music: ibid., p. 288

323 For a dozen years or so: Giuseppe Tomasi di Lampedusa,
The Leopard, trans. Archibald Colquhoun (Harvill Press,
1996), p. 164

324 on the contrary this imperceptible loss: ibid.

324 "Unless we ourselves take a hand": ibid., p. 21

325 "We're worn out and exhausted": ibid., p. 122

326 "Tumeo was right": ibid., p. 84

327 For the significance of a noble family: ibid., p. 169

327 "really become too moth-eaten": ibid., p. 189

327 During the flight down: ibid., p. 190

333 the sun just *shone*: Marilynne Robinson, *Gilead* (Virago,
2004), p. 32

333 I told you last night: ibid., p. 3

334 I do regret that I have: ibid., p. 5

334 put an end to all of this writing: ibid., p. 272

335 lived seventy-six years: ibid., p. 10

335 I want your dear perishable self: ibid., pp. 60–61

335 I can't believe that: ibid., p. 65

336 rainbow colors: ibid., p. 75

337 enlarged my understanding of hope: ibid., p. 231

337 Wherever you turn your eyes: ibid., p. 280

Bibliography

The Novels

James Baldwin, *Go Tell It on the Mountain* (1953) (Penguin, 2001)

Elizabeth Bowen, *The Death of the Heart* (1938) (Vintage, 1998)

Charlotte Brontë, *Jane Eyre: An Autobiography* (1847) (Pan, 1967)

Lewis Carroll, *Alice's Adventures in Wonderland and Through the Looking-Glass* (1865/1871), ed. Peter Hunt (Oxford University Press, 2009)

Roddy Doyle, *Paddy Clarke Ha Ha Ha* (1993) (Vintage, 1994)

George Eliot, *Middlemarch* (1871) (Penguin, 1985)

F. Scott Fitzgerald, *The Great Gatsby* (1925) (Penguin, 2008)

Johann Wolfgang von Goethe, *The Sorrows of Young Werther* (1787), trans. Michael Hulse (Penguin, 1989)

Christopher Isherwood, *A Single Man* (1964) (Vintage, 2010)

Kazuo Ishiguro, *Never Let Me Go* (Faber, 2005)

Henry James, *The Portrait of a Lady* (1881) (Penguin, 1986)

D. H. Lawrence, *The Rainbow* (1915) (Penguin, 1986)

Harper Lee, *To Kill a Mockingbird* (1960) (Vintage, 2004)

William Maxwell, *They Came Like Swallows* (1937) (Vintage, 2001)

Sylvia Plath, *The Bell Jar* (1963) (Faber, 2012)

Marilynne Robinson, *Gilead* (Virago, 2004)

Sally Rooney, *Conversations with Friends* (Faber, 2017)

Vita Sackville-West, *All Passion Spent* (1931) (Virago, 1983)

Muriel Spark, *The Prime of Miss Jean Brodie* (1961) (Penguin, 2000)

Stendhal, *The Red and the Black* (1830), trans. and ed. Roger Gard (Penguin, 2002)

Giuseppe Tomasi di Lampedusa, *The Leopard* (1958), trans. Archibald Colquhoun (Harvill Press, 1996)

Ivan Turgenev, *First Love* (1860) in *First Love and Other Stories*, trans. Richard Freeborn (Oxford University Press, 2008)

John Updike, *Rabbit Is Rich* (1981) (Penguin, 2006)

Virginia Woolf, *Mrs. Dalloway* (1925) (Oxford University Press, 2000)

Other Literary Texts

Franz Kafka, *The Castle* (1926), trans. Willa and Edwin Muir (Minerva, 1992)

———, *Letters to Friends, Family and Editors* (1902–24), trans. Richard and Clara Winston (Schocken Books, 1977)

Stendhal, *The Life of Henry Brulard* (1890), trans. John Sturrock (New York Review Books, 1995)

Wallace Stevens, *The Collected Poems of Wallace Stevens* (1954) (Vintage, 1990)

Leo Tolstoy, *Anna Karenina* (1877), trans. Richard Pevear and Larissa Volokhonsky (Penguin, 2012)

Walt Whitman, *Leaves of Grass*, ed. Sculley Bradley and Harold W. Blodgett (W. W. Norton, 1973)

Non-fictional Texts

Nicolas Abraham and Maria Torok, *The Shell and the Kernel: Renewals of Psychoanalysis* (University of Chicago Press, 1994)

Hannah Arendt, *On Revolution* (1963) (Penguin, 1990)

Simone de Beauvoir, *Old Age* (1970) (Penguin, 1977)

Christopher Bollas, *The Shadow of the Object: Psychoanalysis of the Unthought Known* (Columbia University Press, 1987)

———, *Forces of Destiny: Psychoanalysis and Human Idiom* (Free Association Books, 1989)

César and Sára Botella, *The Work of Psychic Figurability: Mental States Without Representation*, trans. Andrew Weller and Monique Zerbib (Routledge, 2004)

Ralph Waldo Emerson, "Self-Reliance" (1841), *Essays and Lectures* (Library of America, 1983)

———, "Old Age," *Atlantic Monthly*, January 1862, https://www.theatlantic.com/magazine/archive/1862/01/old-age/518679/

Erik H. Erikson, *Identity and the Life Cycle* (1961) (W. W. Norton, 1980)

Erik H. Erikson and Joan M. Erikson, *The Life Cycle Completed: Extended Version with New Chapters on the Ninth Stage of Development by Joan M. Erikson* (W. W. Norton, 1998)

Sándor Ferenczi, "Confusion of Tongues Between Adults and the Child" (1933), *Final Contributions to the Problems and Methods of Psycho-Analysis*, trans. Eric Mosbacher et al. and ed. Michael Balint (Routledge, 1994)

Anna Freud, "Adolescence," *Psychoanalytic Study of the Child*, Vol. 13 (1958)

Sigmund Freud, *Three Essays on the Theory of Sexuality* (1905), *The Standard Edition of the Complete Works of Sigmund Freud*, trans. and ed. James Strachey, Vol. 7 (Vintage, 2001)

———, "On Narcissism" (1914), *Standard Edition*, Vol. 14

———, "The Unconscious" (1915), *Standard Edition*, Vol. 14

———, "Mourning and Melancholia" (1917), *Standard Edition*, Vol. 14

———, "Humour" (1927), *Standard Edition*, Vol. 21

———, *Civilization and Its Discontents* (1930), *Standard Edition*, Vol. 21

Byung-Chul Han, *The Burnout Society* (Stanford University Press, 2015)

Melanie Klein, "The Role of the School in the Libidinal Development of the Child" (1923), *Love, Guilt and Reparation* (Vintage, 1997)

Patricia Lockwood, "Malfunctioning Sex Robot," *London Review of Books*, Vol. 41, No. 19, 10 October 2019

Joyce Schaverien, *Boarding School Syndrome: The Psychological Trauma of the "Privileged" Child* (Routledge, 2015)

D. W. Winnicott, *The Maturational Processes and the Facilitating Environment: Studies in Emotional Development* (1965) (Karnac, 1990)

———, *Playing and Reality* (Routledge, 1971)

Virginia Woolf, *Selected Essays*, ed. David Bradshaw (Oxford University Press, 2008)

About the Author

Josh Cohen is a psychoanalyst in private practice and professor of modern literary theory at Goldsmiths, University of London. He is the author of books and articles on modern literature, cultural theory, and psychoanalysis, including *How to Read: Freud, The Private Life: Our Everyday Self in an Age of Intrusion,* and *Not Working: Why We Have to Stop.* He lives in London.